The Final Countdown:

Where Will You Spend Eternity?

by

Dr. Mike Letterman

© 2024 All Rights Reserved

For my son, Brett! May God continue to bless you and guard your walk with him!

Love,
Dad
(A.K.A. Mike)

THE FINAL COUNTDOWN: Where Will You Spend Eternity?

⁷ Many waters cannot quench love, neither can the floods drown it: if a man would give all the substance of his house for love, it would utterly be contemned.

Song of Solomon 8:7 KJV

For Jan, my wife, partner, and best friend, who always pushes me to reach for the heavens.

If it were not for your courage and support, this book might have never been written.

I love you,

Mike

Special thanks to my friend and mentor
Rev. Rick Talent
who taught me how to accept the forgiveness already offered by Christ Jesus, our Lord.!

and

My dear friend Greg Combs, and his fabulous team at WXRQ radio, 1460 AM, Mount Pleasant, TN!

Table of Contents

INTRODUCTION **11**

HOW TO STUDY THE BIBLE **16**

THE APOSTLE JOHN **22**

THE TRUTH ABOUT HELL **31**

UNVEILING REVELATION **45**

LETTER TO THE CHURCHES **54**

CHURCH AT PHILADELPHIA **63**

THE THRONE ROOM OF GOD **70**

WORTHY IS THE LAMB **84**

HORSEMEN ON THE HORIZON **94**

THE MYSTERY OF THE 144,000 .... **105**

A MULTITUDE NO MAN COULD NUMBER **113**

HEAVEN FALLS SILIENT **123**

WHEN HELL COMES CALLING **134**

A WORLD AT WAR **143**

THE BEGINNING OF THE END **153**

THE TRIBULATION TEMPLE **161**

STANDING ON THE EDGE OF ETERNITY **172**

TWO WITNESSES **179**

THE WOMAN AND THE DRAGON **187**

THE WAR IN HEAVEN **196**

THE BEAST FROM OUT OF THE SEA **203**

THE BEAST FROM THE EARTH	211
THE MARK OF THE BEAST	216
AFTER THE STORM	223
WHEN THE END COMES	230
WHEN THE JUDGE CALLS HIS COURT TO ORDER	241
THE BOWL JUDGMENTS	248
THE FINAL JUDGEMENT	256
THE JUDGMENT OF THE BABYLONIAN HARLOT	274
THE KING	290
THE 1000 YEAR REIGN	298
THIS EARTH IS NOT OUR HOME	319
THE END OF THE FINAL COUNTDOWN	326
THE INVITATION	335

PROLOGUE

This is not an in-depth theological discussion of every aspect of Revelation. I will leave that to other leading theologians like John Walvoord and Robert Thomas, upon whose shoulders I stand and whose commentaries I have frequently consulted. Indeed, if one attempted to document every facet of this topic, it would fill many more volumes with theological and historical information and interpretation, as it already has.

The purpose of this book is to ask a question and beg a response from the reader about a theme God placed on my heart at the beginning of 2023: *The Final Countdown: Where Will You Spend Eternity?*

This book reveals many major points of the Book of Revelation as they have been revealed to me and, I hope, demonstrates the depths of God's love.

It is important to note that while God is judging the world, he is still in the business of saving souls. We often speak of God's love, but we must also be assured of God's judgment. Both are very real.

This book culminates over seven months of sermon preparation and a year of research and study. I hope you find this information valuable. God certainly blessed the sermons that circulated the world and the people who received them. It is my sincere prayer that it blesses you as well.

If you make a decision due to God's influence through this book, I would sincerely like to know about it. Please send an email to *ministry@christ-lives.org* or visit our website at **https://www.christ-lives.org**. From here, you may hit our contact page and leave us a message. This site also gives you access to our most recent sermons and library. Our live broadcast is at 6:00 a.m. CST every Sunday on 1460 AM radio. If you are outside the broadcast area, you may also listen to the sermon live through **http://www.thewxrq.com**.

Our internet and podcast sites are well documented at the end of this book.

Blessings!

THE MIRACLE
December 7, 2020

She fell. How is she, doctor? Well, we really don't know. If she survives the night . . .

Not everyone falls eighteen feet onto concrete. With seventeen broken bones, compound fractures of the femur and tibia, seven skull and jaw fractures, broken ribs and seven brain bleeders, two of which were serious, the outcome was very bleak.

Tonight, my wife, the love of my life, was lying in a hospital bed on life support. Her situation was very serious, and she was on the brink of death. This evening, I was out of options. I finally realized how insignificant we puny humans are. You would think that someone like me, who has seen so much death, would better understand the intricacies of life.

I had nothing left to give, nothing to trade. You can't barter with God. How can you barter when your life is not your own, and your next breath is not promised?

How many times had He called me to His service? My response was always, *give me ten more years.* I think He became tired of waiting.

In the darkness of Jan's CDU room, I knelt beside her bed and took her precious little hand in mine. Emotion swept over me, and I did one of the things I don't often do. I cried. I could not feel the cold, hard surface of the concrete floor beneath me. Usually, my knee replacements would have screamed at the abuse from this evening's actions. But tonight, I could not feel the physical pain from that and my other injuries. Suddenly, I felt very old. So, I offered God the only thing I had left, which in reality was not mine give. I offered him my life in exchange for hers. I prayed.

"Dear God. I don't have anything to offer you except myself. Lord, make this my last prayer. If you require a soul or a life tonight, take mine and let her live. The boys still need a woman's touch, a mother's love. I've taught them what I can about what it means to be a man. I am offering all I have left, and even that belongs to you. God, please take my life and let her live. I am ready. In Jesus' holy name, I pray. Amen!"

* * * *

I was allowed to stay beside Jan on the night of the accident until after midnight. Visiting hours were long since over, but Jan's nurse, Casey, had a kind heart. All I could do for Jan was to stroke her hair, hold her hand, and talk to her. I picked things I knew she would remember. I spoke to her about our first date, the night I proposed at Valentino's in Nashville, and other aspects of our life together as if this conversation could somehow shake her from the comatose prison in which she was now locked.

The following day was a morning like no other. There were no peals of thunder during the night, and lightning didn't strike nearby. But the next morning, when I rushed into Jan's room, things had changed dramatically. Jan was no longer on life support, and she was awake.

I know some of you will say this was all just a coincidence. But you don't go from *"if she makes it through the night"* to no life support without the mighty hand of God intervening.

During the night, God answered my prayer. He did what I asked him to do. However, God, being God, did it in an entirely different way. I asked him to take my life and let her live. That was exactly what he chose to do. He took the remainder of my life in service to him and gave Jan her life in return as my partner in the ministry.

I would add three seminary degrees to my Ph.D., MCS, and MBA. These were a Doctorate in Education and biblical exposition, preceded by Divinity and Christian Leadership degrees. Although some will try, knowledge is one of those things people can never take from you!

Today, Jan still suffers from injuries related to the fall. However, the doctors said she might never walk again. They were wrong. They were wrong about a great many things.

God still works miracles. I am convinced of it. He does it in His time and His way to further His glory!

And so began our ministry and insight into *The Final Countdown!*

INTRODUCTION

It was March of 2023. I was driving down the road, listening to my car stereo, and enjoying life. It was a cool morning. The music changed, and an old song from 1986 by a Swedish rock group, *Europe*, began to play. The song was *The Final Countdown*.

The song's opening was intriguing, and the drum intro was reminiscent of helicopter blades from my past as they churned the air. For a moment, the memory made me shiver. A memory of a much younger man carrying a highly modified XM24A1 sniper rifle came forward.

"Let go of the past," I whispered to myself. I reached toward the tuner and started to change the channel. A voice spoke to my heart. I hesitated.

They must know. I want you to preach the Book of Revelation and the Final Countdown.

I have to say I listen to God when he speaks. And quite honestly, we have some very candid conversations. This one was the same. Let's face it. There are certain things many preachers shy away from in today's feel-good society. Today, many church members want to be told how good they are so they can *feel* they are not like the man who smites his breast, saying *God be merciful to me, a sinner!*

Today, many preachers and TV evangelists coax their congregations the way a man coaxes a pet. The name of Jesus never leaves their lips.

Many preachers have been reprimanded because of God's words on their hearts that they voice from the pulpit, and many pastors have lost their jobs preaching the word of God. It is unfortunate, but it is true.

Please remember that at the time of this event, I was a relatively new evangelist preaching to a small audience on a local radio station that streamed into 136 countries and all 50 states. God would later bless my faith and His Word by increasing our Sunday morning listeners from about 250 to over 1.6 million over the space of 7 months.

So, God and I began our non-verbal conversation.

God spoke to my heart, saying, "I want you to preach on the Final Countdown. I want you to preach the Book of Revelation!"

"God, are you sure this is what you want me to do?" I must admit somewhere in my mind, I was hoping I had misread Him.

God answered in the affirmative. The feeling was overwhelming. Some of you wonder why I would question God this way. I can tell you we have had some fascinating conversations. But to have these conversations where God speaks to your heart in less than an audible fashion, you must be receptive and listen with your heart and faith!

I was an obedient child. Well, most of the time.

"Ok, God. If this is what you want, I'll try to do it and do it justice. Are you sure this is what you want?" Again, I was secretly hoping I had read him wrong. Let's face it. It is human nature (and a human failing) that we all want to be liked. That is natural. And telling someone they are going to Hell is one of those little no-no things that isn't well received. Again, this goes back to our feel-good society. It also goes back to our sinful nature. If we don't want to do something, we try to find every excuse because in our mind, we should not have to do it. And while God is speaking, we are shouting our reply on the matter so loudly we can't even hear ourselves think, let alone God's voice!

God answered in the affirmative again, which left me a perplexed and a little frustrated. Then God added his next instruction.

"I want you to baseline The Final Countdown. I want you to start by preaching about Hell!"

On this next thought I choked and hit my brakes to avoid running over an unlucky squirrel that darted across the road. Ok, well, that was it. God wants me to preach a sermon on Hell to baseline *The Final Countdown!*

"God, are you sure? I mean, preaching on the Book of Revelation will be difficult. But do you (really) want me to start by preaching about Hell? Did I read you right?"

God was emphatic at this point. I started to feel like Jonah. And I remembered how that story ended. There wasn't any big fish out here in this country woodland that I was driving through. But I was sure, with God being God, he could figure out a way to get my attention in some other meaningful fashion.

"God, they will kick me off the air if I start this new series on Revelation with a sermon on Hell!"

God reassured me that was not the case. I was running out of excuses. Isn't God Kool? He has this unique way of peeling you back like an onion to get to your heart. Often, he does it one layer at a time. *God, here is excuse number one. Ok, God, you took care of that one. God, here is excuse number two. Well, you took care of that one too. Ok, God, I'm not even going to offer excuse number three. You have my attention!*

Well, I told you God and I have a special relationship. I tell him what I think, and he tells me what I should think and then what to do. Pretty Kool, right? Sometimes, he is straightforward in his instruction. Other times, I feel He wants me to learn something while I wait for His final direction. Sometimes, He wants me to search for the answer. As far as hearing voices, I am not *Joan of Arc*. But He speaks to my heart, nonetheless. It is up to me to be receptive to his will during these conversations.

When I was a child, my dad used to tell me that *Anything worth having is worth working for!* There is so much wisdom in that statement. Dad used it to apply to daily life, and he believed that i*t was a privilege for a man to be able to work for his family.* I think the same applies to the Kingdom of God. While we are saved through faith, the gardens and vineyards of the Kingdom still need tending. It is certainly something worth working for!

"God, if I preach this sermon on Hell, I am done. I am finished. And I just got started. God, I want to serve you and your kingdom."

In his somewhat dry way, God seemed to point out that if I wanted to serve him, I would do as He asked. Sometimes, I hate it when He pulls the "G" card out on me! Now, some of you may think this is a bit much. But I told you, God and I speak very candidly to each other. I pray to him with respect. But, when we get to this point, this is where he speaks, and I listen. After all, he is God! And remember, the "G" card trumps everything else. I hesitate. He answers. I push back. Then BAM! Out comes the "G" card. Once that one is played, there isn't much else I can say to God when he says to jump. My only acceptable reply is *how high!* I must confess I thank God he is so very patient with me!

"*The Final Countdown? God, are you sure? And you want me to start with Hell, right?*"

I got the good, warm fuzzy!

"*Ok, God, you are the boss! Whatever you want, I will do. Please find a way for me to serve you after I get kicked off the air! And please help me. The Book of Revelation is hard to understand.*"

I later learned that understanding the Book of Revelation, while not always easy, isn't always *that* difficult! We will get into the who, what, when, and where questions used to better understand this book of prophecy. And yes, a few small things may need to be clarified. However, these few things pale compared to the knowledge one can attain through the study of this book. Just remember the rest of the Bible supports the Book of Revelation. And the Old Testament is a great help! Why? Because the Old Testament consistently points its way to the New Testament. It always points to our Lord and Savior, Jesus Christ!

Looking back, I must admit God has to have a sense of humor because he knows me better than anyone. I could almost hear him chuckling as I turned up the radio to an astonishing level, reminiscent of my college days.

The lyrics of *The Final Countdown* resounded through my psyche and seemed to become more intense.

> "*We're leavin' together*
> *But still it's farewell*
> *And maybe we'll come back*
> *To Earth, who can tell?*
> *I guess there is no one to blame*
> *We're leavin' ground*
> *Will things ever be the same again?*
> *It's the final countdown*
> *The final countdown.*

That song would become my battle song for the next seven months. I know. I hear you. Some of you think or praise songs by Hillsong Worship, Elevation Worship or Southern Gospel from WXRQ radio would have been much more appropriate. Don't get me wrong. I listen to these, too, and usually every day! But when I wanted to start prepping for a new sermon, I put in that song and cranked it up. If it was good enough for God to use as a theme to get my attention, it was enough to pump me up to prepare for the next sermon. Also, please note the number of months I have preached on this subject. It was the number seven. The idea of resting and the number seven are intimately connected. God rested on the seventh day. In Hebrew, "seven" has the same consonants as the word for completeness or wholeness. Seven is God's perfect number of completions, and the sermons were finished in a seven-month series. It was not by my design. I honestly did not realize it until I began this book.

    I continued my drive down the narrow country road with the music blaring to my already dilapidated hearing, shattered by small arms fire as a young man carrying an XM24A1 sniper rifle in two countries far away from Tennessee. The music of *The Final Countdown* reverberated through the car, and my spirit rose with it. God had given me a new mission. I was going to preach *The Final Countdown.*

HOW TO STUDY THE BIBLE

I included this chapter because of the diverse population that will read this book. Many of you already know how to study the Bible and the questions you must ask yourself as you read the scripture passages. I'll touch on some great ways to approach your next study session. I am going to keep this simple. These are the basics, and I hope you find this information beneficial!

Pray

One of the first things I do before I study the Word of God is praying. I pray for several things. And no, this prayer doesn't have to be long and flowery. In the introduction of his letter to the Colossians, the apostle Paul tells the church that he and his companions have been praying specifically for them. What were they praying for? He writes, *"We have not ceased to pray for you and to ask that you may be filled with the knowledge of His will in all spiritual wisdom and understanding"* **(Col. 1:9)**. Paul knows that the Christians in Colossae desperately need spiritual wisdom and discernment.

Just like with understanding, we are also told to ask the Lord for wisdom. What is wisdom? One definition I've come to love is that WISDOM IS THE PROPER APPLICATION OF KNOWLEDGE. It's taking what you have learned and putting it to good and proper use. This is an essential component of studying the Bible. But how important?

Scripture specifically tells us that we should pray for wisdom. James writes, *"But if any of you lacks wisdom, let him ask of God, who gives to all generously and without reproach, and it will be given to him"* **(James 1:5)**. We see this demonstrated by King Solomon in **1 Kings 3:2–15**, where the Lord told him in a dream, *"Ask what you wish Me to give you"* **(v. 5)**. Solomon could have asked for anything: health, status, power, money, and more. But instead, he asked the Lord to give him wisdom. The Lord granted his request (and more), which eventually bore fruit on the pages of Scripture in the book of Proverbs. **Proverbs 3:5** specifically tells us, *"Do not lean on your own understanding,"* instead, trust the Lord to give us all we need.

Desire

I also pray for desire! A prayer for desire is both an earnest prayer and an honest prayer. It's earnest because it asks the Lord to give you a longing and a desire to hear directly from Him in His Word. It's also an honest prayer because it admits that you don't have the level of desire that you know you need to have. How do you pray for this? It could be as simple as, LORD, I DON'T DESIRE YOU THE WAY I OUGHT TO. BUT PLEASE GIVE ME A GREATER DESIRE FOR YOU AND YOUR WORD. I've prayed this prayer many, many times. But it's not magic. There's no formula. It's not about the words; it's about the heart behind it! God desires our joy and delight to be in His revealed Word.

I've been through dry seasons in my spiritual life when I've become so desperate for the Lord that I feel like Jacob in **Genesis 32** when he wrestles with the Lord, saying, *"I will not let you go unless you bless me"* (v. 26). At times, my prayer has been, I WON'T STOP PRAYING UNTIL YOU GIVE ME DESIRE FOR YOUR WORD! But God is not stingy or ungracious; He is faithful. I genuinely believe that this is one prayer that God WILL answer favorably. If you *"pray without ceasing"* **(1 Thess. 5:17)**, God will eventually ignite a spark in your heart that will cause it to burn with fresh desire for His Word. How long will it take until you begin to experience it? It's hard to say. But don't stop praying until He grants your desire.

People do what they enjoy. All too often, we tend to treat our Bible study like a laborious, joyless exercise. It almost becomes like penance for us, a self-flogging exercise that pleases God at the expense of our pain. But may it never be! **Psalm 1:2** notes that a person is blessed whose *"delight is in the law of the Lord, and His law, he meditates day and night."* God desires our joy and delight to be in His revealed Word.

Remember, during Job's sadness and despair, his friend Elihu ministers to him in four speeches. Designed to correct Job's faulty theology, he encourages Job to *"pray to God, and He will accept him, that he may see His face with joy"* **(Job 33:26)**. In many ways, we behold the Lord God as

He reveals Himself in Scripture, and we would do well to pray that when we see Him, we would have joy.

Another aspect of prayer is praying for change. We don't want it to be merely an intellectual exercise when we read and study our Bibles. Indeed, we want to gain understanding and wisdom, but we also need to have the truth and wisdom of Scripture permeate our souls and change us from the inside out. In His High Priestly Prayer, Jesus specifically prayed to the Father for His disciples. Of the many things He asked, He prayed, *"Sanctify them in the truth; Your word is truth"* **(John 17:17)**. To be SANCTIFIED means to be changed and conformed to the image of Christ; it's growing in personal holiness. We understand Jesus' prayer for God to change the disciples from the inside out using His Word.

We would pray for the same thing Jesus prays for—that we would be sanctified, changed from the inside out. We also pray that God would identify sinful behaviors and offenses, bring them to our minds, grant us repentance, and then begin to transform us by renewing our minds with the Scriptures **(Rom. 12:1–2)**. This is what David prays for in **Psalm 139**: *Search me, oh God, and know my heart; try me and know my anxious thoughts; and see if there be any hurtful way in me, and lead me in the everlasting way (Verses 23-24).*

This is nothing short of David's prayer for God to change him. It's an earnest prayer; it's the right prayer. And it's a prayer that can be answered through a deep devotion to studying God's Word.

Interpret

2 Timothy 2:15-16 states, *"*[15]* Study to shew thyself approved unto God, a workman that needeth not to be ashamed, rightly dividing the word of truth.* [16] *But shun profane and vain babblings: for they will increase unto more ungodliness."*

This study process brings us into the world of hermeneutics, exegesis, and the like, along with the dangers of eisegesis. I will do my best to lightly touch on some of the basic theological principles that make up the process of interpretation.

First comes hermeneutics, which is the field of study concerned with the philosophy and science of *interpretation* -- especially the interpretation of *communication*. "Biblical hermeneutics" is specifically concerned with the philosophy and science of interpreting the *Biblical text*. So Biblical hermeneutics would cover all the following sorts of inquiries and more:

- (Theory:) What role does Divine illumination play in the interpretation of Scripture?
- (Methods:) What process can we follow to determine whether an apparent chiasm was intentional by the author?
- (Principles:) What are the limits of the Christocentric Principle?
- Exegesis of the Word.

What is exegesis? This may be a new word to many of you, so let's break it down. Exegesis, as indicated by its *etymology*, is critically interpreting a text to draw the meaning out of it. (This contrasts with what has come to be known as *eisegesis*, where one reads his or her meaning *into* the text. We will discuss that in the following paragraphs.) "Biblical exegesis" is drawing the meaning out of a *Biblical* text. So Biblical exegesis would cover all the following sorts of inquiries and more:

- (Grammar:) Who is it that *"wills"* in 1 Corinthians 12:11?
- (Terminology:) What does *"Under the Sun"* mean in Ecclesiastes?
- (Referent Identification:) Who is the author of Hebrews quoting in Hebrews 10:38?
- (Literary Criticism:) What significance does John perceive in the piercing of Christ's side and the flow of blood and water?

So, what is the relationship between hermeneutics and exegesis? The distinction boils down to this (as it pertains to the Bible): ***Hermeneutics is the field of study concerned with how we interpret the Bible. Exegesis is the actual interpretation of the Bible by drawing the meaning out of the Biblical text.***

The distinction is not quite as simple as "theory vs. application," though, since hermeneutics is not **just** concerned with the philosophy of exegesis, and exegesis is not **merely** the application of hermeneutical theory -- even if we restrict our comparison to *Biblical* hermeneutics and *Biblical* exegesis. Here are a couple of examples to illustrate this:

- Hermeneutics also studies the role of *eisegesis* in interpretation, which is not part of exegesis.
- Hermeneutics considers the role of church doctrine and theology in interpretation -- both are (often) irrelevant to exegesis.

The focus of exegesis is the text. The focus of hermeneutics is stuff *like* exegesis... Why do we do it? How do we do it? How should we do it? As far as sequence, I suppose it could be argued that since exegesis is "critical" in nature, it implies some scientific method, which suggests some prior hermeneutic.

This brings us to eisegesis, the downfall of many students of the Word. In recent decades, a new type of preaching, eisegesis, has cropped up in churches worldwide. Eisegetical preaching is when the preacher or the individual reads **their** ideas into the text, ensuring they find what they seek in a passage of scripture. My brothers and sisters, this is dangerous theology! We must find what God says in the Word, not what we want to be there! To replace the Word of God with our own is theological suicide and comes with severe warnings! **Revelation 22:18-19** is very explicit, *"18 For I testify unto every man that heareth the words of the prophecy of this book, If any man shall add unto these things, God shall add unto him the plagues that are written in this book: 19 And if any man shall take away from the words of the book of this prophecy, God shall take away his part out of the book of life, and out of the holy city, and from the things which are written in this book."*

There is no room for doubt. There is a severe consequence of changing God's Word in any way to fit our wants, needs, and desires. As I state in subsequent chapters of this book, I am not concerned with what you believe. I am not worried about what the world believes. It doesn't even matter what I believe. What matters is what God believes; his Word has endured since the beginning and will endure through the end of the age! That is a fact, not fiction!

Notes

It always helps me to write down some notes or bullet points, especially if I need to be better versed in a given topic. I am not saying you should rewrite the book or chapter you just read; far from it. However, a few carefully placed notes can come in handy when you cross this topic again or come across it in the Bible in some other form.

I want to be very clear here. The Bible does **not** contradict itself. You will find the Word of God always compliments itself, beginning with the Old Testament and following through the end of the book of Revelation. The Old Testament is a compass. It points to the New Testament and our Lord and Savior, Jesus Christ. Take notes! I would be heartbroken if I lost my Bible. It is starting to get that worn leather look, and a few pages are creased. But it contains notes and observations from some of the best sermons I have ever heard and notes to prepare for my sermons.

Now that we have laid the groundwork, let's examine one of the most controversial books in God's Word!

THE APOSTLE JOHN

While the book of Revelation is a book of prophecy that extends all the way into eternity, it is also a highly personal book. John has already given us a brief glimpse of what we can expect as we move through this great book. Now, he begins to record the events and circumstances behind how he obtained the Revelation. In these verses, we are given some insight into the Apostle John and what he was going through when the Lord came to him with this vision.

Let's read from God's Word, starting with **Revelation 1:9-11**.

⁹ I John, who also am your brother, and companion in tribulation, and in the kingdom and patience of Jesus Christ, was in the isle that is called Patmos, for the word of God, and for the testimony of Jesus Christ.
¹⁰ I was in the Spirit on the Lord's day, and heard behind me a great voice, as of a trumpet,
¹¹ Saying, I am Alpha and Omega, the first and the last: and, What thou seest, write in a book, and send it unto the seven churches which are in Asia; unto Ephesus, and unto Smyrna, and unto Pergamos, and unto Thyatira, and unto Sardis, and unto Philadelphia, and unto Laodicea.

As we look at these verses, please keep this thought in mind. People matter to God. This book deals with complex prophecies, extraordinary judgments, and profound truths, yet God still takes the time to give a glimpse of John. So, for just a few minutes, John takes the spotlight in the book of Revelation. Let's examine these verses as we seriously look at John the Apostle. As I do, I want you to see some of the facets this passage reveals concerning John.

The first verse tells us a great deal about the author of this book. This verse answers three great questions concerning the Apostle John or John the Saint. Let's look at these three questions and the answers to them!

As humans, one of the first questions we always ask is, *who is this person?* If we want to know something about the man who wrote this book, this verse gives us some precious insight into who John was.

This is *John the Saint,* and he is none other than the great Apostle himself. John left his father's fishing business to follow Jesus as a teenager (**Matt. 4:21-22**). John followed Jesus throughout the years of His earthly ministry. John was there on snow-capped Mount Hermon when Jesus was transfigured (**Matt. 17**). He was there when Jesus raised the daughter of Jairus from the dead (**Mark 5**). John was so close to Jesus that he laid his head on the Lord's breast at the Last Supper (**John 13**). He was there when Jesus was arrested (**John 18**). He was there as Jesus was tried before the High Priest (**John 18:16**). He was there as Jesus died on the cross (**John 19:26**). John was the recipient of some of Jesus' last words as Jesus died on the cross. He was given the care of the Lord's earthly mother, Mary (**John 19:25-27**). John was at the empty tomb and among the first to believe (**John 20:8**). He was known as the "*beloved disciple*" or "*the disciple whom Jesus loved.*"

For nearly 70 years, John has been a faithful servant to Jesus. He has been a great Pastor to God's people. The Lord has used him to pen the Gospel with his name and three epistles. John is a precious, remarkable man of God. At the writing of Revelation, John is possibly the only living connection to the Lord Jesus Christ (**1 John 1:1**), and this is the man we discuss in this chapter. This is the man God chose to be the conduit through which He would send His Revelation of the end times.

Yet, when the Word of God begins to come his way, John says, "*I, John!*" It is as if he is humbly amazed that God would speak to him, much less through him. Yes, John is a remarkable man! One of the things that made him special is that after all he has seen and experienced, he is still humble and amazed by the grace of God.

The second point here is that he considers himself just a man! While John was the great Apostle and unquestionably one of the greatest Christians alive, he did not view himself in those terms. He addresses his readers as

"*John…your brother.*" Isn't that a blessing? After everything he has seen and been a part of, he still sees himself as just another saint of God.

Take note! This is a lesson for the saints of God! We have been saved by grace and allowed to experience some of the greatest blessings known to man. God has been good to us, and He has even used some reading this book for His glory. When that happens, there is a human tendency to want to glory in who we are and what we have done. We must remember that we were nothing when Jesus found and saved us, and we will never be anything apart from Him. Paul said it well: "***But by the grace of God I am what I am***" (**1 Cor. 15:10**).

One of the reasons the Lord used John in such a grand fashion was because John remained a humble servant. He will use us if we can remember where we came from and the source of our power (**James 4:6; 10; 1 Pet. 5:5-6**.)

Take note here. These verses remind us that the preacher is not greater than the people! I believe the man of God ought to be respected for the sake of his call and for the Word he preaches, but he is not above the rest of the church's members. Far too many congregations have degenerated into a cult of preacher worship. When that happens, and a man is given absolute power in a church, the result is sin. The 19th-century British politician Lord Acton is credited with saying, "***If power corrupts, then absolute power corrupts absolutely.***" The Lord must remain the Head of His church because He is incorruptible.

The third point is that John also identifies himself as a "*companion in tribulation.*" John is writing to saints who are suffering for the cause of Christ. They are being smitten by the harsh lash of their Roman rulers. True believers in that day paid a terrible price for their faith in the Lord Jesus Christ. It must have comforted their hearts to know that even the greatest among them was also bearing his cross for the glory of the Lord. No one said serving Jesus would always be easy. Jesus said exactly the opposite. The average Christian life is described as a life that includes self-denial, self-death, and cross-bearing (**Matt. 16:24**). Believers of all ages are warned about the cost of serving Jesus (**2 Tim. 3:12**).

We are living in a blessed time. Yet, Christians are being persecuted for their faith. If you will keep your eyes on the world news, it is becoming increasingly clear that Christianity is under attack. Every year in our world, thousands of Christians are still being martyred for their faith. In our own country, our government continues to push morality to the back burner, and in its place is socially inclusive behavior that violates the Word of God and makes a mockery of Christianity. Christians may yet pay the price for their beliefs in America. It's up to us as the people of this great nation to make our opinions and beliefs known and to support those who support the Word of God. However, the day of persecution could come sooner than later for America. We must ensure we are ready to pay the price.

Finally, as we discover who John is, we see he is also a servant. When John uses the phrase *"companion ... in the kingdom and patience of Jesus Christ"*, he uses language that identifies him as one who is waiting and watching for the coming of the Lord Jesus Christ. The word *"kingdom"* refers to the work. The word *"patience"* refers to the wait. John is faithfully working for Jesus and waiting for Him to return. Just because John is an elderly man does not mean that he has stopped serving. He is still working for the Lord. He is still looking for the Lord. He is still a witness to the Lord. This is an example of how we should live our lives. There is no place to stop, no place to quit, no place to sit down and do nothing. Until the Lord comes for us, we must be determined to live every moment for His glory, in His service, and looking for His appearance. After all, that is why He saved us (**Eph. 2:10**).

Now that we understand who John is, let's answer the question of where John is. After telling us who he is, John tells us where he is when this Revelation comes his way. He is *"in the isle that is called Patmos."* Patmos is a small island in the Aegean Sea, about 30 miles from Ephesus. The island is about 10 miles long and 6 miles wide. It is formed from rough, volcanic rock and was used by the Romans in John's time as a prison. Prisoners were sent there to work in the copper mines.

Patmos was not an ideal destination. Those sentenced there suffered horribly! They did not have adequate clothing, food, or shelter. They were forced to sleep out in the open on the bare rocks. They were forced to work in the mines, and they suffered terribly under the brutal whip of their Roman guards.

That is where John is when he receives the Revelation. This

reminds us that God can use even the most terrible circumstances in our lives for His glory and our good (**Rom. 8:28**).

Then comes the question of Why? The Bible tells us that John was banished to Patmos. Tradition also tells us before Emperor Domitian banished John to Patmos, he tried to kill him by placing him in boiling oil. John survived that and was sent away to eliminate him (and his message). They couldn't kill him, so they tried to get rid of him, not realizing that God was going to go with him and use him in the greatest possible way.

Why was this poor man, who is at least 90 years old, sent to that harsh island prison camp? For several reasons, believers in that day were hated and treated so viciously by the Romans. Let's look at a few of them.

- **They were hated for Political reasons** – The Roman Emperors were worshiped as gods by their citizens. Romans were required to enter a temple dedicated to the Caesars, and they were required to take a pinch of incense, place it on an altar, and say, "*Caesar is Lord!*" Christians refused to do this, and they were persecuted as a result.
- **They were hated for religious reasons** – The Romans also worshiped a pantheon of gods represented by idols. Christians refused to recognize the Roman gods. The superstitious Romans believed that Christian refusals were to blame for natural disasters, plagues, wars, famines, etc. For the first few decades after the death of Jesus, Christians were seen as being just another branch of Judaism. But, when the Romans saw the hatred the Jews possessed for the Christians, the Romans saw Christianity as a distinct religion. Since it was against the law to form a new religion, Christianity was outlawed, and Christians became outlaws and the targets of intense persecution.
- **They were hated for Social reasons** – Roman society was built on a very rigid class system. The upper crust had little to do with the lower classes. Christians taught that all men were equal in the eyes of God. This threatened to undermine the social structure of Rome, and Christians were persecuted for it, too. Christians also refused to

attend the Roman games, festivals, and other functions of that pagan society. The fact that they chose to be a separate people marked them for hatred.

- **They were hated for economic reasons** – Because the Christians did not worship idols and even preached against idols, their doctrine hurt the business of the priests, craftsmen, and merchants who made their living from idol worship.

John was singled out for persecution by the Roman Emperor Domitian because of the words John preached. John preached the truth instead of preaching a message pleasing to the Romans. He condemned sin, and he preached the Gospel. Both brought the fury of Rome down upon him. The thorn in their flesh was John's insistence that Jesus Christ was the Son of God. He preached Jesus crucified and risen from the dead. John preached Jesus as the only way to salvation. He condemned the Roman gods, the Roman way of life, rulers, and society. He pointed men to Jesus, and he was hated for it!

Today, we enjoy the freedom to worship in this nation. A preacher can step into a pulpit and preach anything they want from the Bible and are protected under our nation's laws. But there is a day coming in America when it will be considered illegal to preach against certain sins and when it will be unlawful to condemn society, government, and false religion. There is a day when it will be a crime even to quote **John 14:6**. I pray those saved by Jesus will have the courage to face it like John and the rest of the Apostles did!

We have seen the testimony of *John the Saint*. Now, let's look at *John the Worshiper*. John is 90 years old, banished to an island prison, forced to labor in the mines, and subjected to the most horrible of circumstances. But what is John doing? He is worshiping! Let's look at three points about *John the Worshipper*!

He is 90 years old, and he is still worshiping! A lesser man might have said, *"I've paid my dues! Let somebody else carry the load for a while. I've preached the gospel. I've visited the sick. I've taught Sunday School. I'm done!"* Let me tell you right now: if you are a child of God, you need to know that there will not come a day when you can stop being a worshiper. God expects us to come into His presence to worship for as long as He gives us the ability to do so. If you don't like worshipping God, you are going to be very miserable in eternity.

I praise God for older Christians. You are an inspiration and a challenge to those who may be just starting their walk with Christ. Regardless of age, arthritis, and adversity, you are so faithful to come to the house of God. We can learn a lot from senior saints! When you prioritize Jesus, worship will come easy to you!

Let's look at John's circumstances. John is not staying at the Ritz Carlton in Pentagon City! It is the Patmos Motel where he humbles himself in worship. He is not sitting on a padded pew in a heated, air-conditioned building. He is in prison! He is suffering. He is cold. He is hungry. But, despite all that he is facing, he is still worshiping! Some might have said, "Serving the Lord doesn't pay off. I have been faithful to Him and look at where it got me. I am going to quit! There is no use!" But not John! Despite his condition, he goes before the Lord in worship.

Modern believers could use a dose of John's faith and commitment! It doesn't take a lot to keep the modern Christian out of church. A little pain, a little problem, a little hurt feeling, and they are gone! They can lay out of church and not think a thing about it!

Many years ago, in a place far away from Tennessee, I had an *MH-6 Little Bird* helicopter shot out from under me. Most of my family, except for my wife and mother, don't know about some of the things I did for our nation. I was young. We were taught ways to suppress what we did and I didn't think as much about it then. But as I became older and suffered other injuries, the reality of some of my injuries (physical and spiritual) began to sink in. There are some Sunday mornings when my back feels like it is screaming as the pain shoots down my spine and into my legs. Even as I write this book, I am facing surgery on my right ankle that will take many months to completely heal. Somehow, I make it to church anyway. My logic has always been this. If Jesus can suffer all the pain, injustice, and suffering for me and walk *The Way of Sorrows,* I will go to church to worship him if I can get inside. This isn't about how great I am! It is about how great HE IS, so let's keep our eyes on him!

I praise the Lord for those saints who are determined to worship God at every opportunity. I appreciate those saints who are not looking for what they can *"get"* at church but are interested in what they can *"give"*. Thank God for those who love to worship their Lord.

Let's consider the commitment that John had toward the Lord! Look at what the verse says, *"I was in the Spirit on the Lord's Day"* and what that means. Some refer to "the Lord's Day" as *"the day of the Lord"* when Jesus will come to this earth in power and glory. They take it to mean that John was *"transported"* into the future to the very day of the Lord. Jesus said to Peter, *"If I will that he tarries till I come, what is that to thee?"* (**John 21:22**). Some people think this is a reference to that verse. I think it refers to *"the Lord's Day."* I think the Bible says that John found a place to worship on Patmos. Then, one Sunday, when John was in worship, this Revelation came to him. We never know what the Lord is going to do and when He is going to show up.

Despite everything John faced on that remote island, he rose above it all and found himself in the presence of the Lord for worship. We are told that he was *"in the spirit."* John's physical location was the island of Patmos, but his spiritual location was in the presence of the Lord. John occupied two worlds at once.

Now, let's visit *John the Writer*. As John worshiped, the Lord Himself visited him. When the Lord spoke, His voice sounded like a "trumpet." It was a sound that got John's instant attention. As we move through the pages of Revelation, we will hear more trumpets sounding. Each one introduces some solemn event. This particular voice summons John to listen and to write down what he hears.

This heavenly visitor and the words He says reminds us that what we are reading and studying together is not a book written by a man. John was merely the penman. The author of this book, along with every other book in the Bible, is the Lord Himself. (**2 Tim. 3:16**).

If we examine the destination of his writing, we see that Revelation is to be sent to the seven churches named in this verse. Let me remind you that these churches are fundamental, literal churches. John was to send his letter directly to them. These churches are also representative of THE CHURCH as a whole. This Revelation is not just for those churches that existed in that age; they are also a message to us in our day. While we are here, let me remind you there were never supposed to be multiple denominations or versions of religion. From the beginning, there was to be only one. It was mankind that split the churches like a ripe southern watermelon dropped from the back of a pickup truck!

God has something to say to every church that has ever existed in this letter, to every individual in those churches, and to you and to me.

If you look at the divisions of his writing, we see the divinely inspired outline of the book of Revelation. This verse reveals how we are to divide and interpret this book. To refresh our memories, this verse breaks the book of Revelation into three clearly defined divisions. They are:

- *The things which thou hast seen* – The events of **chapter 1**
- *The things which are* – The events of **chapters 2-3**
- *The things which shall be hereafter* – **The events of chapter 4-22.**

Now, some of you may wonder where I got the idea that **chapter 4** marks a major division of this book. The answer is found in the word *"hereafter."* This word translates into two Greek words. They are *"meta"* and *"tauta"*. *"Meta"* means *"after,"* and *"tauta" means "these."* This two-word combination is also found in the first verse of chapter 4, where the Bible says, "After this..." In other words, the Bible indicates, that chapter 4 is the dividing line between *"the things which are"* and *"the things which shall be hereafter."*

As we study, I want you to keep a general timeframe in mind that divides the book. This is an important view to remember as we move forward and one that is referred to consistently!

	Four Ages in Revelation	
Chapters	**Age**	**Years**
Chapter 1-3	Church Age	7 years
Chapter 4-19	Tribulation Age	7 years
Chapter 20	Kingdom Age	1000 years
Chapter 21-22	Eternal Age	Endless

I hope you have enjoyed this background on the Apostle John from the biblical passage. It lets us glimpse the work he is being called to do. Understanding who John was, why he did what he did, and the kind of heart he possessed for the Lord Jesus will help us as we continue our study of *The Final Countdown*!

THE TRUTH ABOUT HELL

God had a reason for wanting my first sermon on The Final Countdown to be a study on Hell. There is good cause. A 2023 Gallup Poll reveals earth-shattering (literally) information about Americans and who they believe in, or more concisely, what they do NOT believe in. Consider the chart below.

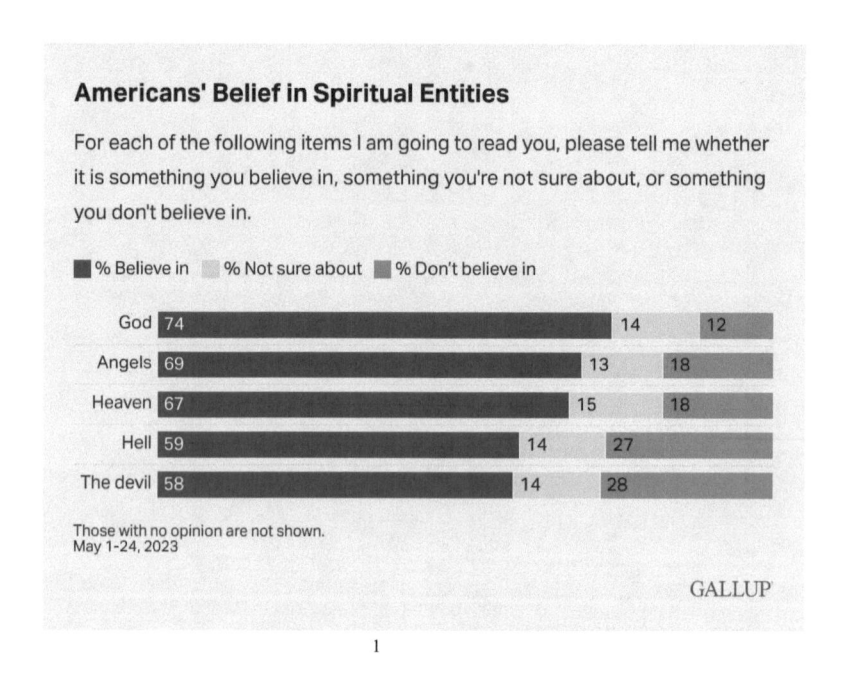

Americans' Belief in Spiritual Entities

For each of the following items I am going to read you, please tell me whether it is something you believe in, something you're not sure about, or something you don't believe in.

	% Believe in	% Not sure about	% Don't believe in
God	74	14	12
Angels	69	13	18
Heaven	67	15	18
Hell	59	14	27
The devil	58	14	28

Those with no opinion are not shown.
May 1-24, 2023

GALLUP

The percentages of Americans who believe in each of five religious' entities—God, angels, heaven, hell, and the devil—have edged downward by three to five percentage points since 2016. Still, majorities believe in each, ranging from a high of 74% believing in God to lows of 59% for hell and 58% for the devil. About two-thirds believe in angels (69%) and heaven

---

[1] Gallup Poll July 20, 2023

(67%).

Gallup has documented sharp declines in church attendance, confidence in organized religion, and religious identification in recent years. Americans' beliefs regarding God, angels, heaven, hell, and the devil have also fallen by double digits since 2001. Still, U.S. adults believe in each entity at the majority level, and regular churchgoers remain largely unwavering in their beliefs. **Look at this poll! Only 59% of Americans believe in hell.** God knew what he was doing when he asked me to establish this baseline. I'm going to go one step further here. If you do not believe in hell, why would you need salvation? You would have nothing that you need to be saved **from**! I strongly encourage you to ask the question of your family members gently. Do 41% of your family members deny the existence of hell? Just a thought!

Our text for this chapter comes from Luke 16:19-31. We will look at this scripture in detail! As we enter this chapter, you must understand the Final Countdown has already started and the clock has been ticking since roughly 4 or 6 BC. The clock began ticking with the birth of Jesus Christ.

In this chapter, I will discuss one of today's most tiptoed-around topics in theology. By the time we are finished, some of you will close this book and never reread it. Others will come back for more. I pray you will listen with an open heart as God speaks to you through me.

In this chapter, I will let you in on a little secret!!! HELL IS REAL!

Imagine life if you had none of the beautiful things that accompany our modern world. This world is a wonderful place, and this is an awesome time to be alive, but along with our blessings and the things we enjoy here, some things in our modern world are anything but good. One of the worst things that have come about in the modern world is skepticism concerning the things of God, especially those things written in the Bible. Many today have no confidence in the truth of the Word of God. **Be that as it may, the Bible is still God's Word; it is still divinely inspired and believable in every aspect.**

Perhaps no other teaching has received more doubt than the one you are reading about today, the doctrine of Hell. If someone still believes in Hell, they may be called old-fashioned, out of touch, out of step with reality, foolish, and ignorant. Many, appealing to rationality and reason, tell us that the concept of an eternal hell where sinners burn forever is ludicrous and demeaning. Others appealing to the nature of God will say that it flies in the face of everything God is to teach that He will consign some people to Hell.

Still, others turning to religion tell us that man can redeem himself, and therefore, every man is working out his heaven, and there will be hell for no one. The cultists, without exception, have all concocted a plan whereby they and their followers can escape eternal damnation and live joyfully in a better world. That sounds pretty good, but it is a lie!

Today, I am not concerned with what you believe about Hell. I am not concerned with what the world believes about Hell. I am not concerned even with what the church I attend <u>believes</u> about Hell. Our focus today will be this, **"What does God believe about Hell?"** Because in the end, it won't matter what we think; the Scriptures will be proven correct, and every philosophy and opinion of man will perish.

Therefore, we will discuss The Truth About Hell as God gives liberty. If you are going there, this is your wake-up call and your opportunity to do something about it. If you are saved, this is a reminder that billions are hell-bound. Here is the truth about Hell. And amidst all of this, the FINAL COUNTDOWN has begun. The clock is ticking!

Our core text in this chapter is taken from the book of **Luke, Chapter 16:19-31.**

> *[19] There was a certain rich man, which was clothed in purple and fine linen, and fared sumptuously every day:*
> *[20] And there was a certain beggar named Lazarus, which was laid at his gate, full of sores,*
> *[21] And desiring to be fed with the crumbs which fell from the rich man's table: moreover the dogs came and licked his sores.*
> *[22] And it came to pass, that the beggar died, and was carried by the angels into Abraham's bosom: the rich man also died, and was buried; [23] And in hell he lift up his eyes, being in torments, and seeth Abraham afar off, and Lazarus in his bosom. [24] And he cried and said, Father Abraham, have mercy on me, and send Lazarus, that he may dip the tip of his finger in water, and cool my tongue; for I am tormented in this flame. [25] But Abraham said, Son,*

remember that thou in thy lifetime receivedst thy good things, and likewise Lazarus evil things: but now he is comforted, and thou art tormented. [26] And beside all this, between us and you there is a great gulf fixed: so that they which would pass from hence to you cannot; neither can they pass to us, that would come from thence. [27] Then he said, I pray thee therefore, father, that thou wouldest send him to my father's house: [28] For I have five brethren; that he may testify unto them, lest they also come into this place of torment. [29] Abraham saith unto him, They have Moses and the prophets; let them hear them. [30] And he said, Nay, father Abraham: but if one went unto them from the dead, they will repent. [31] And he said unto him, If they hear not Moses and the prophets, neither will they be persuaded, though one rose from the dead.

Look at **verses 23 and 28** from the scripture. Hell is a real place. This text treats Hell as being as real as any other geographic location. It is as accurate as "Abraham's bosom" – Heaven! You cannot have one without the other! Refer to the Gallup poll I included in this chapter. that showed 67% of Americans believed in Heaven, while only 59% believed in Hell! Can you believe that? At the risk of being repetitious, you cannot have one without the other.

It is important to understand that Jesus believed in Hell. Read **Luke 16:19-31** and **Mark 9:43-48**. **Mark 9:43-48** says:

[43] If your hand causes you to stumble, cut it off. It is better for you to enter life maimed than with two hands to go into hell, where the fire never goes out. [44] [b] [45] And if your foot causes you to stumble, cut it off. It is better for you to enter life crippled than to have two feet and be thrown into hell. [46] [c] [47] And if your eye causes you to stumble, pluck it out. It is better for you to enter the kingdom of God with one eye than to have two eyes and be thrown into hell, [48] where the worms that eat them do not die, and the fire is not quenched. [49] Everyone will be salted with fire.

Oh yes, JESUS believed in HELL!

Where is Hell? What is the difference between Hell, Hades, and Gehenna? Let's look at the differences between these. The god (little g) Molech and the valley of Himmon play a significant role in our understanding.

Molech (or Moloch) was the national god of the Ammonites, whose land bordered Israel's territory east of Jordan. A well-known feature of the worship of Molech was the sacrifice of children by fire. This practice in Israel carried the death penalty **(Leviticus 18:21, Leviticus 20:2-5, 2 Kings 23:10, Jeremiah 32:35)**. The Valley of Hinnon, Gehinnom, or Gehenna is a historic valley surrounding Ancient Jerusalem from the west and southwest. King Ahaz of Judah sacrificed his illegitimate sons in the valley. The phrase used to describe the sacrifice in the Bible is *"cause his children to pass through the fire."*

The valley of Gehenna is where Israel sacrificed their children to the god Molech. Later, after God outlawed the practice, the Israelites continued to burn their trash and the carcasses of dead animals in this valley. It was said this was where the fires never went out due to this practice. Gehenna would have been a place where the target audience would have understood the practice of burning. Gehenna was perpetually on fire, and thus, Jesus uses it as an image of hell. It was an illustration his target audience would have understood. Many English translations recognize the place as obviously referring to hell, and thus, if you look in your ESV, you will see it even translated as "hell." **James 3:6** uses "Gehenna" as a prominent idiom for hell.

In the Old Testament, the righteous and unrighteous went to Sheol, which contained realms of suffering for the unrighteous and rest/worship for the righteous. The New Testament refers to this as Hades. However, when Jesus rose from the grave, he emptied Sheol/Hades of the righteous, and now, when Christians die, they do not go DOWN to Sheol/Hades but UP to heaven. Meanwhile, the unrighteous are left in Hades until the final judgment, when they are then resurrected, given new bodies, and cast into the fires of hell/Gehenna forever.

So now that we have established the Valley of Gehenna, let's look at the differences between the Old Testament and New Testament views of Hell. Take note of the following passages **(Matt. 8:12; 22:13; 25:30; 2 Pet.**

2:17; Jude 1:13.) You can read these at your leisure. All these verses teach that Hell will be outer (away from) darkness. This is the reality of Hell – It is absolute, eternal separation from the presence of God.

2 Thessalonians. 1:8-9 says, *"[8] He will punish those who do not know God and do not obey the gospel of our Lord Jesus. [9] They will be punished with everlasting destruction and shut out from the presence of the Lord and from the glory of his might (NIV)."* I think this scripture is clear. Those in Hell will be separated from God for all eternity. Can you imagine your body burning for eternity but never being consumed by fire? There is no hope. All you have is eternal, unbelievable anguish! To make matters worse, there is nobody you can pray to, nobody to offer you salvation from this anguish, because the time for redemption is now past.

To understand what Hell is, we must understand the differences between the Old and New Testament views of HELL.

SO WHAT IS SHEOL (SHE-OLL)? The Old Testament speaks of Sheol as the "realm of the dead," including both the saved and the lost. Consider these Bible verses:

Genesis 37:35 NIV
All his sons and daughters came to comfort him, but he refused to be comforted. "No," he said, "I will continue to mourn until I join my son in the grave." So his father wept for him.

Ecclesiastes 9:10 NIV
Whatever your hand finds to do, do it with all your might, for in the realm of the dead, where you are going, there is neither working nor planning nor knowledge nor wisdom.

Psalm 16:10 NIV
because you will not abandon me to the realm of the dead, nor will you let your faithful one see decay.

Acts 2:31 NIV
Seeing what was to come, he spoke of the resurrection of the Messiah, that he was not abandoned to the realm of the dead, nor

did his body see decay.

Psalm 55:15 NIV
Let death take my enemies by surprise; let them go down alive to the realm of the dead, for evil finds lodging among them.

Jonah 2:2 NIV
He said:"In my distress I called to the LORD and he answered me. From deep in the realm of the dead I called for help, and you listened to my cry.

Luke 16:23 NIV
In Hades, where he was in torment, he looked up and saw Abraham far away, with Lazarus by his side.

Psalm 86:13 NIV
For great is your love toward me; you have delivered me from the depths, from the realm of the dead.

Hosea 13:14 NIV
I will deliver this people from the power of the grave; I will redeem them from death. Where, O death, are your plagues? Where, O grave, is your destruction? I will have no compassion,

Job 14:13 NIV
If only you would hide me in the grave and conceal me till your anger has passed! If only you would set me a time and then remember me!

There are more, but that is a good start. For example, consider the patriarch Jacob, who thought of himself as going to *Sheol* when he died. *Sheol* is not only where patriarchs go, but it is also spoken of as the realm to which those who die, absent saving faith, descend. For example, Moses declared that when people who "***despised Yahweh***" descend into Sheol **(Numbers 16:20). Deuteronomy 32:22** speaks of Sheol as the realm of the fire of God's judgment. It is best to understand Sheol as the term for "realm of the dead," where both righteous and unrighteous went when they died. The best proof for this inclusive concept of Sheol is that David thought of himself going to Sheol **(2 Sam 22:6)**, and yet he also taught that the wicked go there as well **(Psalm 31:17)**. Thus, Sheol refers to the realm where the souls of all dead went at death.

You'll notice I said, "went." I used the past tense because, for the righteous, Sheol was an Old Testament concept. Because Jesus is truly human, he experienced death as all humans do. He, too, descended to Sheol and proclaimed victory over the grave by liberating the souls of the righteous and bringing them to heaven. Thus, when church-age believers die, they do not go to Sheol but rather to heaven to be with the Lord forever **(1 Thess 4:17)**.

HADES is a New Testament (Greek) term used to refer to Sheol. Hades/Sheol refers to the same place, but there is a noticeable difference in how the Old and New Testaments speak of Sheol/Hades. The Old Testament speaks of Sheol inclusively, and even the righteous dead descend there. However, because of Jesus' victory over death and the liberty he brings to the righteous in Sheol, Jesus does not teach that believers go to Hades, but rather that believers will be with him in heaven **(John 14:2-3)**.

For that reason, the New Testament emphasizes Hades as a place of suffering and judgment **(Matt 11:23, Luke 10:15, Luke 16:23)**. Even so, it is still the same location as Sheol and does refer to the place where the righteous Old Testament saints went at their deaths. This is made clear when Peter says that Jesus descended to Hades when he died, while the Old Testament speaks of him descending to Sheol (compare **Acts 2:27 and 31** with **Psalm 16:10)**.

Let's look at them again.

Acts 2:27 — The New International Version (NIV)
^{27} because you will not abandon me to the realm of the dead, you will not let your holy one see decay.

Acts 2:31 — The New International Version (NIV)
^{31} Seeing what was to come, he spoke of the resurrection of the

Messiah, that he was not abandoned to the realm of the dead, nor did his body see decay.

Psalm 16:10 — The New International Version (NIV)
[10] because you will not abandon me to the realm of the dead, nor will you let your faithful one see decay.

Don't tell me the Old Testament has no bearing on the New Testament, as some religious theologians say. The Old Testament points the way to the future, the future that brings in the Lord Jesus Christ!

Ultimately, Jesus has authority over Sheol/Hades. **Revelation 1:18** says, *[18] I am the Living One; I was dead, and now look, I am alive for ever and ever! And I hold the keys of death, and Hades.*

Do we need to read that passage again? Christ *"has the keys to death and Hades,"* which is another way of saying he can bind or free people from there as he pleases. Of course, he frees all the saints there at his resurrection and then uses his keys again to empty Sheol by casting the damned souls there into the lake of fire. **Revelation 20:13-14** demonstrates this as it notes, *[13] The sea gave up the dead in it, and death and Hades gave up the dead that were in them, and each person was judged according to what they had done. [14] Then death and Hades were thrown into the lake of fire. The lake of fire is the second death.*

Another image to keep in mind is that Hell will be filled with real people. In verse 22 of **Luke, Chapter 16:19-31**, we see an image of a wealthy man. This man was some mother's son. Possibly, he left a wife and children behind. We don't know. He certainly had brothers who were on his mind, as we can see from verse 28. So, we know he was a mother's son. He was a father's son. He may have been a father. He was someone's brother. Here is the sad fact. People you know, and people I know will populate Hell. It may be those of your household that die and go there.

Hell wasn't made for men, as we see in **Matt. 25:41**, but those who reject Jesus Christ as their personal Savior will go there! Matthew illustrates this in **Matt. 7:21-23**. It is illustrated again in **Revelation 15:11-15**. Hell will be filled with real people. These will be people who said no to God.

Will you be among them? Who do you know that will be? These are tough questions. I hope you have the right answers. Eternity is a long time!

In **verse 22 of Luke, Chapter 16:23-25** we see that Hell contains real punishment. *[23] And in hell he lift up his eyes, being in torments, and seeth Abraham afar off, and Lazarus in his bosom. [24] And he cried and said, Father Abraham, have mercy on me, and send Lazarus, that he may dip the tip of his finger in water, and cool my tongue; for I am tormented in this flame. [25] But Abraham said, Son, remember that thou in thy lifetime receivedst thy good things, and likewise Lazarus evil things: but now he is comforted, and thou art tormented.*

Look at the language that is used. It couldn't be any plainer that Hell is a place of pain and torment. I have heard some very educated men claim this language is symbolic —They had better hope not! Symbolism is only used when conventional language is inadequate to describe something. The reality is always much worse than the symbol!

Here are some reminders about the real torments that Hell contains:

1. **Unquenchable Fire** – Mark 9:43; Luke 16:24
2. **Memory and remorse** – Ill. Rich man – "Son remember" 25, 27-28
3. **Intense, unsatisfied thirst** – Luke 16:24-25
4. **Misery and pain** – Luke 16:24-26; Rev. 14:10-11
5. **Frustration and anger** – Luke. 13:28; Matt. 24:51
6. **Eternal separation** – Rev. 21:8 – From what? Everything beautiful!
7. **Undiluted wrath** –Hab. 3:21 In Hell, God's fury will be unleashed!

Hell is a permanent sentence. There is no parole. Once you are in Hell, you can never be released. The rich man was told that he had to stay there. He is still there today! If you die without Jesus Christ, you will most certainly go to Hell! If you go to Hell, you will be there forever, with one little exception. That is the Judgment of the Dead and The Great White Throne Judgment.

Revelation 20:11-15 gives us a detailed view of this event. *[11] Then*

I saw a great white throne and him who was seated on it. The earth and the heavens fled from his presence, and there was no place for them. [12] And I saw the dead, great and small, standing before the throne, and books were opened. Another book was opened, which is the book of life. The dead were judged according to what they had done as recorded in the books. [13] The sea gave up the dead that were in it, and death and Hades gave up the dead that were in them, and each person was judged according to what they had done. [14] Then death and Hades were thrown into the lake of fire. The lake of fire is the second death. [15] Anyone whose name was not found written in the book of life was thrown into the lake of fire.

Can you imagine standing before Christ at that moment, viewing His glory as He sits on His throne, seeing these pitiful people screaming and crying because they know what is coming? Some may be cursing, aware that soon, searing flames will scorch their body. Some may be waiting anxiously as they are judged, *hoping* there was a mistake, and their name will be written in *The Book of Life*. After all, compared to the works of some of these that stand in judgment, perhaps you weren't *that bad*. Sometimes, you give money to homeless people on the street. You were good to your children. You went to church. You sang in the choir.

The judgment is done. You may have a chance to plead your case. I don't know if you will or not. But think about it. It's your turn. You say, "*Lord, Lord, have I not prophesied in your name? And in your name have cast out devils? And in your name done many wonderful works?*"

There is silence. You think about the times God called you to the altar. How many times did he plead for you to accept his son Jesus? You knew it was many. But something stopped you each time. You depended on your good deeds to balance your life. After all, you didn't want to be embarrassed or people to *think* you weren't the Christian man or woman you portrayed yourself to be. You were a Sunday School teacher, for goodness' sake!

And then the silence is broken. The figure on the throne prepares to speak. You know who it is. This is the Lion of Judah. This is the lamb slain from the foundation of the world. This voice does not sound like a lamb. Instead, it is the voice of a king. It is a king offering a sentence on a condemned subject. The voice is authoritative and intense. Maybe you think you hear a little pain in the voice. After all, He remembers what it is like to be human and tempted. **Yet he committed no sin.** You remember **Romans 8:34**, where the writer says, *"⁴ Who then is the one who condemns? No one. Christ Jesus who died—more than that, who was raised to life—is at the right hand of God and is also interceding for us"*. You think to yourself, "Is he still interceding for me?"

He says, "Depart from me, ye that work iniquity. I never knew you!"

And then there is that final agony where you know you have been tried, sentenced, and found guilty. All you had to do was to accept Jesus Christ as your Lord and Saviour. You refused. You will now spend eternity in hell in everlasting torment and without God!

Let's look at what hell is not! Hell is not annihilation! Look at **Rev. 19:20**. *²⁰ But the beast was captured, and with it the false prophet who had performed the signs on its behalf. With these signs, he deluded those who had received the mark of the beast and worshiped its image. The <u>two of them were thrown alive</u> into the fiery lake of burning sulphur.*

Hell is not a temporary place of purging (i.e. purgatory). And no, you cannot buy a shorter time in hell by giving money to the church. Hell is not the grave. Hell is not a parable, and it is not a scare tactic. It is reality, and it is waiting on you if you are outside Jesus Christ today!

We have discussed this terrible place that was never designed for mankind to go. But there is a bright place in all this. Hell can be avoided through an absolute promise. The rich man is told the Word of God holds the answer. It still does. It tells us of God's love for sinners. John 3:16 says, *"¹⁶ For God so loved the world that he gave his one and only Son, that whoever believes in him shall not perish but have eternal life."*

God's word shows us Christ died to save us. **Romans 5:8** tells us, *"⁸ But God demonstrates his own love for us in this: While we were still sinners, Christ died for us."*

God's word continues to tell us of Christ's resurrection that guarantees eternal life to all who come to him by faith. **John 11:25-26** says, *"²⁵ Jesus said to her, 'I am the resurrection and the life. The one who believes in me will live, even though they die; ²⁶ and whoever lives by believing in me will never die. Do you believe this?'"*

The Bible tells of a God who will save all who come to Him by His grace.

The subsequent chapters will discuss more of The Final Countdown, as God laid on my heart to share. But to get there, we had to establish a common ground. HELL IS REAL! PEOPLE YOU LOVE WILL GO TO HELL UNLESS YOU ARE WILLING TO DO SOMETHING ABOUT IT!

Are you outside God's will? Have you accepted Jesus Christ as your saviour and Lord?

I read this chapter to a friend of mine. He momentarily contemplated and said, "Preacher, I think you are just trying to scare me! I replied, "I pray to God that this chapter did scare you! I pray it scared you enough to turn to repentance and salvation!"

Are you already a child of God? Are you? Or are you one of those who doesn't believe in hell? If so, I would ask you to rethink your salvation. Logic says there is no need to accept Jesus as Lord and Saviour when there is nothing to save us from! If you don't believe in hell, do you believe in Jesus? I think not!

If you are truly a child of God but have not followed Him and told others of the message of salvation, I would ask that you rethink HIS plan for YOUR life. I hope you read through the rest of this book. I pray it will bless you!

UNVEILING REVELATION

Well, the previous chapter gave you your baseline. This is precisely how God placed it on my heart and how I preached it across the United States and in 136 countries. Hell is a real place, and people **you know** are going there. Some of you still wonder why I gave Hell such an essential part in this book. It's the **G card.** Remember what I told you in the first chapter? God is God, and if he wants Hell placed first, then that is the way it's going to be. One listener told me he thought I was trying to scare him. I replied that I was trying to scare him and prayed this message did just that. I don't understand how a lost individual could read the things in Revelation without shaking or quaking from fear.

Now that we know where we do not want to spend eternity, let's look at the Book of Revelation. In this study, we are going to embark on an exciting adventure. We are going to study the book of *The Revelation of Jesus Christ*. This is a beautiful book. It has been misunderstood, misrepresented, and misinterpreted by many. The book of Revelation has been avoided because many seem to believe that it cannot be understood and that reading, studying, and preaching from it will only lead to confusion. That is sad because anyone who studies the Revelation will soon discover that it is not hard to comprehend. The book will only be unclear to the unbeliever, **Luke 8:10; 1 Cor. 2:14.** The diligent student will soon discover that Jesus Christ is more clearly revealed here than He is anywhere else in the Word of God. This is not a book to be avoided; it is a book to be read and studied.

So, beginning today, I want us to take a trip. Not a trip to any geographical location but a trip to the future. I intend to move through this beautiful book paragraph by paragraph and bring you a series of truths about your future.

As part of our introduction, I want to call to your attention the four methods of interpretation people take when they approach the book of Revelation. How you approach this book will determine how you interpret it, and how you interpret it will determine what you will receive from it. There are four primary interpretations of the Book of Revelation. They are:

The Preterist Interpretation – This view sees the events recorded in Revelation as a historical record of the events of the first century. This view requires a belief that Jesus has already returned to the earth, and it ignores the fact that Revelation claims that much of its content is prophetic. **(Rev 1:3; 22:7, 10, 18-19.)**

The Idealist Interpretation – This is the liberal view. The idealist looks at the Revelation as a collection of allegories and stories designed to depict the struggle between good and evil. This view does not see the events of the Revelation as actual events but as mere myths and fables.

The Historicist Interpretation – This view considers the Revelation a sweeping overview of church history. It sees this book as a church history timeline from the apostolic era to the present. Most of the events in the book under this interpretation are viewed as past events. Those who hold to this school of interpretation often spiritualize the text and view it as a pure allegory. This view ignores the book's claims to be prophecy and offers odd interpretations and strange applications of the text.

The Futurist Interpretation – This view looks at the book of Revelation and sees most events as future in nature. This view holds that the book of Revelation is primarily prophetic in nature. This view takes a literal approach to interpretation. The futurist interpretation allows all the events of the Revelation to be actual events. The people, places, and occurrences are not spiritualized and relegated to allegory and myth. Everything the book says, from the church's rapture to the Lord Jesus's second coming to a literal millennial kingdom, is seen as a natural, actual, future event. This is the only school of interpretation that allows the book of Revelation to be considered as it is written and for the clearly stated purpose for which it was written. **(Rev 1:1, 3.)** This is the path of interpretation that we will follow for our study. Here are a few quick thoughts to set the stage for studying this book.

Date: **95 AD** – Many liberals try to date it later, but there is no evidence for their claims and strong evidence to date this book in the first century.

Author: **John the Beloved**, the same Apostle who penned the Gospel and the three epistles with his name. This is not disputed as it is clearly stated several times: (Rev **1:1, 4, 9; 22:8**.)

Title: *The Revelation of Jesus Christ* (Not *"Revelations"*.) Revelation translates the Greek word *avpoka, luyij apokalupsis* {*ap-ok-al'-oop-sis*} which means *"an unveiling"*. More will be said about that in a moment.

Key Verse: **Revelation 1:19** – This verse offers a clear, three-part outline of the events of the Revelation. This verse is also the key to understanding the book. The Revelation is the Bible's only book with its divinely inspired outline. That outline is as follows:

I. **The Things Which Thou Hast Seen** – Chapter 1
II. **The Things Which Are** – Chapter 2-3
III. **The Things Which Shall Be Hereafter** – Chapters 4-22

Ok, let's take a moment to set the stage. Remember, when studying the Bible, one of the most important things to understand is the setting under which the chapter was written. This applies not only to Revelation but also to the rest of the Bible!

This book was written during some dark days for the early church. They were suffering terrible persecution under the iron hand of the Roman Emperors. This book was written to give them hope, comfort, and encouragement in their daily struggles. This book was also given to them to let them know how the plan of God would eventually play out. They are made to understand that God has a plan and that His plan includes the destruction of Satan, sin, and this wicked world; the redemption of creation and God's people; and the exaltation of the Lord Jesus Christ. This great plan will take shape far more clearly as we move through the pages of this book.

This book is a book of prophecy. It speaks of future events in what is often symbolic language. That language, however, is clearly defined and explained.

This is a book closely tied to the Old Testament. Of the 404 verses in Revelation, 278 somehow refer to the Old Testament. Of those 278 verses, over 800 allusions to Old Testament events exist. So, a working knowledge of the entire Bible is necessary to understand everything in this book.

The Book of Revelation and the Book of Genesis stand like the great bookends of God's creation. Many things that commence in Genesis have their conclusion in Revelation. Things like sin, Satan, creation, the curse, Heaven, earth, redemption, etc., come full circle by the time you reach Revelation. Now, that is a lot of introductory material. I hope I haven't lost you already. Let's begin our journey through this beautiful, vitally important book. Let's unveil the book!

In **Revelation 1:1-3**, we are given a solid introduction to the content and purpose of this book. Let's dig into these words for a few minutes and try to understand this excellent book better! These three little verses reveal some of the essential principles that govern the content of the book of Revelation.

First, there is the person of the Revelation. This book is a book about Jesus! Your Bible might title this book "***The Revelation of Saint John the Divine.***" That is the title given to this book by some man. However, the accurate title of this book is given in **verse 1**. It is called "***the revelation of Jesus Christ.***" That is what this book is.

Jesus Christ is the theme of the Bible. You might say that the Bible is a "***Him***" book. It is a book about Him! Everything in the Bible points to Jesus in one way or another. You can find Him on every page, every chapter, and every event. But, the book of Revelation, more so than any other book, is about Him! It is a "*revelation*" or an "*unveiling*" of the *Person*, the *Purposes*, the *Plans*, the *Power*, and the *Promotion* of the Lord Jesus Christ.

When Jesus was here the first time, He was veiled. Most people did not recognize him as God, even though He was and is God in the flesh, **Phil. 2:5-8**. The Bible tells us in **1 Cor. 2:8** that they would not have crucified

Him if they had known Who Jesus was. On one occasion, the veil of His flesh was pulled aside, and His glory appeared. This happened on the Mount of Transfiguration, **Matt. 17:1-8**. There, the heavenly glory concealed beneath the flesh of His humanity burst forth. However, only Peter, James, and John witnessed that event. The rest of the people did not see His glory.

When the world looked at Jesus all they saw was His poverty, His humanity. They saw a carpenter from Nazareth. Some saw him as a revolutionary with strange and dangerous teaching. The last view the world had of Jesus was that of a convicted criminal dying in sorrow, shame, and suffering on a Roman cross.

The book of Revelation tells us that the world has not seen the last of the Lord Jesus! He is coming again. When He comes the second time, He is not destined for a cross but a crown. He is not coming as a suffering Lamb but as a Sovereign Lord. He is not coming in shame and poverty but in splendor and power. There is a day when Jesus Christ will be revealed to the whole world. They will see Him as He truly is. This is the clear teaching of the Scriptures, **1 Cor. 1:7** (The word "*coming*" is "*apokalupsis*".); **2 Thes. 1:7** (The word "*revealed*" is "*apokalupsis*".); **1 Pet. 1:7**. (The word "*appearing*" is "*apokalupsis*".) Do you get the picture? Jesus is coming, and the world will see Him as He is. (**Rev. 1:7**.)

As the chapters of this book unfold, we see that Jesus is the solution to all the world's problems. We see that He is the only hope for fallen man. We see a world in turmoil and tribulation and that Jesus is the answer to the need. We see that when everything else is gone, when sin, Satan, and sorrow have all been defeated, Jesus will still be Lord. Regardless of what you might be facing today, remember that Jesus Christ is the answer. He is your only hope. He is "*the way, the truth and the life, and no man cometh unto the Father but by*" Him.

We see God's promise to Jesus in **Phil. 2:9-11** fulfilled in this book. Jesus came to this world to give His life for humanity. He came to reveal God and redeem God's elect. He did give His life for us, and God has promised to exalt Him because of that. We will see that accomplished in this book.

Verse one says, "*which God gave unto Him.*" This reminds us that when Jesus became a man, He voluntarily gave up the independent use of some of His divine prerogatives. When Jesus was here, He plainly said that He did not know the hour of His coming, **Mark. 13:32**. Some believe that the Revelation is God giving this information to Jesus. However, this view has a problem; this book does not tell us of the day and the hour when Jesus will come. However, it fully reveals the glory He will display and receive.

The purpose of this book is clearly stated in **verse 1**, *"to shew unto His servants things which must shortly come to pass."* This book is given to the people of God so they can comprehend God's master plan for the future. **Verse 3** reminds us that this book is a book of *"prophecy."* There are two types of prophecy. One meaning of the word is to *"forth tell."* That is what I am doing right now. I am taking the Word of God and "forth-telling" that Word. There is a sense in which preaching is prophecy. The other word used carries the idea of "foretelling". That is, revealing truths and events before they occur. Both types of prophecy occur in the book of Revelation. **Revelation 1-3** are "forth-telling" chapters. **Chapters 4-22** are "foretelling" chapters.

This revelation of Jesus is given to *"His servants"*. Servant is the word *dou/loj* (doulos {doo'-los}). This word refers to *"one who gives himself up to another's will; a slave"*. It suggests the law of the bondservant in **Exodus 21:1-6**. If a man became indebted to another, he was to work off that debt through seven years of servitude to the debtor. The debt was paid at the end of the seven years, and the servant could go free. If, however, he wished to remain with his master and spend his life serving him, then a hole would be bored through his ear, and he would become a bond slave. The hole in his ear would mark him as one who served the master by choice, out of love.

This book is for the people of God! The lost man or woman will have trouble grasping the truths in this book because they are words intended for those who serve the Lord from a heart of love. As I said earlier, these are things *"spiritually discerned."*

We are told that another purpose of this book is to reveal *"things which must shortly come to pass"*. Many people read this and think of the shortness of time. If that is the case, then we have a problem. It has been 2,000 since these things were written, and most have yet to be fulfilled. This phrase means that when these events begin, they will happen quickly. So, the events of Revelation were made clear 2,000 years ago, but once the events begin to unfold, one will follow the other in rapid succession. The word *"shortly"* translates two Greek words. They are: *"en"* (*en*), which means "in" and "tachos" (tachos), which means *"quickness; swiftness"*. We get our word *"taxi"* from this word. You need to get somewhere in a hurry, so you flag down a taxi, and hop in, a takeoff. That is the way the end-time events will take place. Once they begin, they will *"take off like a speeding taxi."* (Ill. My experience with an Iranian taxi driver in Washington, DC.)

Verse one says He "sent and signified it by His angel." The word *"angel"* refers to a *"messenger."* Jesus sent this word to John by a heavenly messenger service, much like the virgin birth was announced to Mary. However, the word "signified" is significant in understanding this book. The literal translation means *"to give the sign."* We could read the word *"Sign-I-Fied"*. In other words, the Lord is letting us know He will speak in symbolic language and word pictures in Revelation.

Why would the Lord use sign and symbols? There are a few reasons. *These symbols are a spiritual code*. The Church was under intense persecution that day. The language would have been clear to the redeemed but a riddle to the lost who might desire to use the book's message to attack the saints. *Languages change; symbols do not*. John was trying to write about events, images, and people far into the distant future. He did not possess the vocabulary to describe what he was seeing adequately. He used the language of his day to describe events in our day and beyond. That is why the Lord sent this message in signs and symbols. As the language has changed, the symbols retain their power and speak today. Don't worry about the signs and symbols we will encounter in this book. They are all carefully and wholly explained for us. Remember, this is not a hidden book but a revelation, an unveiling of eternal truth. We will encounter significant symbolic numbers 3, 4, 6, 7, 12, and 666, all explained in the book. We will read about trumpets, bowls, and seals; they are all explained. Every symbol we will encounter is defined for us.

This chapter would only be complete if we considered the man who put the words of Revelation onto paper. John is designated to be the human author. This is the son of Zebedee. He is known in **John 20:2** and **21:20** as *"the disciple whom Jesus loved"*. He is the one who rested his head on the breast of the Lord Jesus at The Last Supper, **John 13:23**. (Note that even here, he was privy to divine secrets.) It pays to be close to the Lord. He reveals things to His friends, **Gen. 18:17; John 15:15**.) He is the one who left everything to follow Jesus, **Matt. 4:22**. He is the one who stood by the cross of Jesus as the Lord hung there dying, **John 19:26-27**. He was the one who stared into the empty tomb on the morning of the resurrection and believed. (**John 20:8**.) That is the penman of this book! He was a faithful friend to the Lord Jesus and a faithful scribe of the Word of God.

John tells us that he faithfully recorded everything that was revealed to Him. Just as John had faithfully recorded an accurate record of the first advent of the Lord Jesus, **John 19:35; 21:42; 1 John 1:2; 4:14**, he tells us that he is doing the same with this revelation that He has been given. These visions must have overwhelmed the old Apostle. But he gives us a faithful record of the Revelation of the Lord Jesus Christ.

Now we come to the promise. This is another book in the Bible with a built-in promise to those who read, hear, and heed the message. God promises a special blessing to those who spend time reading this book. Three present-tense words describe who can expect to receive this blessing: *readeth*, *heard*, and *kept*. Let's examine these words!

1. **He that readeth** refers to the one who would read these words in public gatherings. In those days, copies of the Scriptures were rare. Usually, there was one copy per congregation, and one person would stand and read so that all could hear the words. The one who reads the book is promised a blessing.
2. **They that hear** refers to the congregation hearing the words as they are read. There is a special blessing attached to hearing this book read.
3. **They keep** speaking to those who will take this message to heart. Those who hear, believe, and live it can expect the Lord to bless them for their efforts in this book.

We can expect the Lord to feed and teach us as we read this great book. But we can also expect the Lord to bless us because we are taking Him at His word and reading, hearing, and keeping the words of this prophecy. I encourage you to invite lost people to study with you. I believe the Lord will save them! Invite other believers! if they come, they will be blessed along with us.

Now, we are told why this book is so important. Look at the last phrase of **verse 3**. It says, *"for the time is at hand"*. The word *"time"* in this verse does not refer to the time on a clock; it means "due time; a season; an era of time." God is telling us that we are nearing the end of these things, and this book will give us help and hope as we see the end approaching.

If the time was nearly 2,000 years ago, why haven't these things come to pass? First, God's clock does not operate like our clock. Read this verse. (**2 Pet. 3:8**.) *"But, beloved, be not ignorant of this one thing, that one day is with the Lord as a thousand years and a thousand years as one day."* God does things in His Own time and on His schedule. Second, God is giving lost sinners time to be saved in this age of grace. Read **2 Pet. 3:9**. *"The Lord is not slack concerning his promise, as some men count slackness; but is longsuffering to us-ward, not willing that any should perish, but that all should come to repentance."* And finally, (**2 Pet. 3:15**). *"And account that the longsuffering of our Lord is salvation…"*

My dear brother or sister, if you are here lost today, I urge you to come to Jesus and be saved. One day, He will return, and it will be too late then. Now, if the Lord has spoken to your heart on any level during the reading of this chapter, I invite you to come before Him and do whatever He is leading you to do. If you listen carefully, you, too, may hear approaching hoofbeats!

LETTER TO THE CHURCHES

The book of Revelation is impressive. It is also a very complex book. There are many twists, turns and rapid plot developments in its pages. This book contains all the elements of a great thriller. In its pages, you will find action, suspense, mystery, wonder, fear, drama, horror, and excitement. While it takes 22 chapters for all the action to develop, John gives us a preview at the very beginning. He gives us a vision to show us what is coming our way.

Revelation 1:4-8 introduces the material that will be developed as we move through the verses of Revelation. Let's look at this preview, starting with God's Word.

> *⁴ John to the seven churches which are in Asia: Grace be unto you, and peace, from him which is, and which was, and which is to come; and from the seven Spirits which are before his throne;*
> *⁵ And from Jesus Christ, who is the faithful witness, and the first begotten of the dead, and the prince of the kings of the earth. Unto him that loved us, and washed us from our sins in his own blood,*
> *⁶ And hath made us kings and priests unto God and his Father; to him be glory and dominion for ever and ever. Amen.*
> *⁷ Behold, he cometh with clouds; and every eye shall see him, and they also which pierced him: and all kindreds of the earth shall wail because of him. Even so, Amen.*
> *⁸ I am Alpha and Omega, the beginning and the ending, saith the Lord, which is, and which was, and which is to come, the Almighty.*

Let's look at the destination of this letter. This letter was to be sent to seven specific churches in Asia Minor. These churches are mentioned in **verse 11** and dealt with in detail in **chapters two and three**. We will consider each of these congregations when we get to those verses. For the time being, there are several things we need to remember about these churches. First, they were real, literal congregations that existed when John penned this book. Jesus spoke to them about real saints, real sinners, real situations, and real solutions. Second, these churches represent every Christian church that has ever existed. Every church contains some of the characteristics that marked these early churches. So, while this letter was not addressed to your respective church, this book has as much to say to your church as if it was included explicitly in the passage.

This letter was sent to *"the seven churches."* This is the first use of the number seven in Revelation. This is a number that will show up time and time again as we study the book. Seven is a number that suggests *"perfect, completion, and fullness."* So, when the Bible mentions seven churches, it refers to the church in its fullness. That is why I am saying that even though this book was not explicitly written to us, it still speaks to us as though it were.

Seven is a prominent number in our world. Seven colours make up the light spectrum. There are seven notes in the musical scale. There are seven days in one week. Seven appears frequently in the Bible. God commanded seven feats in the Law. There are seven secrets, or mysteries, in Christ's parables of the kingdom. There were seven sayings of Jesus on the cross. At Jericho, seven priests carrying seven trumpets marched around the city for seven days. On the seventh day, they marched around the city seven times.

In this book, seven is used forty-nine times, seven times seven. (I love numbers!) Here are some of the sevens in Revelation:

1. Seven Churches – **1:4**
2. Seven Spirits – **1:4**
3. Seven Stars – **1:16**
4. Seven Seals – **4:5**
5. Seven Horns – **5:6**
6. Seven Eyes – **6:6**
7. Seven Trumpets – **8:2**
8. Seven Angels – **8:2**
9. Seven Thunders – **10:3**

10. Seven Heads – **12:3**
11. Seven Crowns – **12:3**
12. Seven Plagues – **15:1**
13. Seven Vials – **17:1**
14. Seven Mountains – **17:9**
15. Seven Kings – **17:10**

There are many other sevens in this book. These are just a tiny sample of the many we will see.

Let's look at the desire of the letter. The scripture says, "Grace unto you and peace." This is the classic New Testament dedication. John greets them with the prayer that they will continue to enjoy the all-sufficient grace of God and peace, which passes understanding. While the book of Revelation is a problematic book filled with scenes of judgment and condemnation; it is a book of joy. It reveals God's grace in the lives of His people, and it points to a coming world where grace and peace will reign forever. This is a fitting way to introduce the book.

Then, there is the deity of the letter. This great promise of grace and peace comes from the Holy Trinity. Notice the word *"from"* in **verses 4-5**. This word is used three times. Each time it appears, it introduces another member of the Godhead. God is the source of all grace and peace.

These two verses remind us that this book was not the creation of a man. It is the Words of God to man! Therefore, it carries with it tremendous power and ultimate divine authority. Let's examine the Deity behind this letter.

This deity is the sovereign father. This identifies God, who is *"the self-existent One."* This is the God Who called Himself *"I AM"* in **Exodus 3:14**. This is God who has always existed in the source of grace and peace. This is the God Who is the eternal One. This is the God who lives in three dimensions, past, present, and future, all at the same time. He is the source of grace and peace. This God, the One Who has always existed, who exists, and who will always exist, is the source of this grace and peace. This is the God Who never changes. Look at **Mal. 3:6, Heb. 13:8, and James 1:17**.) He is our source!

Then we come to the sufficient spirit. The phrase *"the seven spirits which are before His throne"* speaks of the *"fullness, the perfection, the completeness"* of the Spirit of God. It refers to His ministry in our lives. He can give us His grace and peace because He is perfect and complete. He is all we need as we pass through this life. He is sufficient! This phrase may also reference **Isa. 11:2**, where the Bible says, *"And the spirit of the LORD shall rest upon him, the spirit of wisdom and understanding, the spirit of counsel and might, the spirit of knowledge and of the fear of the LORD."*

John tells us that there is a third source of grace and peace. He tells us that these things come from *"Jesus Christ."* When John mentioned the Father and the Spirit he spoke of them symbolically. When he speaks of Jesus, he uses straightforward language and sets Jesus on center stage. Why? Well, the purpose of this book is to reveal and unveil Jesus.

So, in the beginning, John tells us exactly Who Jesus is. He does not want any confusion about Jesus, who He is, or what He is about. John knows that believing right about Jesus is critical to getting everything else right. If you get your beliefs about Jesus messed up, you are going to be off base in everything you believe. John gives us a three-fold description of the Person and work of the Lord Jesus Christ. This brings us to His Revelation. Jesus is called *"the faithful witness"*. This little phrase calls to mind His coming to the world for the first time. Jesus came to reveal the Father. (**John 14:7-9; John 12:45; Col. 1:15; Heb. 1:3**)

Jesus is the only person in history with the right to bear the title of *"Jehovah's Witness."* In the Old Testament, Israel was God's witness to the world. (**Isa. 43:10**.) In this age, the church is His witness to the world, **Matt. 28:19-20; Acts 1:8**. However, neither the church nor Israel is a faithful witness. The best we can be is a mere reflection of God and His grace. Jesus Christ was and is God in human flesh. He is more than a reflection. He is God! Therefore, He gave a *"faithful witness"* to the Person and work of the Father, **John 18:37; 1 Tim. 6:13**.

Now we come to His Resurrection. Jesus is called *"the first begotten of the dead."* Understand that Jesus was not the first to get up from the dead. There were some in the Old Testament and several in the Gospels. But Jesus was the first one to get up and stay up. The rest died again.

The word translated as *"first begotten"* comes from the word that gives us the word *"prototype."* Jesus sets the standard that the rest will eventually follow. When the Bible says that Jesus is the *"first begotten of the dead"*, it does not mean He is the first One to get up. It means that He is first in preeminence. In other words, He set the standard! He is the prototype. He is an example of what will happen to all those who believe in Him. Just as He got up to stay up from the grave forever, those who trust in Him will also experience a resurrection one day. Because He lives, those who have faith in Him have *"passed from death unto life"*, **John 5:24**, and they *"will never die"*, **John 11:25-26**.

This brings us to His Royalty. In this verse, the third title given to Jesus is *"the prince of the kings of the earth."* This establishes Jesus as the *"King of Kings and Lord of Lords."* This phrase pictures Him as the One Who is in absolute control. We will see Satan sent his king, the Antichrist, into the world. He will rampage and exalt himself above *"all that is called God."* But even he will have a Master, and His name is Jesus. One day, every ruler, every tyrant, every dictator, every king, potentate, etc., who has ever lived will bow before the nail-pierced feet of the Lord Jesus Christ and call Him "Lord, to the glory of God the Father," **Phil. 2:9-10**. He is the ultimate Ruler!

Now comes the praise of the Revelation. Having told us about the Godhead, the source of grace and peace, John gets so caught up in Who Jesus is that he offers us a hymn of praise to the Lamb of God. Let's take a minute to listen to John's song of praise.

First, He Is Praised for His Loving Ministry. We see the words *"Unto Him Who loved us."* Don't let that past tense verb throw you. John reminds us that Jesus loved us despite what we were and still are. His love is unceasing, unfailing, and unconditional. He loves us, and that is cause enough for loud and long praise to be offered to Him. His love for us brought Him to the world, **John 3:16**. His love for us bound Him to the cross. (**Rom 5:8**.) His love for us is a guarantee that can never fail. (Rom. **8:38-39**.)

He Is praised For His ministry – "and washed us from our sins in His blood." – The word translated *"wash"* means to *"cleanse*! Jesus shed His blood on the cross, and when we trust Him, His blood washes us whiter than snow and cleanses us from every stain of sin, **1 John 1:7**. Did you know what each of us brings to this thing called salvation? The text says, *"our sins"* and *"His blood."* All we had to contribute to our salvation was sin. He contributed His blood. And His blood washes away all our sins. **(Eph. 1:7)**.

He Is Praised for His lifting ministry – *"And hath made us kings and priests unto God and his Father."* – This phrase tells us that Jesus is to be praised because He refused to leave us as He found us. He found us in sin; He loved us; He washed us in His blood and saved us; then He lifted us out of that condition and changed us for the glory of God, 2 Cor. 5:17. He takes old hell-bound sinners and makes them "kings and priests." As kings, the saints will reign with Jesus one day, **2 Tim. 2:12**. As priests; we are given direct access to the throne of God **Heb. 4:16; 10:19**. He deserves to be praised for caring for us, cleansing us and changing us for His glory!

Look at the words *"Hath made us."* The Prodigal son left home saying, "Give me." He returned home, broken, dirty, defeated, crying, "Make me." When the Lord touches your heart just right, you will be willing to let God make of you just what He pleases. And, my brother or sister, He never wants to make anything bad out of you. He wants to make you a king and a priest. He wants to make somebody out of you!

John tells us all this about Jesus and then breaks out in praise. He says, *"to him be glory and dominion for ever and ever. Amen."* This is the book of Revelation's first doxology or song of praise. But it will not be the last. As the book progresses, the doxologies get longer and more detailed. Each time, Jesus is exalted more and more. The more He is revealed in this book, the more He is praised. That's the way it ought to be! The closer we get to Him, the more we should praise Him. The more we learn about Him, the more our hearts should be stirred to give Him praise, honor, and glory.

This brings us to the promise of the Revelation. These last two verses give us a little glimpse of what we can expect as this book unfolds. They offer a bit of a promise to us that some exciting things are going to be happening in this book. Let's examine the promise of the revelation.

First, we have the promise of a coming one! The world has waited for 6,000 years for the Redeemer to come. He came the first time, was born of a virgin, and died on the cross to purchase redemption. He is returning in the clouds above this earth to catch away His Bride in the Rapture. Then, one day, Jesus will return to this earth in power and glory. He will defeat the enemies of God, and He will establish His kingdom here, and He will reign here for 1,000 years. This verse is about that event. This does not speak about the Rapture but of His Revelation.

Then, we see the method of His coming. "He cometh with clouds." This is not the first time Jesus clothed Himself in this fashion. He led Israel through the wilderness in a pillar of cloud, **Exodus 13:21-22**. He ascended back into Heaven, riding a chariot of clouds. (**Acts 1:9**) When He comes back, He will again surround Himself with clouds and appear in glory and power. He is coming!

Then, we see the manifestation of His coming. The Word of God tells us that "every eye shall see Him." The thought of everyone being able to see the same thing at the same time all over the world was considered impossible just a few decades ago. But, with the advent of satellite technology, people worldwide witness the same event simultaneously. But, when Jesus comes, He will not need Fox News or CNN to broadcast His coming. He will appear in the clouds, and the whole world can see Him simultaneously. This tells us that His presence and glory will be undeniable in that day.

Unfortunately, we see the misery of His coming. The Bible clarifies that the Second Coming of the Lord Jesus will not be pleasant for the world's people. Jew and Gentile alike will wail when they see Him coming. The Jews will weep because their fathers rejected Him, and their people paid a high price for their rebellion. The Gentiles will wail because He comes to judge sin and sinners alike. When Jesus comes there will be horrible judgment as He treads the *"winepress of the fierceness and wrath of Almighty God"*.

John hears this and says, *"Amen!"* that is, *"So be it; or may it come to pass."* This is a prayer that every saint should echo. Let us pray that whatever the cost, Jesus will come and set this world as it should be.

Then we see the promise of a final conclusion. Yes, Jesus is coming, and it will signal awful judgment for this wicked world. But it will also signal the culmination of all things. He will conclude what began in Genesis, in the Revelation.

During this process, we hear the Lord's Announcement. *"I am Alpha and Omega, the beginning and the ending, saith the Lord"*. As *"Alpha and Omega"* Jesus is the One Who knows everything. Alpha is the first letter of the Greek alphabet, and Omega is the last. Those letters and the others in between can be used to express all the ideas and knowledge of mankind. Jesus lets us know that He is the omniscient one. He sees all, and He knows all. The phrase *"beginning and ending"* reminds us that He is the one who started this universe on its present course and is the one who pilots it to its proper conclusion. In other words, He declares Himself to be the one who is in control! He is the *"Lord," The Lord's Authority – Jesus also calls Himself "which is, and which was, and which is to come."* With this phrase, He proclaims His deity! After all, this is the title used to describe the father in **verse 4**.

As God, Jesus is the all-present, all-knowing, all-powerful being, transcending time and space. He has the authority to do everything He says will come to pass in this book. In other words, He will see that everything goes as He has planned and that everything foretold in this book will pass just as He has said! So, don't worry, saint of God, our Savior is in control! But, if you are not saved, you need to be! After all, just as surely as there is a Heaven for the redeemed ones, there is a Hell for the lost ones.

During all this, we see the Lord's ability. Jesus declares Himself to be *"the Almighty"*. This word means *"the one who holds sway over all things"*. It proclaims Him to be the sovereign Lord of the universe. He is the one who can bring everything He has planned and promised to pass. He will do it, and no one can stop it!

Reaching into our English history, some stories tell us of the conquests and crusades of Richard I, the Lionhearted. While Richard was away trouncing Saladin, his kingdom fell on bad times. His sly and graceless brother, John, usurped all the king's prerogatives and misruled the realm. The people of England suffered longing for the king's return and praying that it might be soon. Then, one day, Richard came. He landed in England and marched straight for his throne. Around that glittering coming, many tales are told, woven into the legends of England. (One of them is the story of Robin Hood.) John's castles tumbled like ninepins. Great Richard claimed his throne, and none dared stand in his path. The people shouted their delight. They rang peal after peal on the bells. The Lion was back! Long live the king!

One day, a King greater than Richard will claim a realm greater than England. Those who have abused the earth in His absence, seized His domains, and mismanaged His world will all be swept aside. That, my brothers, and sisters, is a lot to look forward to! And every bit of it will happen, just as He promised. What are we to do in light if his coming again? Allow me to offer a few thoughts about what we should do with a message like this.

- We should be sure we are ready to meet Him when He comes. (**Matt. 24:44**)
- We should pray for those who are not ready and tell them how to be ready. (**Mark 16:15**)
- We should realize that our time is short in this life and commit ourselves to doing all we can for Him while there is still time. (**John 9:4**)

Will you be ready? Where will you spend eternity?

CHURCH AT PHILADELPHIA

We continue to move through our Lord's letters to the seven churches of Asia Minor. We have covered five of the seven churches thus far and will soon pass into the heart of the book of Revelation. Let me remind you that these letters can be viewed from three different perspectives.

1. *Practically* – These letters were written to real churches functioning in that day.
2. *Prophetically* – Each church represents a different period of church history from Pentecost to the Rapture. This church represents the period between *1,700 AD and 1,900 AD*. The true Christian churches, though weak numerically and financially, began the modern mission movement during this period. This period also saw the *"Great Awakenings"* and revivals in America and Britain.
3. *Personally* – These churches have something to say to every individual believer and to every church in existence.

In this chapter, we will consider the church in Philadelphia. Let's look at God's Word! The text comes from **Revelation 3:7-13**.

> *⁷And to the angel of the church in Philadelphia write; These things saith he that is holy, he that is true, he that hath the key of David, he that openeth, and no man shutteth; and shutteth, and no man openeth;*
> *⁸I know thy works: behold, I have set before thee an open door, and no man can shut it: for thou hast a little strength, and hast kept my word, and hast not denied my name.*
> *⁹Behold, I will make them of the synagogue of Satan, which say they are Jews, and are not, but do lie; behold, I will make them to come and worship before thy feet, and to know that I have loved*

thee.

¹⁰ Because thou hast kept the word of my patience, I also will keep thee from the hour of temptation, which shall come upon all the world, to try them that dwell upon the earth.

¹¹ Behold, I come quickly: hold that fast which thou hast, that no man take thy crown.

¹² Him that overcometh will I make a pillar in the temple of my God, and he shall go no more out: and I will write upon him the name of my God, and the name of the city of my God, which is new Jerusalem, which cometh down out of heaven from my God: and I will write upon him my new name.

¹³ He that hath an ear, let him hear what the Spirit saith unto the churches.

Philadelphia was the youngest and smallest of the cities addressed in these letters. It was in a narrow pass between two mountain ranges, a literal doorway between Asia Minor and Asia. Because of its strategic location, Philadelphia was used as a military buffer city. A small force at Philadelphia could delay enemy armies passing through the narrow pass.

The city was named for King Attalus II, the king of Pergamum. He was renowned for his love of his brother Eumenes and became called **"Philadelphos"**. The word means **"one who loves his brother."** Thus, Philadelphia became known as **"The city of brotherly love."**

Philadelphia was built on a geological fault. As a result, the city was plagued by frequent earthquakes and tremors. The citizens were often forced to flee the city to avoid being injured or killed by falling buildings. Philadelphia was also the home to numerous temples desiccated to the gods and goddesses of ancient Greece. Philadelphia was the last of the seven cities to lose its Christian testimony. There was a thriving Christian community there as late as 1000 AD when the Muslim armies of the Middle East captured the city.

Jesus speaks in these verses to the church in Philadelphia. He comes to them with no words of complaint but words of praise and promise. I think the Lord's words, to this weak but faithful church, have much to say to us today. It should be this church if we model ourselves after any of these seven churches. Let's examine our Lord's words and discover why.

First, we must pay careful attention to the church and its master. If you look again at verses seven and eight, Jesus identifies Himself in two powerful ways. He comes to us and the sinless one! The word *"holy"* tells us that Jesus is sinless and pure. Jesus speaks to a church striving to be holy in a corrupt and sinful world. He says to them: *"It is possible to live for God! I am holy, and I can help you be holy too."* This word of encouragement is one we all need from time to time. This world is against us, and sin and Satan are pressing us in on every side. Jesus has the power to help us to live the holy lives He desires us to live!

Secondly, he is sincere. The word "true" means "that which is genuine." We know that His Word is accurate. Now, He tells His people that He is the real Saviour. He is the only genuine Lord.

These early believers were surrounded daily by that which was false. False gods and false worship abounded in that time. Jesus wants them to know that He is the real deal. They are not wasting their time serving Him. They did not make mistakes when they turned their back on their idols and pagan gods. When they came to Jesus Christ, they came to the only Saviour. If you doubt the veracity of this statement, read **Acts 4:12** and **John 14:6**.

We live in an age when many things are mere imitations. We are surrounded by that which is fake and pretend. Remembering that at least one thing is real is a comfort! Jesus is the real deal! Jesus is not a substitute for anything! When you trust Jesus Christ, you get in on something real! Salvation is real! Prayer is real! Grace is real! Heaven is real! His presence is real! His Word is real! His power is real! I am just saying that Jesus is the real thing!

Thirdly, Jesus identifies Himself as the One Who is in control! He has the keys, and He opens and closes the doors. Jesus says that He has *"the key of David."* Look at **Isa. 22:20-25**. This passage speaks of a man named Eliakim. This is an Old Testament prophecy that the glory of God, the power of God, and the authority of God will rest on his shoulders. Then, we are told that he will be set as a nail in a sure place and that he will be cut off after a while. This ancient prophecy is a picture of the coming of the Lord

Jesus Christ.

God placed on His Son His kingdom and His government, **Isa. 9:6**. He set Him *"as a nail in a sure place."* But, after a time, He was cut off. This is a clear picture of the cross of our Lord. We are told that He will have the *"Key of David."* What does this mean?

Keys grant you *authority, access, and availability*. Jesus comes to this ancient church and says, "I have the keys!" He is telling you today that He "has the keys." What kind of keys does Jesus have?

1. **He Has the Keys of Sleep – Rev. 1:18**. Jesus alone is the Master of death. You can't even die until He opens the door! You can't stay dead if you know Him, **John 11:25-26**.
2. **He Has the Keys of Suffering – Rev. 1:18** - Only He can open Heaven and shut Hell. Jesus is the Key to Heaven!
3. **He Has the Keys of Salvation – John 4:12; John 14:6; John 10:9**. Only He can open the door into eternal life for those who will come to Him.
4. **He Has the Keys of Service - 1 Cor. 16:9** – He decides when we serve, where we serve and how long we serve.
5. **He Has the Keys of Safety – Col. 3:3** – No one can touch those locked away within Jesus Christ.

Fourthly, he controls the doors. Jesus is in the business of opening and closing doors in the lives of His people. We see this truth at work in the life of the Apostle Paul, **Acts 16:6-10**.

When God opens a door of opportunity in your life, run through it as fast as you can. It may be a once-in-a-lifetime opportunity. How tragic it would be to get to Heaven and see what we could have done if only we had trusted the Lord and stepped through the open door He gave us.

By the same token, when He closes a door, don't try to force it open. You don't want to be where God doesn't want you to be. The path to blessing is to be where the Lord wants us to be when He wants us to be there. We must pray that God will give us spiritual wisdom to see the doors when He opens them.

Let's look at the ministry of Philadelphia. It was a small church with tremendous potential for the glory of God. These verses tell us something about their ministry. Verse 8 shows us their ministry had opportunities. In His sovereignty, the Lord had given this church a robust open door of ministry. Jesus says, **"Thou hast a little strength"**. This may mean they were small and lacked political and financial influence. They were weak, but the Lord was using them in a mighty fashion. They were weak but made a tremendous impact on their city! Why the impact?

They had kept His Word. This means that even though they were weak in many ways, they were pure and strong in their doctrine. *They had not denied His Name.* They were not ashamed of Jesus or their relationship to Him. This means that they were not keeping the Gospel to themselves! They were spreading God's Word to a lost and dying world. God had given them an open door of ministry there in Philadelphia and they had stepped through it and were doing what they could.

Because they were faithful to Him, He was blessing them! They were preaching and exalting Jesus, and the enemies of the cross were powerless to stop them. Such was the power of God in their midst! These principles still apply today. Fundamental, Bible-believing churches are in the minority in our world. If we honor God's Word and keep Jesus at the center of all we do, the Lord will honor that by giving us an open door of ministry in this world. But we must do what He says here. We must "*keep His Word*". This means that we are to hear it, love it, do it, and share it.

We must "*not deny His name*". That is, we must not minimize Jesus to draw a crowd. But we must make Him the centerpiece of our church and our worship! God blessed that kind of church 2,000 years ago and He still will today!

If we love the Book and live the Book, if we love Jesus and lift Jesus, God will use us in this world in ways we cannot begin to imagine! He "*opened*" that door long ago, and it remains open today!)

In verse 9, we see their ministry involves opposition. The phrase "*synagogue of Satan*" may refer to the local Jews who were persecuting them. The phrase "*which say they are Jews and are not*" can be interpreted by what Paul said in **Rom. 2:28-29**. This church is suffering at the hands of people who claim to love God but are lying! They have rejected their Messiah, and they are headed to Hell, **Rev. 21:8**.

Jesus tells them that He is aware of their mistreatment. But He wants them to know that a day is coming when they will see those who oppose them bowing before them. He probably refers to that day when *"every knee should bow, of things in heaven, and things in earth, and things under the earth; And that every tongue should confess that Jesus Christ is Lord, to the glory of God the Father."* **Phil. 2:10-11**.

One day, their enemies would experience total defeat. Whatever the Lord is speaking about here, He wants them to know He controls the critics, too. They have endured much but will be spared the horrors that will come upon the entire world and those who dwell in it. Jesus promises them that their faithfulness to them guarantees them deliverance from the terrible time of tribulation that is to come upon this earth.

Take note of the phrase *"them that dwell upon the earth."* This can be translated as *"the earth dwellers"*. We will encounter this phrase several more times in Revelation. It refers to those who are part of this world's evil system. It speaks of those people who do not know the Lord. They will face the wrath of God in the tribulation, but His people will not!

Despite what some may say, the church will not pass through the tribulation. Absolutely not! Jesus is coming, and He will remove His church before God pours His wrath upon this world.

We see in verse eleven their ministry had several obligations. The believers in Philadelphia are told to be on the lookout for two things. First, they are to be watching for the coming of the Lord. Second, they were to watch their walk. Jesus is coming, and His people must be ready to meet Him. That means we are to live as if He might come at any minute, and we are to work like our time is short. But, as we watch and work, we must be careful of how we live our lives. We must not allow ourselves to become like the world around us. We are to live for Jesus, love Jesus, and look for Jesus, guarding everything He has given us so that we can be confident of a reward when He comes. We will face our Lord someday at the Judgment Seat of Christ. That day can be a reward or loss, depending on how we live now.

In **Verse 12**, Jesus closes His letter to this church by giving them hope for the future. This message is just as valid for us today as it was for the people in Philadelphia.

Jesus tells these believers that He will set them as pillars in God's temple and that they will no longer go out. This was a message of hope to the people in Philadelphia. With all the earthquakes the city suffered, they were used to having to evacuate their city. Now, Jesus promises them that they will enjoy stability in His kingdom.

There is also a lesson here for us. This world may knock us about from time, and troubles and trials may assault us day by day, but we have been placed on solid rock, and we are headed to a sure destination. There may be little stability in this world, but the saints of God will be fixed firmly in Heaven above, and they will never be threatened, assaulted, or attacked again! Nothing that troubles the church down here will be allowed to enter over there, **Rev. 21:4, 27.**

This world hates us, the devil hates us, and each day we see the church become the focus of increasing attacks and hatred. But things will be different in heaven! We are the redeemed children of God! We are the spotless, chaste, virgin bride of the Lamb of God! Our names are known over there, and one day, well, enter that city and be firmly fixed there forever!

God puts His name on them to establish ownership. He has redeemed them, and they are His forever! He places the city's name on them because that is their destination. They might live on the earth today but are headed for glory. He writes a new name for Jesus on them because they are special to Him. The name of Christ represents the fullness of His Person. And, in Heaven, they will see Christ in all His fullness! The world might not see their value, but God does and honors His faithful servants. The people in the church of Philadelphia had no security in the city where they lived. But they had eternal security in their relationship with Jesus Christ and His kingdom! And so can we!

THE THRONE ROOM OF GOD

Now that we have looked at the churches, I want to skip forward just a bit to look inside the throne room of God. Remember what a challenge it must have been for John to try to write down what he saw. Even today, with our technology and having seen the miracles of the universe, we would have just as much trouble as John did. We have nothing on this earth to compare these sights of glory! Our text for this chapter comes from **Revelation Chapter 4:2-11**.

> *² At once I was in the Spirit, and there before me was a throne in heaven with someone sitting on it.*
> *³ And the one who sat there had the appearance of jasper and ruby. A rainbow that shone like an emerald encircled the throne.*
> *⁴ Surrounding the throne were twenty-four other thrones, and seated on them were twenty-four elders. They were dressed in white and had crowns of gold on their heads.*
> *⁵ From the throne came flashes of lightning, rumblings and peals of thunder. In front of the throne, seven lamps were blazing. These are the seven spirits[a] of God.*
> *⁶ Also in front of the throne there was what looked like a sea of glass, clear as crystal. In the center, around the throne, were four living creatures, and they were covered with eyes, in front and in back.*
> *⁷ The first living creature was like a lion, the second was like an ox, the third had a face like a man, the fourth was like a flying eagle.*
> *⁸ Each of the four living creatures had six wings and was covered with eyes all around, even under its wings. Day and night they never stop saying:*
>
> > *"'Holy, holy, holy*
> > *is the Lord God Almighty,'*[b]

who was, and is, and is to come."
⁹ Whenever the living creatures give glory, honor and thanks to him who sits on the throne and who lives for ever and ever,
¹⁰ the twenty-four elders fall down before him who sits on the throne and worship him who lives for ever and ever. They lay their crowns before the throne and say:
¹¹ "You are worthy, our Lord and God, to receive glory and honor and power, for you created all things, and by your will they were created and have their being."

Here, we see John lifted to the heavens. He is told he is about to receive a revelation of "things which must be hereafter." As we study **Revelation 4:1**, we understand that John was a representative man. He represents all true believers in Jesus Christ who will be taken out of this world at the end of the church age in the event called *"The Rapture."* I praise the Lord for that blessed hope!

[2]1 Thessalonians 4 contains one of the outstanding eschatological passages in the New Testament. This section, along with John 14:1-3 and 1 Corinthians 15:50-58, is one of the key New Testament passages on the church's rapture. A new topic is introduced in 4:13. Here, the focus of the letter shifts from the present to the future resurrection of the dead and rapture of the living at the *parousia* (second coming) of Christ.

John Walvoord notes that Paul spoke of the certainty of the rapture in 1 Thessalonians 4:13-14, *But we do not want you to be uninformed, brothers, about those who are asleep, that you may not grieve as others do who have no hope.*

Since we believe that Jesus died and rose again, even so, through Jesus, God will bring with him those who have fallen asleep. One of the great facts of the Christian faith is that we have hope when our loved ones in Christ are taken away from us in death. Christians often fail to realize the hopelessness and despair that characterizes people in pagan religions. No hope in the future life exists apart from the Lord Jesus Christ.

---

[2] John Walvoord – The John Walvoord Prophecy Commentaries (1 & 2 Thessalonians Commentary) Moody Publishing

Verse 13 refers to "those who are asleep," and verses 14 and 15 repeat the phrase "those who have fallen asleep." Sleep is a softened expression or euphemism for death, which for a Christian is very much like sleep (Matt. 27:52; John 11:11; Acts 7:60). The word "sleep" (*koimaomai*) was used in the early church of a corpse since it looks like it is asleep and will be awakened at the resurrection. We get our word "cemetery" from the Greek word *koimeterion*. As John Stott says, "Cemeteries are dormitories for the dead."[3] We understand from Scripture that "sleep" refers to bodies laid in the grave. But our souls and spirits go immediately into God's presence and the conscious enjoyment of heaven, for to be "away from the body" is to be "at home with the Lord" (2 Cor. 5:8), as noted above. Paul also described a believer's death as "to depart and be with Christ" (Phil. 1:23). We believe in the sleep of the body. Still, we do not believe in teaching something called "soul sleep," which says that the soul is unconscious during the interim period between death and the Lord's coming.

A believer's soul or immaterial part immediately goes to the Lord. The body sleeps in the grave but will be resurrected when Christ returns. A problem exists in verse 14 in the statement, "through Jesus, God will bring with him those who have fallen asleep." Some translations connect the words "through Jesus" with "those who have fallen asleep." This carries the idea that believers fall asleep or die "through Jesus." But what does it mean to sleep "through Jesus"? The meaning is that when a Christian dies, his hope of being in the presence of God is made possible through Jesus. Our loved ones are asleep through Jesus' sleep in the hope of waking. Other translations, such as the ESV, take the expression "through Jesus" to go with "God will bring with him." This is also true and could be the meaning of the expression. Either way, our hope in living and dying is certainly "through Jesus" (cf. 1 Cor. 8:6).

John Walvoord also notes that whether we are young or old, whether well or in poor health, we do not know how much time God will give us to serve Him in this world. Those in the Thessalonian church who had already died in Christ were illustrations of the uncertainty of human life.

We should live every day so that if it is our last day on earth, it will have been well spent in the Master's will. We must count our days to ensure our days count (Ps. 90:12; Eph. 5:16). The question had also been asked,

"When will the dead in Christ be raised?" Paul gave the answer in verse 16: "The dead in Christ will rise first," followed by the living (v. 17). Both groups will be "caught up together" or raptured to be with Christ. This passage teaches that when Christ returns, He will return to atmospheric heaven. When that and the other events pictured here occur, Christians whose bodies have been in the grave will be resurrected, their bodies will be transformed into resurrection bodies, and they will meet the Lord in the air. All of this will take place in a split second. Then, living Christians, will be translated from their bodies of flesh into resurrected, immortal, imperishable, incorruptible bodies.

1 Thessalonians 4:16-17 says, *For the Lord himself will descend from heaven with a cry of command, with the voice of an archangel, and with the sound of the trumpet of God. And the dead in Christ will rise first. Then we who are alive, who are left, will be caught up together with them in the clouds to meet the Lord in the air, and so we will always be with the Lord."*

At the risk of jumping around between books of the Bible, let's look at 1 Corinthians 15:50-53 which reads: *I tell you this, brothers: flesh and blood cannot inherit the kingdom of God, nor does the perishable inherit the imperishable. Behold! I tell you a mystery. We shall not all sleep, but we shall all be changed, in a moment, in the twinkling of an eye, at the last trumpet. For the trumpet will sound, and the dead will be raised imperishable, and we shall be changed. For this perishable body must put on the imperishable, and this mortal body must put on immortality.* Here, the order of the resurrection of Christians is taught very plainly. Christians who have died will be resurrected just a moment before the rapture of living saints.

One reason so many people these days do not seriously consider the coming of Christ is that they have not been at His cross enough. Pulpits that do not proclaim the death of Christ and His resurrection can hardly be expected to preach the coming of the Lord. All these events are tied together. If we accept what the Scriptures teach about the first coming of Christ and put our trust in Him, then an earnest desire to see the Savior will be planted in our hearts and the truth of His coming for us will be exceedingly precious.

As we move deeper into this chapter, we are given a glimpse inside the very throne room of God Himself. We can view some of the activities in Heaven before God's judgment is placed upon the world.

The scene that is described in these verses is almost beyond comprehension. But, in these verses, John gives us a small glimpse of what those who are saved will do someday! Let's join John in God's presence and try to grasp what occurs in these verses. I want to take us to Heaven and look inside the throne room of God.

You see, we need a heavenly perspective on this world. Taken by themselves, the events, the trials, and the problems of this world often make no sense. From an earthly perspective, this world appears to be out of control today: war, disease, crime, wickedness, ungodliness, etc. But, when you understand that God is on His throne and in control, and when you think He has a perfect, eternal, good plan, it all falls into place.

So, today, let's move up to Heaven and glimpse what is happening around God's throne. I want us to understand the scenes John saw when he went up to Heaven.

In **verses 2 and 3**, the very first thing John sees is God Himself sitting on a throne in Heaven. What a thrill that must have been!

Many years ago, I was honored to meet and have a long conversation with George W. Bush at a reception at the Governor's Mansion in Austin, Texas. It was also an honor to meet him again as President of our great nation and to later sit on his Small Business Advisory Council. Meeting the President of the greatest nation in the free world was exciting! But, to walk into the very throne room of God and see Jesus sitting on His throne would be glorious beyond description! Yet, that is the honor John was given, and it is an honor we will also enjoy! Let's listen in as John describes his encounter with Sovereign God.

In verse two, we see that He is the ruling one! The first thing John sees is a *"throne set in Heaven."* A *"throne"* speaks of *"sovereignty and authority."* We are viewing One Who occupies the place of absolute authority over all the affairs of Heaven and Earth. (**Psa. 47:8; 103:19**)

God's throne is eternal! No foe can ever force Him down from where He rules and reigns. (**Psa. 45:6**). *Your throne, O God,[a] will last for ever and ever; a scepter of justice will be the scepter of your kingdom.*

This world may not recognize God's authority and rule today, but He reigns nonetheless! Men do not give a second thought to the existence of God, but He notices all, controls all, and He will ultimately judge all. Men may not give Him the time of day now, but we will all face Him someday. Man may not bow today, but they will one day. (**Phil. 2:9-11; Rom. 14:12**).

In verse three, John attempts to do the impossible. He attempts to describe God. The One on this throne is God the Father. How do we know? God the Son takes the seven-sealed books out of His hand in **Rev. 5:5-7**. The verses say "*⁵ Then one of the elders said to me, "Do not weep! See, the Lion of the tribe of Judah, the Root of David, has triumphed. He is able to open the scroll and its seven seals." ⁶ Then I saw a Lamb, looking as if it had been slain, standing at the center of the throne, encircled by the four living creatures and the elders. The Lamb had seven horns and seven eyes, which are the seven spirits[a] of God sent out into all the earth. ⁷ He went and took the scroll from the right hand of him who sat on the throne.*

John describes God as a "*jasper and a sardine stone*". The word "*like*" lets us know we have encountered symbolic language. God is not a mineral or a stone, but His appearance reminded John of these two precious stones. The "*jasper*" is clear and bright. It may be the same as a diamond. A diamond is a hard stone. It speaks of "*firmness*". This comparison reminds us that our God is "*firm and unchanging.*" Since we are in a throne room where sovereign authority is about to be exercised, this tells us that God's laws, like God Himself, are firm and unchanging.

There are specific laws in nature that are firm and unchanging. Take gravity, for instance. God has established the ***Law of Gravity***; it is firm and unchanging. If you place a pot of water on a stove eye and turn on the heat, you need not expect to find ice in the pot when you return. God has established the ***Law of Thermodynamics***. It is unchanging.

The same is true concerning God's moral law. He is unchanging and inflexible there, too. Men kick against God's moral laws. They call the Bible out of date and old-fashioned. They do their own thing, thinking that God will let them slide. They are sinning against a God, who is firm and unchanging in His moral law.

The *"sardine"* stone is a blood-red stone. It reminds us that while God is a God of sovereign rule and absolute authority, who holds men to a high standard of holiness, He is also the God of redemption! He is a God who saves all who will turn to Him by faith.

Thank God He is a saving Lord as well as a Sovereign Lord. If He weren't, then we wouldn't have a chance! But it was this holy, righteous God of judgment and wrath Who was moved by mercy, love, and grace to provide a way of salvation for all who will come to Him!

As we remember these two stones, it is worth noting that the *"Sardius"* and the *"Jasper"* were the first and last stones in the breastplate of the High Priest (**Ex. 28:17-21**). The *"sardius"* represented the tribe of Reuben, and the *"jasper"* represented the tribe of Benjamin. These two stones represented all twelve stones and were a reminder that God always kept His people and covenants with His people close to His heart. In other words, these stones were a constant reminder that God would keep His Word and do everything He had promised.

Judgment will come, but it will be carried out by One Who has walked among us. His judgment has a human side. He will judge, but His compassion and mercy will temper it.

In verse three, we see he is a restraining one. An emerald rainbow encompasses God's throne. This rainbow is not like those we see here on Earth. We only see half the bow; in Heaven, it will all be visible. We also know that the rainbow signals that the storm has ended. We also know that the first rainbow was given to Noah as a visible sign that God would never again destroy the earth by a flood. (**Gen. 9:11-17**).

This rainbow in Heaven reminds us that the storms will be over for the children of God when we arrive there. It reminds us that while we may not understand everything that happens here, we will when we get there. It is also a reminder that God will judge the earth, but He will keep His promises and covenants.

You see, the rainbow speaks of God's mercy. Even as the wrath of God is about to fall on this doomed world, God is still moving in restraint and mercy. Every person reading this chapter is headed for an encounter with God! You might have parked your car and walked into Wal-Mart today, but you were headed toward God. You might have parked your car at Waffle House and headed into that building, but you were headed straight toward God. One day, we will all be face-to-face with Him. We will meet Him in scenes of glory or the halls of judgment, but we will meet Him just the same. Be ready for that moment! I want you to begin to think about YOUR Final Countdown with God. Will it be one of mercy and rejoicing? Or will it be anguish and fear because you know what will come?

Has it dawned on you yet that you will see Him one day? Has it become apparent that you will stand in His throne room and see His face? One day, the long road of life will end, and we will be home. Our journey will be complete, our burdens lifted, our tears dried away, our questions answered, our broken hearts healed forever, and we will be home! Praise God, there is a better day coming! Those of you who saved will experience this. Those of you who are not will still see him. You will see him as you are judged and sent weeping and screaming into eternal damnation. Too harsh? I am sorry. I am only telling you the truth.

In verse four, we see the assembly around the throne. Who are these individuals? Some people think they are angels or cherubim. I have never seen the word "*elders*" used to refer to angels in the Bible. Others think they represent some other group. From my research, they represent all the redeemed children of God. Let's examine the evidence. They are sitting on "*seats*". This is the same word translated as "*throne*" in verse two. Thus, they are seen to be reigning with God. The saints will reign with Him someday. **(2 Tim. 2:12; Rev. 1:6; Rev. 2:26-27)**.

They seem to be representative people. In **Rev. 21:12-14** the New Jerusalem is described as having twelve gates named after the twelve tribes of Israel. It is built on twelve foundations, which contain the names of the twelve Apostles. Twelve plus twelve equals twenty-four! these twenty-four elders represent the redeemed people of God in both the Old Testament and the New Testament.

In the Old Testament (1 Chron 23), David appointed twenty-four Levites to represent the entire priesthood. When a meeting was necessary, gathering every one of the thousands of Levites together would have been impossible. Still, when the twenty-four came together, they represented the whole body. The same is true of these Elders. They represent the entirety of the redeemed saints of God! These elders represent us!

If we look at their activity, we see they are at rest. They are *"sitting"*. This signifies rest. Their labors are over, and they are resting in the presence of God in Heaven. One day, we will be where God has already positioned us.

I want to remind you that one day, this life, with all its burdens, cares, worries, and problems, will be behind us forever. We will go to a new home where those things can never hinder or bother us again. (**Rev. 21:4**). We will enter His rest in Heaven!

Let's look at how they are clothed. They are *"clothed in white raiment"*. White garments in the Bible speak of *"the righteousness of the saints."* (**Rev. 19:8**). When God saved us He forgave our sins and forever cleansed every sin stain away from us. He declared us to be forgiven and justified in His eyes. (**1 Cor. 6:11; Rom. 5:1**).

How are they adorned? They have *"on their heads crowns of gold."* There are two words for crown in the New Testament. One is the word *"diadem"*. This is a word used to describe the many crowns Jesus will wear when He returns in power and glory to reign on the earth. This is the kingly crown, the crown of glory. The other is the word *"stephanos"*. It refers to *"a victor's crown."* It speaks of the crown given to victors in athletic contests.

The *"diadem"* is worn by Jesus by divine right. The *"stephanos"* is earned by the saints. We are told of at least five crowns that the people of the saints of God can win. These are as follows:

1. **The Crown of Life – James 1:12; Rev. 2:10** – This crown is given to those who demonstrate their love for Jesus by successfully enduring trials and temptations.
2. **The Crown of Righteousness – 2 Tim. 4:8** – This crown is given to those who live in the light of His coming. The saints, who long for, live for and love the coming of Jesus, can receive this crown.
3. **The Crown of Glory – 1 Pet. 5:4** – This crown is the reward of the faithful Pastor.
4. **The Crown of Rejoicing – 1 Thes. 2:19** – This crown is a reward for those who faithful share the Gospel message and point others to Jesus.

5. **The Imperishable Crown – 1 Cor. 9:25** – Awarded to those who battle the flesh and seek to live holy lives.

You need not worry that your service for the Lord Jesus will go unnoticed. He sees everything you do for His glory. He knows about every sacrifice. He sees every effort. He takes note of every prayer, every witness, and every secret thing you do to bring glory and honor to His Name. He will reward your faithful service one day. You may not receive recognition here, but you surely will in Heaven. If you do what you do for the praise of men, you have already received your reward. (**Matt. 6:1-6**)

In **verses 5-11** look at the praise before the throne of God. In verses 5-6, John watches, and amazing things begin to take place around the throne of God. This had to be hard for the old man to understand. Yet he does a great job of explaining what he saw! Let's break down the verses.

1. **Verse 5a He Speaks of Wonders** – "*Lightenings, thunderings and voices*" – The things speak of approaching judgment. Heaven booms with the warning signals that judgment is on the way. These same things are seen in **Exodus. 19:16-19**. The heavenly noises then warned the people of Israel to keep their distance from God's holy mountain. The sounds warned that men had better reverence God, or they would face Him in judgment.
2. **Verse 5b He Speaks of A Witness** – "seven lamps of fire" – This is the Spirit of God in His fullness, **Isa. 11:2**. The Spirit is no longer a "**Comforter**", **John 14:16, 26**; He is now an instrument of God's judgment. He is there to witness to the righteousness of the judgments that are about to fall on the earth.
3. **Verse 6a He Speaks of Waters** – "*a sea of glass like unto crystal*" – This crystal sea speaks of God's judgment as being form and fixed. On this earth, there is nothing more constantly changing or in motion than the ocean. The sea is never still, and it is never the same. This sea is solid and unmoving! Judgment is fixed, and it cannot be altered! If you will remember, there was a "*sea of brass*" called "*the laver*" outside the tent of the Tabernacle. Before the priests entered the tent, they were required to wash in the laver. It

symbolized cleansing and forgiveness of sin. How many times have I stopped at the laver of **1 John 1:9** and washed my sins and stains away? I thank God that there is a place of forgiveness and restoration today. In Heaven, that sea of brass has become a sea of glass. There will be no more need for the saints to come to God for cleansing. We will never fail Him again! That will be a blessing. But, for the lost sinner, this sea reminds us that it has become too late for repentance. Judgment is set and fixed. Man has reached his limit and God is about to pour out His wrath on a lost and sinful world. What a horror awaits the *"earth dwellers"*!

Then suddenly, in verses 6-11, there are shouts in Heaven! This throne room is a place of judgment, but it is also a place of praise. There are two groups involved in the praise of God on this occasion. Verses 6b-9 speak of the shouts of the beasts. The word *"**beasts**"* comes from the Greek word *"**zoon**"*. We get the words *"**zoo**"* and *"**zoology**"* from it. The word has the idea of *"**living ones.**"* John sees these four *"**living ones**"* and attempts to describe them for us.

1. He says that they are *"**full of eyes before and behind**."* This speaks of complete intelligence.
2. **One was like a lion**, which represents wild animal life.
3. **One was like a calf**, which represents domesticated animal life.
4. **One was like a man**, which represents intelligent life.
5. **One was like an eagle**, which represents bird life.
6. These four beasts represent the entirety of God's creation gathered before Him.
7. They are *"**full of eyes**"* – perfect intelligence; They have *"**six wings**"* – speaks of swiftness; They *"**rest not**"* – speaks of ceaseless activity.
8. These representatives of all creation stand in God's presence and lift their voices in praise to the Creator.
9. He is the Creator, and everything that was made exists for Him and His glory.

Then, in verse 8, we see their declaration! They declare His holiness, eternal nature, sovereignty, and control over all things. All of nature is involved in praising the Lord. You need to understand that the rain, the sun, the birds, the animals—everything but man—exists to glorify God. Everything but man glorifies Him by doing what He formed them to do!

Before we leave these beasts behind, we should also note that they represent different sides of the Lord Jesus. The Lion pictures Jesus as He is portrayed in the *Gospel of Matthew – The Lion of the tribe of Judah*. As a Lion, Jesus possesses majesty, power, and authority. The Calf pictures Jesus as He is portrayed in the *Gospel of Mark – The Suffering Servant*. As a servant, Jesus demonstrated service and strength. The Man pictures Jesus as He is portrayed in the *Gospel of Luke – The Son of Man*. As the Son of Man, Jesus possesses perfect intelligence and moral righteousness. The Eagle pictures Jesus as He is portrayed in the *Gospel of John – The Son of God* come down from Heaven. As the Son of God, Jesus possesses majesty and transcendence.

We aren't finished yet! Not even close! Starting in verse 9, we see **The Shout of The Believers**. It isn't just the four living creatures that lift their voices in praise. When the four beasts praise the Lord, the 24 elders join right in. Pay close attention to the content below.

1. Verse 9-10a Their **Praise Is Voluntary** – Nobody is seen forcing them to praise the Lord. When they hear their Lord exalted, they join right in. They fall before Him and worship their Redeemer!
2. Verse 10b Their **Praise Is Visible** – They don't just praise the Lord *"in their hearts."* They fall before Him and offer the Lord visible, open, unabashed praise.
3. Verse 10c Their **Praise Is Valuable** – They take the crowns they have been given and cast them at the feet of the Lord God. They acknowledge that where they are, when they have, and all they have accomplished is a direct result of His power, grace, and love. They owe it all to Him and offer Him everything they have. They are not concerned about their glory but are lost in **His** glory!
4. Verse 11 **Their Praise Is Vocal** – On top of everything else, they open their mouths and loudly proclaim their love and adoration for the Lord.
    - They declare His *"worthiness."*

- They declare His power.
- They declare His right to rule and reign.
- They agree with what He is about to do in the world.
- They declare the fact that He made the world and all that is in it. It is His, and He can do with it as He pleases!
- Heaven will pulsate with the praises of God!

Anytime man enters the presence of God, man always falls in worship. **(Isa. 6:5; Eze. 1:28; Dan. 7:15)**. Man is terrified in the presence of God and always falls in humble worship.

Do you want to know what we will be doing in Heaven? We will not be floating around on a cloud, strumming a harp. Neither will we be fishing, hunting, sleeping, or any of the foolish things we hear from time to time. If you want to know what we will be doing, look no further than this passage.

When we leave here, we will be called up, cleaned up, and caught in His praise and worship. When we arrive there, we will see what we were, where we were headed, and what He has done for us in saving our souls. We will not be able to restrain our praise! If we want to praise Him, let's do it here as we will there! Our praise should be *voluntary, visible, valuable, and vocal*.

I am excited about going to Heaven. How about you? I look forward to seeing my Lord and my God. I look forward to joining my voice with the other redeemed saints and praising the One who sought, bought, and delivered me from my sins. I want to live here as an expression of praise to the Lord who loves me. I want to be found glorifying Him by my life and how I praise Him. He is worthy of our love, devotion, adoration, and praise. He deserves it as much today as He will when we are with Him in glory. Let's give Him everything He deserves, and let's not wait for Heaven to do it!

As we leave this chapter, I want you to think about something. If you are not saved today, I want you to know that you will face the Lord in judgment. You need to come to Jesus for salvation. If you are saved and you want to thank Him for what He has given you, there is no time like the present.

Heavenly Father, we thank you for all the blessings of life, our homes, our food, our families, our friends, and our church home. Father, most of all, thank you for your son Jesus and what he did for us on the cross. It can't be bought, and we can do nothing to earn it. Father, I ask any of those reading this book to seek your face and accept the salvation you freely offer. In Christ's holy name, I pray. AMEN.

I must add one very proud note at the end of this chapter. I want to add that almost exactly 4 hours from finishing the end of this chapter; I baptized my seven-year-old granddaughter. She gave her life to the Lord Saturday, April 15, 2023, at 10:00 am. I ask you to rejoice with me and pray for Melettie Ann Letterman and her journey with Jesus.

WORTHY IS THE LAMB

As we enter this fifth chapter, let's look back! In **chapter 4**, John is caught up in Heaven. When he arrives, he sees God Himself sitting on a glorious throne. John sees Heaven arrayed as a courtroom. God is preparing to unleash His wrath on the inhabitants of the earth.

Amid this awesome scene, we also see Heaven filled with Jehovah's praises. Heaven understands what the Lord is about to do, and the inhabitants of that city praise the Lord for His glory, power, and creation. They also acknowledge His right to judge the earth.

Let's look at the scripture of **Revelation 5:1-7**.

5 And I saw in the right hand of him that sat on the throne a book written within and on the backside, sealed with seven seals.
² And I saw a strong angel proclaiming with a loud voice, Who is worthy to open the book, and to loose the seals thereof?
³ And no man in heaven, nor in earth, neither under the earth, was able to open the book, neither to look thereon.
⁴ And I wept much, because no man was found worthy to open and to read the book, neither to look thereon.
⁵ And one of the elders saith unto me, Weep not: behold, the Lion of the tribe of Judah, the Root of David, hath prevailed to open the book, and to loose the seven seals thereof.
⁶ And I beheld, and, lo, in the midst of the throne and of the four beasts, and in the midst of the elders, stood a Lamb as it had been slain, having seven horns and seven eyes, which are the seven Spirits of God sent forth into all the earth.
⁷ And he came and took the book out of the right hand of him that sat upon the throne.

John is taken to Heaven to give him a heavenly perspective concerning what will happen on the earth. I mentioned this before, and it is still true. When the events of this earth are viewed from a purely earthly perspective, they can cause fear, doubt, and confusion. But when all the events of history are viewed through the eyes of Heaven, everything makes sense!

So, **chapter four** ends with God receiving the praise of His created ones and of His redeemed ones. Heaven throbs with the voices of those caught up in their love for Almighty God. **Chapter five** finds us in the same courtroom in Heaven. Now, praise has ceased for a moment, and heavenly business is about to be transacted, and we will have front-row seats as it is acted out.

We are about to find out that, in Heaven, Jesus is the central Figure. He is the center of attention. Heaven will be a glorious, wonderful place. There will be streets of gold, walls of jasper, gates of pearl, and more glory than you and I can imagine. Seeing Abraham, Moses, Paul, and the rest will be great. But the main attraction of Heaven will be Jesus Himself. In this passage, we will see Jesus in His rightful place, glorified, and exalted in Heaven.

This passage sets the stage for the judgments during the Tribulation. It reveals Jesus in His heavenly glory. Let's look at these verses and consider ***Worthy Is the Lamb***.

Verse 1 shows us a mysterious scroll. As this chapter begins, God is said to be holding a book. This is not a book like we think of a book. It is a scroll. Paper was made in long sheets, and as it was written on, it would be rolled up. A portion would be written, and it would be rolled up and sealed. Another portion would be written, and then that portion would be rolled up and sealed. This scroll God holds has seven seals on it. This is a mysterious scroll. Let's see if we can unravel the mystery of the scroll.

As we read these verses, the character of this scroll becomes clear. In Verses 2-4, it has something to do with *"man."* It has something to do with the *"earth."* In **Revelation 6**, the seals of this scroll begin to be opened, and the scroll's contents are read. When they are, they reveal what will happen on the earth during the Tribulation Period. It seems that this scroll has something to do with *"redemption"*. When Jesus takes this scroll, He is praised for His redemptive work. (**Rev. 5:9-10**). This is a book of redemption. Redemption is something we talk about a lot. It is an important truth. Understanding redemption is vital to understanding God's great plan for the ages. Everything He does and has ever done is related to His redemptive work. To understand redemption, we need to look back to Old Testament times. In that time, three things could be redeemed.

A Slave could be redeemed – If a master lost a servant, he could pay a redemption price and buy that servant back. Jesus did that when He came to die on the cross for us. (**Rev. 5:9, Gal. 4:5, 1 Pet. 1:18-19**). We have been *"bought with a price."* (**1 Cor. 6:19-20.**) **A Wife could be redeemed** – If a woman was left as a widow with no male children, a close kinsman of her dead husband could redeem her and her husband's inheritance by paying a redemption price. This is seen in the book of Ruth when Boaz pays the price to redeem Ruth and her dead husband's inheritance. Jesus died on the cross to redeem a Bride unto Himself. (**Eph. 5:25-27**).

Land could be redeemed – If a man lost the land he had been given as an inheritance, he could buy his property back by paying a redemption price. This truth is demonstrated in **Jeremiah 32**. Jeremiah's uncle had lost a piece of property. Jeremiah's cousin comes to him when he is in prison and asks him to buy back the property in **verse 8**. Jeremiah does this and records the transaction on a scroll and seals it up, **verse. 10**.

History shows us they recorded the information related to redemption on both sides of a scroll. On the inside, they would write the reason the land was forfeited. On the outside, they would write the terms of the redemption.

They kept two copies of this transaction; one was open to the public for all to read, and another was kept sealed. These scrolls were laid up in the Temple in earthen jars for safekeeping. Jeremiah serves the function of a kinsman redeemer for the property that belonged to his uncle. What we are witnessing in **Rev. 5** is the heavenly version of what men did in Old Testament times. If you will notice, the book God holds is written on both sides. It is written up and sealed just like a deed.

When Jesus died on the cross, He did not just die for us. He also died for a ruined creation. (**Rom. 8:22-23**).

One of my professors once pointed out that the scroll we see here could be titled The Deed to Earth. When man sinned in Eden, sin entered this universe. Mankind fell that day, and God's creation came under a tragic curse. We will never know the extent to which sin has ruined creation, but we do know that when Adam fell, creation also fell.

Here is the problem. When God made man and placed him in the Garden of Eden, God gave man dominion over all of creation. **(Gen. 1:27-28)**. When man fell, he gave away his dominion, and Satan became the god of this world. **(2 Cor. 4:4)**. When God sent Jesus to redeem mankind on the cross, the blood of Jesus redeemed fallen sinners. But it was and is also sufficient to break the bondage of sin over creation. The Second Adam bought back everything the First Adam gave away.

So, this scroll in the hand of God is written within and without. On the inside is the tragic story of sin, tragedy, death, failure, and defeat. On the outside are the terms of redemption. If we could read these terms, we would find that the redeemer must be willing to redeem and one who is worthy to redeem.

Verses 2-4 give us a little information regarding the character and the content of this mysterious scroll John saw in the hand of God. For the next few verses, this scroll is front and center in Heaven, as a search is made for one worthy to break the seals and read the scroll's contents. In verse 2, an angel asks the all-important question, *"Who is worthy to open the book?"* In modern language, the question is more like, ***"Who is morally fit to read the text of this scroll and carry out all necessary to redeem the earth?"***

Notice that the angel did not ask who would like to open the book! Many men throughout the ages were more than willing but could not. More than one ruler has determined he will have dominion over the earth.

Alexander the Great conquered the known world by age 33 and wept because there were no more lands to conquer. He did not redeem the world. He left it worse than he found it! Before him, Nebuchadnezzar saw himself as the greatest ruler ever. He was not worthy to take dominion either. Julius Caesar, Napoleon Bonaparte, Charlemagne, Adolph Hitler, Vladimir Putin, and scores of others were more than willing to have dominion over the earth, but they were not worthy.

Soon, the world will see the rise of a demonically charged madman called the Antichrist. He will come far closer than any mortal man to ruling the world. But in the end, he will merely ruin the world. He will also prove that he is unworthy to possess the title deed to this planet and rule.

Thank God there is one who is worthy of taking the book and opening its seals. Later in this chapter, we will discover why He is worthy.

In verse 3, we see the reach of this search! A search is made throughout the universe for one worthy man to take the book and open it up. They searched Heaven above, Hell beneath, and Earth in between. They could find no one worthy to take the book!

No saint in Heaven was found worthy, not Abraham, Moses, David, or Paul. Gabriel, Michael, and all the angelic hosts of Heaven were not worthy to take that book. No one living on the earth, no king, no president, no ruler, no billionaire, no politician, no scientist, no preacher, no one was worthy to take the book. No one in Hell, no demon, no doomed sinner, not even old Satan himself, was worthy to take that book.

They searched high and low, but no man was found who was even worthy to look upon the book that rested in the hand of Almighty God!

In verse 4, we see the results of the search are made public, something happens in Heaven that had probably never happened before or since: John burst into tears! There are two words used for weeping in the New Testament. One is used in **John 11:35**, where the Bible says, "*Jesus wept.*" That word refers to "*silent weeping*". Jesus stood there at the tomb of His friend, and He wept in silence. The other word is used when Jesus wept over Jerusalem. (**Luke 19:41**). This word refers to "*uncontrollable sobbing.*" It is a small child's crying when its little heart is broken. It is the weeping you see when someone loses a loved one unexpectedly. It is open, unabashed weeping! It is the same word used in John's weeping in this verse. John is in Heaven, weeping out loud because no one is worthy to open the book, or even to look upon it.

Why is John weeping? John knows what that book represents. He knows that if no one can open the book, creation will feel the effects of sin for eternity. John's tears represent the tears of all humanity since man fell in Eden. John weeps for us all!

Now, in verses 5-7, we see the mighty power of the Lord Jesus Christ as it begins to be revealed in Heaven in all its magnificence. In these verses, we meet the One Who is worthy to take the book, to look on the book and to open the book. We are introduced in these verses to our magnificent savior!

John is weeping, but one of the elders comes to him and gives him some encouraging news. He tells John to wipe his eyes and stop his crying because, while no mere man is worthy, one has been found worthy who is! Notice the elder's words, *"**Weep not, behold...**"* Then, he points John to Jesus! That is the message the church has been preaching for 2,000 years, *"**Weep not, behold...**"* Regardless of the problem, Jesus is the solution! Weep not! Look to Jesus, and He will meet your needs! What a Savior!

In verse 5, the elder tells John that *"**the Lion of the tribe of Judah, the Root of David hath prevailed...**"* When John hears the title *"**Lion of the tribe of Judah,**"* he immediately knows that the elder refers to the Messiah. In **Gen. 49:8-10**, the Jews are promised that a great ruler will arise out of Judah. Like a lion, He will be powerful, strong, brave, and majestic. He will be a mighty conqueror! The Jews were looking for a Messiah who would throw off the yoke of their oppressors and give them liberty. They were looking for a military leader to lead them to victory over their enemies.

This person is also called *"**the Root of David.**"* This title reflects the humanity and the deity of the Messiah to come. He will raise up the withered branch of the line of David and bring it to power once again. That is the human side of the Messiah. But He was also the *"**power behind the throne.**"* The Messiah was the root out of which David sprang!

When Jesus came to this world, claiming to be the Messiah, He did not fulfill the expectations of the Jewish people. Instead of delivering the Jews from their bondage in a great military victory and establishing the Kingdom of Heaven on earth, Jesus went around healing, preaching, and performing miracles. As a result, the Jews rejected Him and their Messiah and crucified the *"**Lion of the tribe of Judah and the Root of David.**"*

When John hears of Jesus in Heaven, He is described as a mighty Lion and as a King and as the King of Kings. John is told that this Lion has prevailed. So, Jesus is described as a **Conquering Lion**.

But in verse 6, we see him as a crucified lamb. When John turns around to see this mighty, conquering Lion, he sees a *"**lamb as it had been slain.**"* The word *"**lamb**"* means *"**a little lamb, a pet lamb**"*. When John looked, he expected to see a great and powerful Lion; instead, he saw a little Lamb.

Of course, this scene is also wrapped up in Jewish symbolism. This image of the "little Lamb" reminds us of the Passover lamb. In **Exodus 12**, the people of Israel were instructed to select a perfect lamb, one without blemish and spot. They were to take that lamb into their home and nourish it and care for it for several days. During that time, you know what happened, that little lamb became like a pet lamb to that family. Then, on the prescribed day, they were to take that lamb, kill it, apply its blood to the doorposts of their home, roast its little body, and eat it. When the people did this, they were promised to be spared when the Lord came to judge the Egyptians. Don't you know that it broke the hearts of that little family to kill that pet lamb?

In that little dead lamb, the Israelites were given a powerful picture of what the Lord would do someday through the Redeemer He would send into the world. Just as that family would kill their pet lamb, God would judge His precious Son on Calvary's cross for **our** sins. Oh, how it must have broken the Father's heart to send His Son into a world filled with people who would hate Him, reject Him, and crucify Him. How it must have broken the heart of the Father to judge the Son in the place of sinners and to smell the sour stench of the sin of Man, all man, from the beginning of time to the end of the age!

But it was on the cross that Heaven won the most significant victory of all time and eternity! We are told that the Lion Lamb has *"prevailed."* This word means *"to carry off the victory."* Just because Jesus is a Lamb does not mean He is weak! Jesus carried off the victory at every possible turn. We see this in his victories on the Mount of Temptation, the Garden of Gethsemane, the victory on the cross, and the ultimate victory when He rose from the dead.

Satan must have thought he had defeated Jesus when Jesus died on the cross. Hell must have celebrated their perceived win, as the broken, bleeding body of Jesus was removed from that cross and placed in that borrowed tomb. For three days, the demons and devils of Hell must have cavorted in glee as they celebrated what they thought was Satan's victory over the Lord Jesus Christ.

What Satan thought was his most significant victory was his greatest defeat! The cross was one of God's most outstanding accomplishments! On the cross, God displayed more power and glory than He did in creation. When Jesus cried, "It is finished," it was a far more significant achievement than when He said, *"Let there be!"*

Jesus is called *"Lamb"* 28 times in the book of Revelation. Satan, the Lamb's enemy, is described as *"a great, red dragon."* **(Rev 12)**. Satan's power is defined as massive. He masses a great human army and a great demonic army, all intent on defeating God. Heaven's response to this vast display of infernal power is to send *"a little Lamb."* When a nation chooses a symbol, it usually selects an animal that suggests power and authority. The Lion is the Symbol of Great Britain. The Bear is the symbol of Russia. The Eagle is the symbol of the United States of America. When Heaven looked for a symbol, it displayed a *"slain Lamb," symbolizing humility, submission,* and gentleness. Jesus conquered Satan's kingdom not by military might but by humility, compassion, love, and submission!

So, a *"little Lamb"* won the victory, and because of that, He is worthy of taking the book. Before we leave this thought, let's take a moment to examine this Lamb in a little more detail. This little lamb is in Heaven. He is not in a dirty manger. He is not on a dusty road in Galilee. He is not on a ship in a storm. He is not sitting wearied and dirty on the rim of a well. He is not hanging in shame and agony on a cross. He is not lying in a cold, sealed tomb. He is where He deserves to be. He is on the throne. He is in Heaven! He is glorified and exalted.

This Lamb had been in the middle of the action all along. John had not seen Him until now, but He had been there the whole time. Just remember that Jesus is always in the midst when we gather. We might not recognize Him, but He is always here (**Matt. 18:20).**

This Lamb still bore the marks of having been slain. When we see Jesus in Heaven, we will see the marks of His suffering in His body. For all eternity, Jesus will bear the wounds of the cross as a constant reminder of what He did for us. There will be no room for pride in Heaven! No one can brag about how he/she got there. When we see Him, we will see His love on permanent display.

We also see this lamb standing. When Jesus ascended back to Heaven, we are told that He sat down at the right hand of God (Hebrews 1:3). He sat down because His work of redeeming sinners was complete. He stands in these verses because His work of delivering the earth is about to begin!

We also see that this Lamb has seven eyes. He is wise and all-knowing. This Lamb is omniscient. Nothing escapes His gaze.

What we see in verse 7 is a completing Lord! He finishes what he starts. We see the Lamb take the book out of the hand of God. When He does, Heaven breaks out in an anthem of praise. Heaven knows that Jesus is about to do the work of the Lion and deliver the earth and all of creation from the bondage of Satan and the blight of sin. He is about to complete His redemptive work.

The Lamb is worthy to take the book and open the seals. If this scroll is the title deed to the planet Earth, what right does He have to open it? There are at least three reasons why He has this right. I want you to remember all three!

1. The world is His *by right of Creation* – He made it!
2. The world is His *by right of Calvary* – He redeemed it!
3. The world is His *by right of Conquest* – He will retake it!

One day in Heaven, the Lamb will take the seven-sealed scroll out of the Father's hand. When He does, it will signal the beginning of the end for sin and Satan. On that day, Jesus will receive the glory the world has denied him for so long. He will be shown to be worthy of worship, rule, and reign over all creation. He has earned the right because He squared off against all of Hell and carried off the victory!

Jesus is a Winner! Those who know Him as their Savior are winners too. When Jesus stands, takes that scroll, and opens it up, we will be standing there watching, rejoicing, as He takes the world by force.

As you study this chapter and the verses we have discussed today, consider who Jesus is to you. He will be who you let Him be! He will be a Lion who will come to judge you someday if that is what you want Him to be. Or He will be a Lamb who will conquer your sins and save your soul. I am glad I know the Lamb! And because I do, I will never have to face the Lion!

HORSEMEN ON THE HORIZON

Revelation 6:1-8 is a shock to the senses. In the past two chapters, we have been allowed to witness scenes of heavenly *worship*. In this passage, we are going to see images of divine *wrath*. We have been to a place where there is *praise and shouting*. We are about to examine a scene filled with *pain and suffering*. We have been seated in "heavenly places" in chapters four and five, observing *"scenes of joy."* In chapter six, we are brought down to "earthly places" to observe *"scenes of judgment."* Let's read the scripture!

> *I watched as the Lamb opened the first of the seven seals. Then I heard one of the four living creatures say in a voice like thunder, "Come!" ² I looked, and there before me was a white horse! Its rider held a bow, and he was given a crown, and he rode out as a conqueror bent on conquest.*
>
> *³ When the Lamb opened the second seal, I heard the second living creature say, "Come!" ⁴ Then another horse came out, a fiery red one. Its rider was given power to take peace from the earth and to make people kill each other. To him was given a large sword.*
>
> *⁵ When the Lamb opened the third seal, I heard the third living creature say, "Come!" I looked, and there before me was a black horse! Its rider was holding a pair of scales in his hand. ⁶ Then I heard what sounded like a voice among the four living creatures, saying, "Two pounds[a] of wheat for a day's wages,[b] and six pounds[c] of barley for a day's wages,[d] and do not damage the oil and the wine!"*
>
> *⁷ When the Lamb opened the fourth seal, I heard the voice of the fourth living creature say, "Come!" ⁸ I looked, and there before me was a pale horse! Its rider was named Death, and Hades was following close behind him. They were given power over a fourth of the earth to kill by sword, famine, and plague, and by the wild*

beasts of the earth.

Beginning in chapter six through chapter nineteen, we are placed in the middle of the "Tribulation Period," or the time known as the "Great Tribulation." This **period of seven years** is broken down into **two parts**, with **each portion lasting 3 ½ years.** This period is clearly described in the Word of God. The verses below depict just a few references to this terrible period.

1. **Jeremiah 30:7**, "How awful that day will be! No other will be like it. It will be a time of trouble for Jacob, but he will be saved out of it."
2. **Daniel 12:1**, ""At that time Michael, the great prince who protects your people, will arise. There will be a time of distress such as has not happened from the beginning of nations until then. But at that time your people—everyone whose name is found written in the book—will be delivered."
3. **Matthew 24:21-22**, "[21] For then there will be great distress, unequaled from the beginning of the world until now—and never to be equaled again. If those days had not been cut short, no one would survive, but for the sake of the elect those days will be shortened."

In this passage, the seven seals in the book in the hand of the Lord Jesus begin to be broken, one by one. As the seals are opened, a series of divine judgments is poured out upon the earth and those who dwell on the earth. The four seals we will consider in this chapter describe events that will take place during the first 3 ½ year portion of the Tribulation.

We are about to witness a time of destruction, devastation, and death that our mortal minds can hardly comprehend. These verses describe events on Earth after the church has been removed in the Rapture. The world we are about to see has no Gospel witness. There are no Christians, gospel singing, preaching, or peace. This is a world in rebellion against its Maker. It is a world that stands on the brink of terrifying judgments.

In verse one, we are told that when the Lamb opens the first seal, there is "the noise of thunder" in Heaven. Just as thunder signals the approach of a storm, this heavenly thunder indicates that a storm is about to be unleashed upon this world that is almost beyond description.

Let's examine these verses together as we discover what God's Word says about The **Apocalyptic Horsemen and** what a lost world will face when the Tribulation begins.

The White Horse of Deception

Each of the Horsemen of the Apocalypse has a clear and distinct purpose. Let's start with the White Horse of Deception in verse 2. Some read this and say that this rider is Jesus Himself. They cite the similarities between these verses and those in **Rev. 19:11-16**. While there are some similarities, there are many more differences. The man on this horse is not the Christ. He is the Antichrist! There are several reasons why this man cannot be Jesus.

It is Jesus Who is breaking the seals, **Rev. 6:1**. Why would Jesus be in Heaven opening the seals and riding this white horse simultaneously? This rider wears a "*crown*"; Jesus wears "*many crowns.*" This rider wears a "*stephanos*", or a victor's crown. His crown is a prize. Jesus wears many "*diadems,*" the many crowns of the King of Kings.

The rider in these verses has his crown "*given unto him.*" This man was appointed a king by men. This rider is given a crown that he has earned. Jesus wears His crowns because of who He is, not what He has done. He is the King of Kings by birthright. Jesus is not given a crown. He "*gives*" crowns, **Rev. 2:10**. This rider carries a "*bow.*" Jesus carries a "*sword,*" **Rev. 19:15**.

My studies indicate from the similarities between this rider and the Lord Jesus that this man is the Antichrist. Wait, did I say similarities? Yes, I did. Satan is a great imitator! His plan unfolds as he copies that which is holy. In short, he creates his version of the Trinity, albeit unholy! We will learn more about this as our study progresses. For now, it is essential to note that he is not Jesus Christ. Now, we know who this man is not. Now, let's see what we can find about who he is. We immediately know the scene, which implies he is a man bringing peace. You will notice that this rider has a "*bow*" in his hand, but he has no arrows. This implies that he will conquer the world without bloodshed. He will accomplish this by providing the answer to the problems faced by the world today. He comes on a white horse, bringing a promise of peace to this world. When the Antichrist comes, he will come up with solutions for the world's problems. He will come with an explanation concerning the disappearance of all the Christians. He will come up with a plan to bring peace to this world. The world will fall at his feet and honor him as their ruler when he comes.

He comes as a Savior to a world desperate to be saved. Our world is in turmoil, and things will only get worse. Historian Arnold Toynbee said, "We are ripe for someone who can promise peace and tranquility to the earth. *We will deify that individual if he comes.*" Well, he is coming, and the world will love him.

Our world faces many problems today. Most of the turmoil centers on the nation of Israel. Iran, the Palestinians, and the rest of the Arab world desire to wipe Israel from the face of the earth. When the Antichrist comes, he will have the solution to the problem and establish a peace plan that will satisfy the world. (**Dan. 9:27**).

We are told that "*he went forth conquering, and to conquer*", which means he is a man of power. We are also told that "*a crown was given to him.*" The Antichrist will be given the key to the world. The leaders of the nations of the earth will bow at this man's feet and grant him the right to rule over the entire world. They have denied this right to the King of Kings. They have denied it to the Savior of men. They have denied it to the Son of God. But they will grant that privilege to this child of Hell.

The problem with the Antichrist is that he is different from the man he appears to be. He portrays himself as one person when he is, in fact, another person altogether. He comes riding a white horse. Think about this. The world is programmed to trust the man of the white horse! He is a good guy. He comes portraying himself as a man of peace. He will appear on the world stage, promising peace, safety, and prosperity. But he will be the evilest, dictatorial ruler the world has ever seen. Everything he is and says will be a study in lies and falsehoods.

Some would argue that the leaders of this world are too smart to fall for a deception like this. If you watch the news, you will soon realize that it is not always the best and brightest who rule our nation! Add to that the lessons from history, and you will see that this world is ripe for a satanic deception.

Just look at what Hitler did before WWII. Hitler had outlined in detail his plans for conquest in his book ***Mein Kampf***, which was published more than a decade before WWII began. Yet, the Western Allies persisted in believing Hitler's false claim to be a man of peace.

They stood idly by as he reoccupied the Rhineland (demilitarized after WWI), thus abrogating the Versailles Treaty. Then he annexed Austria, the Sudetenland, and Czechoslovakia. British Prime Minister Neville Chamberlain met with Hitler at Munich in 1938.

Upon his return to England, Chamberlain triumphantly waved a piece of paper that contained a pledge of peace from Hitler, which he claimed guaranteed peace. Winston Churchill rose in the House of Commons to declare that England had suffered a total, unmitigated defeat. Angry members of Parliament shouted him down.

The deception was nearly universal. Only after Hitler invaded Poland in 1939 did the Allies acknowledge the truth. By then, it was too late. The anti-Christ will be the same and do the same, only on a worldwide scale. This world is ripe for such a person to step into center stage.

The Red Horse of Destruction

Following the White Horse of Deception comes a second rider. This second horse and rider appears. This horse is red. Red is the color of fire and blood. Fire has the power to devour and to destroy. And when the fires of this war are unleashed upon this earth, there will be bloodshed on an unprecedented level. This seal unleashes a time of war the world has never known. The peace instituted by the Antichrist seems to be short-lived. War breaks out across the globe. Of course, this is what Jesus said would happen during the Tribulation. (**Matt. 24:6-7**). He also warns men about putting too much stock in the cries of peace bantered about by the politicians and rulers of this world. (**1 Thes. 5:3**)

Can you imagine a world that knows no peace at all? In every corner of the globe, violence and war will rage. That is the world that every lost sinner will face during the Tribulation. This rider is given a ***"great sword"*** to ravage the world. The word *"great"* refers to the extent of the warfare. It will be worldwide in its scope. The word *"sword"* refers to the short swords carried by Roman soldiers. These swords were used in hand-to-hand combat and effectively destroyed the enemy.

When Antichrist first steps onto the world stage, he will be hailed as a man of peace. But, after he is given the reins of power, he displays his true colors. He will demand absolute power after men allow him a place of prominence and power. When this happens, many of the powerful countries of this world will rebel, and the world will experience war on a scale that it has never witnessed.

During WWII over 50 million people died worldwide. That number will fall far short of the millions who will die during the wars that will rage during this time. It is during this period that Russia and her allies will invade Israel in fulfillment of **Eze. 38-39**. Their army will be defeated by divine intervention, and Israel will burn the weapons of warfare for seven years. (**Eze. 39:9-10**). The conflicts will not end here. However, the wars spawned by the Antichrist will rage, one after the other, until Jesus, the Prince of Peace, returns in power and glory! Imagine a world consumed by war. Nations will fight against nations. Race wars, class wars, and religious wars will abound. Indeed, many of these have already begun today! Peace will be elusive for everyone everywhere! The world is ripe for war today!

Add to that there will be no mothers, fathers, and churches praying for the soldiers in the wars. There will be no preachers taking the Gospel to men dying on foreign battlefields. This will be a time of war fought without God, Jesus, and hope.

The Black Horse of Destitution

Then, the third seal is broken, and the black horse of destitution appears. Black is a color associated with famine. Famine always follows in the aftermath of war. Thus, worldwide wars will spawn worldwide famines. Jesus spoke of this in **Matthew 24:7**. This will be a time marked by shortages. The rider on this horse has a set of scales in his hands. This indicates that the Tribulation Period will be marked by severe shortages in the necessities of life. The famines will be so severe that food and other necessities must be rationed.

We know very little about that in our day! We can go to a grocery store or a restaurant and buy all the food we can eat. Our cabinets, our refrigerators, and our freezers are filled. We know nothing about doing without or making do with just a little. But that day is coming! Rationing occurred here in America during World War II. When the war began, the military's demand for certain goods increased dramatically, and there were shortages. Ration books were handed out, and people used the coupons in those books to obtain the things they needed. Things we take for granted, like sugar, coffee, butter, meat, cheese, canned goods, shoes, and gasoline, were all carefully rationed. During the height of the war, sugar was limited to 12 ounces per week. Gas was limited to 3 gallons per ration period. Coffee was rationed at 1 pound for five weeks. We saw a small example of what this could be like during COVID. Nobody wanted to get out to pick up the things needed at the store and the shelves were bare. Even the basics like toilet paper could not be found.

I still remember going to a Dollar Tree and purchasing two large bundles of toilet paper. On the way out, I overheard an elderly man tell his wife, "It's OK, mother. We will find some toilet paper somewhere!" My heart went out to them. I immediately handed him one of the bundles I had just purchased. His wife thanked me profusely, tears streaming from her eyes while he fumbled for money. I felt sure he didn't have it. I just smiled and reminded him to pay it forward when the opportunity came.

We will find some good people still willing to share what they have. But I saw how ugly the world can get during the COVID pandemic. World War II shortages will pale compared to the deprivations suffered by those left to endure the Tribulation. **Verse 6** tells us this will be a time marked by starvation. A biblical *"measure"* would be enough food to feed a grown, working man for one day. A *"penny"* refers to the *"denarius"*, which was a day's wages. Wheat is the food from which bread is made. Barley was used primarily to feed livestock; at times, it was consumed by the very poor.

Here's the image. A man will work all day just to be able to buy enough good food to feed him. Or he can work all day to buy enough food fit for an animal to feed three people. Think about what this means! People will have to make some hard choices! People who cannot get out and work for themselves will be left to starve to death so that the workers can eat. It

will be a terrible time, marked by terrible starvation. Most of us have never experienced conditions such as these. But many in our world know the horror of starvation all too well. Consider the following statistics:
- Every 3.6 seconds, someone dies of starvation.
- Every year, 15 million children die of starvation and of hunger-related illnesses.
- 4 million people starve to death every year.
- 1.3 billion people live on less than $1.00 of income per day. Another 3 billion must try and survive on less than $3.00 per day.

As horrible as those figures are, they will be dwarfed by the starvation problem this world will face in the Tribulation.

The phrase *"and see thou hurt not the oil and the wine"* may indicate that the famines will not affect luxury items. Oil and wine have always been the items of the wealthy set. Oil is used in the manufacture of cosmetics, and alcohol has always been associated with the high life. In other words, while most of the world is plunged into poverty and starvation, the rich will continue to get richer and enjoy the extravagant lifestyles they enjoy now. This great divide already exists! Those of us in this room live in the lap of luxury compared to most people worldwide. Consider the following facts:
- The average American puts enough food in the trash can daily to feed a family of six in India.
- For the price of one missile, a school full of hungry children could eat lunch every day for five years.
- Throughout the 1990's, more than 100 million children died from illness and starvation. Those 100 million deaths could have been prevented for the price of ten Stealth bombers or what the world spends on its military in two days!
- To satisfy the world's sanitation and food requirements would cost only $13 billion US dollars. This is what the people of the United States and the European Union spend on perfume each year.
- The assets of the world's three richest men are more than the combined GNP of all the least developed countries on the planet.

The division between the *"haves"* and the *"have nots"* is vast today, but it will only grow wider during the Tribulation.

The Pale Horse of Devastation
Verses 7 and 8 speak of the fourth horse, which is said to be *"pale"* in color. The word pale comes from the same Greek word that gives us the English words *"chlorophyll"* and *"chlorine."* The word means *"Green"*. It refers to the *"sickly, yellow-green pallor of a corpse."*

The events that take place in the wake of this horse and rider also inevitably follow a time of war. However, these events seem to take place independently from those before.

We are told that the rider of this pale horse is *"death."* We are also told that *"hell"* follows behind him. The word *"death"* speaks of the death of the body. The word *"hell"* reminds us that there is a horrible place waiting to receive the souls of lost men when they are taken by death.) We are told that death will claim one-quarter of the world's population. That is one out of every four people living during those days. If you take today's population of eight billion people, you are talking about the death of 2 billion people in a short period!

If you look at the brutality of this devastation, you will see the methods death will use to claim this significant number of people. The four methods mentioned are the sword, famine, death, and beasts.

The **sword** refers to warfare. During this period, it is almost certain that wars will be both conventional as well as nuclear in nature. Someone will use a nuclear weapon in warfare someday. There can be little doubt that some countries will use biological and chemical weapons as well. The numbers that will die in these wars will be astronomical! No preacher, that would never happen! Nobody is going to push the button. I worked in intelligence as a field operator and later in my career in intelligence services. How would you feel if I told you I watched over the space of an hour as our nation climbed from DEFCON 5 to DEFCON 2 because a Soviet truck in the tundra raised a nuclear missile to a firing position, likely for maintenance? A soviet ICBM can reach the U.S in 25-30 minutes, depending on the point of launch and the target. That's not classified. That's Google.

During the Cuban Missile Crisis, U.S. Strategic Air Command was placed at DEFCON 2 while the rest of the military was at DEFCON 3. What that meant for military units: On Oct. 22, 1962, SAC ordered its B-52 bombers on airborne alert. Then, as tension grew over the next day, SAC was ordered to remain ready to strike targets inside of the Soviet Union.

Pilots flew these nuclear-laden airborne alerts, commonly known as Chrome Dome missions, for 24 hours before another aircrew assumed the same flight route," wrote Air Force journalist Stephanie Ritter. "Chrome Dome ensured that a percentage of SAC bombers could survive an enemy surprise attack and that the U.S. could retaliate against the Soviets. At the height of the air alerts, SAC produced 75 B-52 sorties daily.

In addition to the flying sorties, more than 100 intercontinental ballistic missiles were alerted, waiting for the President to release the birds to SAC. Thank God, that didn't happen.

We have already talked about the problem of **famine** and starvation that will become worldwide in its scope during the Tribulation. Many millions will meet their deaths in that fashion.

Death refers to deaths apart from warfare and famine. In **Matthew 24:7**, Jesus said this, "***For nation shall rise against nation, and kingdom against kingdom: and there shall be famines, and pestilences, and earthquakes, in divers places.***"

Here is the opinion of Mike Letterman. I say this because the Bible does not clearly say. So, opinion flame on! The word "***pestilences***" is what I think this word "***death***" is referring to. Pestilence suggests diseases that will run rampant through people during this time. Diseases like the "***bird flu***" will leave millions of dead in their wake. We may think something like that cannot happen. But think back to the Spanish Influenza outbreak during World War I. 25 million people died with the flu in a world without overnight, intercontinental air travel. Three times more people died of the flu during World War I than in battle!

An outbreak of that sort in our world has the potential to kill hundreds of millions of people in just a few short weeks. An outbreak like that would shut down society as we know it and would bring many more to the place of starvation.)

At the end of December 2019, the World Health Organization country office in China was notified of several cases of pneumonia of unknown etiology. These were the first cases of COVID-19. In the three years since, COVID-19 has killed more than 7.3 million people worldwide. In fact, some estimates suggest the total number of deaths could be more two times as large as reported globally—nearly eighteen million deaths—and more than ten times greater than reported in some countries.

Animal attacks or **Beasts** will account for many deaths. The word *"beasts"* can also refer to *"small animals"* or to *"rodents."* We are, once again, in the arena of Mike's opinion. The Bible does not say this specifically, but it could refer to rats with this phrase. Consider this information concerning rats. With all the warfare, the death, and the carnage, the rat population of this world will explode exponentially. One breeding pair can produce five litters of between 8 and 9 offspring annually. If 95% of the rat population in a given area is destroyed, they can replenish their numbers within one year. Rats are nasty animals. They carry some 35 known diseases. They, and the fleas they carried, were responsible for killing 1/3 of the population of Europe during the Middle Ages as the bubonic plague raged. Rats carry typhus, which has killed nearly 200 million people for one 400-year period. Rats destroy some $1 billion in food in the United States every year.

None of us knows how bad things will get before the Lord Jesus comes again. We are already seeing the beginnings of some of these things in our world.

If you listen very carefully, you may hear approaching hoof beats. The time I have tried to describe is coming! Are you ready?

THE MYSTERY OF THE 144,000

In **Revelation chapter 6**, we witnessed a world under a storm of divine judgment. The Lord Jesus took possession of the title deed to this planet in **chapter 5**. He began opening the seven seals of that title deed. He is beginning the process of redeeming this planet out of the hands of sin, sinners, and Satan.

We watched Jesus open six of the seven seals on the scroll. Before He did, there was a great burst of thunder in Heaven. **(Rev. 6:1)**. This thunder signaled the approaching storm of God's wrath. Judgment and wrath began to be poured out as each seal was opened upon the earth. I want to remind you that we haven't seen the worst suffering and sorrow coming upon this world. After the seals, seven trumpets will sound, and seven bowls will be poured out upon the earth. As we move deeper into this book's heart, we will see death, judgment, and sorrow intensify.

Before that happens, we are confronted with a divine parenthesis. **Chapter seven** is a parenthetical passage representing a pause in God's plan to judge the earth. The first part of the storm has passed; the worst part lies unseen in the future. We will examine the events that come later. In this chapter, we will consider the first part of **Revelation 7**.

Let's watch as the Lord extends grace to a select group of people amid the Tribulation Period. Two groups of people are in view here in **Revelation 7**. The first group is identified as the 144,000 in **verses 1-8**. The second group is recognized as a redeemed multitude in **verses 9-17**. We will consider the 144,000 today and, Lord willing, the redeemed multitude next. Let's take these verses and see what God has to say about the Mystery of the 144,000.

In verses 1-3, we see a deliberate pause in the action! There is a reason for this pause! God calls for a momentary peace to fall upon the earth because He has some divine business to transact. As God's wrath is rained down upon the earth, He pauses to answer a prayer that was prayed many centuries ago by the prophet Habakkuk, **(Hab. 3:2)**. By the way, this chapter is a great encouragement! Even during a time when death, suffering, and wrath will reign supreme, God will still be extending grace and saving souls for His glory! This has always been the Lord's method of operation. He remembered mercy in wrath when the blood of the lamb was applied to the doorposts of the houses in Egypt (**Ex. 12**). He remembered mercy in wrath when He delivered Lot from Sodom, (**Gen. 19**). He remembered mercy in wrath when He saved Noah and his family from the flood, (**Gen. 6**). Let's look at this break in the action.

We are told that four angels stand on the four corners of the earth, holding back the four winds of the earth. When I read these verses, some questions immediately began to form in my mind.

1. **Who are these angels?** From verse 2, these angels have been given the power to execute God's judgment upon the earth. The word "hurt" implies "injury without mercy." It is a picture of absolute destruction. These are avenging, judging angels.
2. **What are they doing?** – They are holding back the earth's four winds. When these angels appear, there will not be as much a breeze blowing anywhere on earth. There will not be a cold wind racing over the snowcapped peaks of Everest. There will be no siroccos blowing their scorching breath across the burning deserts of the world. There will be no ill winds or cool, pleasant breezes anywhere. The winds will cease for a time. This is an incredible display of divine power. The winds that race through the atmosphere of this world are driven by tremendously strong forces like the sun and the earth's rotation. Yet, four angels can restrain the winds. The word "holding" translates as a strong word. It was used to speak of horses straining against their bits. These winds are struggling to break free from the hold of the angels.
3. **What is meant by the winds?** – The word winds should be taken literally. As I mentioned, there will be no winds blowing on the earth. However, there is a sense in which the Bible uses wind in a spiritual sense. **Hosea 8:7** says, "*For they have sown the wind, and they shall reap the whirlwind:*" So, these angels are holding back the wind of divine judgment from off the earth as well. There is a

lull in the storm as God cares for His servants. God harnesses the winds of His divine judgment that they should not blow for a season.
4. **What is meant by** *"the four corners of the earth?"* – Does this mean that God thinks the earth is flat? Of course not! He answered that in **Isa. 40:22**. This is an idiomatic expression that refers to the four points of the compass. It is merely a figure of speech. (Ill. The ancient Jews superstitiously believed that winds that blew out of the north, south, east, or west were favorable or good winds. They also believed that winds that came from between these directions, hence from the four corners of the earth, were ill-favored. These winds could undoubtedly be described as ill-favored winds!)
5. **What is the significance of the number four?** – The Book of Revelation uses numbers a lot. Often, these numbers have spiritual meaning attached to them. For instance, the number seven is the number of divine completions. There are seven days in a week and seven colors in the spectrum. Revelation identifies seven churches, seven seals, seven trumpets, seven bowls, seven horns, etc. Four, on the other hand, is the number of the earth. There are four seasons, four elements – earth, wind, fire and water, directions, etc. Here, four angels hold four winds at the earth's four corners. This number lets us know that we are dealing with events happening on Earth. This is a time of earthly judgment!

After this deliberate pause, verses 2-3 show us the emergence of a divine personality. As John watches, a fifth angel appears on the earth. This angel rises from the east like the morning sun. Some have taken this to mean that this angel is none other than the Lord Jesus Christ. However, the word *"another"* translates the Greek word *"allos"* or άλλος, and tells us that this angel is just that, an angel. We may not know who he is, but we do know that he has incredible power. He comes commanding the first four angels to refrain from their mission of destruction upon the earth.

This angel has come to *"seal the servants of God in their foreheads."* If you don't know it by now, Satan is an imitator. Throughout this book, he attempts to duplicate many of the things God has done and is doing. We will see his place a mark on his servants in **Rev. 13:16-17**. He will give them the ***mark of the beast.***" This mark will identify them as his servants. This passage shows the Lord God as He seals His servants. The word "***seal***" refers to an official stamp. It suggests the signet rings used by kings to mark documents as official. A piece of wax would be placed on the document, and the king's signature ring would be pressed into it. This seal signified *possession, protection,* and *preservation.* This is seen several times in the Word of God (**Gen. 41:42; Est. 3:10; Dan. 6:17; Matt. 27:66**).

In the Bible, there are several instances of God sealing His people. Noah and his family were sealed up in the Ark (**Gen. 7:16**). Rahab was sealed by a scarlet thread hanging from her window (**Josh. 2:18**). The blood of the lamb sealed the children of Israel on the doorposts and lintels of their homes, (**Ex. 12:13**). The clearest example of this is in **Eze. 9:3-6**. Just as God sealed His servants in Ezekiel's day and protected them, He will do the same for His servants during that Tribulation Period.

While we are on this subject, let me remind you that if you are saved today, you, too, have been marked by God. He has sealed you. In **Eph. 1:13-14**, the Bible says, "*In whom ye also trusted, after that ye heard the word of truth, the gospel of your salvation: in whom also after that ye believed, ye were sealed with that holy Spirit of promise,* **14** *Which is the earnest of our inheritance until the redemption of the purchased possession, unto the praise of his glory.*"

When you were saved, an invisible mark was placed upon you. No one can see it, but it is there. God sealed you at that instant and marked you as His Own. What does this invisible mark mean?

The mark is a Seal of Possession – God places His seal upon your life and marks you as His possession! He claims you as His very Own. He paid the ultimate price to redeem you from your sins and owns you now, **1 Cor. 6:19-20**. Because He owns you, He will return for you someday. He will not desert you to the enemy.

The mark is a seal of protection. Since we are His, we can expect Him to protect us from the enemy's attacks. Satan would love nothing better than to defeat us and drag our souls to Hell (**1 Pet. 5:8**). But because we are sealed, he cannot get to us. We are "*kept by the power of God*", (**1 Pet. 1:5**). The word "*kept*" means "*garrisoned*". The Lord has set an eternal guard around our souls, and we are sealed and safe in Him!

The mark is **a** seal of preservation. **Eph. 4:30** tells us how long this seal will last. We are sealed until the day we arrive home in glory. Just as a jar of beans is sealed until someone pops that seal, God has sealed us, and we are safe in Him until we make it home to Heaven.

Now, we are introduced to the people the angel has come to seal. He calls them the *"servants of our God"*. The word *"servants"* is the word for *"slaves"*. These people are the saved and sealed servants of Jesus. But who are they, and what do they do?)

Verses 4-8 clearly explain where these people come from. They are from *"**all the tribes of the children of Israel.**"* Over the years, many groups have tried to claim that they are part of the 144,000. Several denominations have tried to make that claim. If anyone ever comes up to you claiming to be part of the 144,000, ask them which tribe they are from. That will usually put them on the run. Others have said that these 144,000 represent the church. The text is clear, however, that these 144,000 are Jewish men, called and saved out of the tribes of Israel.

I have been asked numerous questions about these 144,000 and the significance of 12,000 from each of the 12 tribes. I am going to address that here. Twelve in the Bible is a number associated with Israel. There were 12 tribes in Israel. There were 12 loaves of bread on the table of Shewbread in the Tabernacle. There were 12 gates to the city of Jerusalem. There were 12 stones in the breastplate of the high priest. The Lord is showing us that these men are from Israel. This teaches us a valuable lesson! God is not finished with Israel! He has a plan for their future restoration and redemption (**Romans 9-11).** Some of the tribes are not mentioned. The tribes of Dan and Ephraim are not mentioned, while the tribe of Levi, which did not receive an inheritance among the other tribes is. You will also notice that the tribe of Joseph is mentioned. In **Genesis 48**, Joseph's two sons, Manasseh and Ephraim, were adopted by Jacob and given an inheritance in Israel. It could be that Dan and Ephraim are not mentioned here because they went away into deep idolatry during the kingdom years. Therefore, they appear to have been left out of the list.

How and when will these 144,000 be saved? There are indications they will be saved by the preaching of the Two Witnesses mentioned in Rev.

11:1-12. God will send two preachers to preach the Gospel in Jerusalem. These 144,000 will be converted and sealed to a unique ministry by the Lord.

What makes them so unique? To answer that question, we must fast forward to Rev. 14:1-5. There, we learn that these men are sexually pure. They are virgins. We are also told they are entirely dedicated to the Lamb of God. They follow Him wherever He goes. They do His bidding without question. They are also called the "first fruits" of God and the Lamb. They are the first of many to be saved during the Tribulation's dark, dangerous, deadly days.

Another thing that marks them as unique is that God knows who they are! There is only one Jew in the entire universe who knows which tribe He is from. There is only one Jew who still possesses an accurate genealogy of his ancestry, and His name is Jesus Christ. He is from the tribe of Judah (**Matt. 1**). No other Jew knows which tribe he is from because all the genealogical records were destroyed in 70 A.D. when Titus, the Roman general, destroyed the temple in Jerusalem. The birth records were stored there, and they were destroyed forever. Now, no Jew may know which tribe he is from, but God does. He knows how to find them. He knows how to save them. He knows how to use them.

Now that we have more information regarding these men, let's look at their mission during the Tribulation. **Matthew 24:14 says, "*And this gospel of the kingdom shall be preached in all the world for a witness unto all nations; and then shall the end come.*"** This verse has never been fulfilled despite 2,000-plus years of evangelism and mission work. Hundreds of millions have never heard the name of Jesus, much less the Gospel of Grace.

There are places in our world where missionaries cannot go. During the Tribulation, that will change. The Lord will raise an army of 144,000 converted Jewish evangelists who will take the Gospel to the ends of the earth. They will fulfill the prophecy of **Matt. 24:14**. The Antichrist will try to stop them, but he will be powerless to hinder their ministry. He will be unable to silence, kill, or stop them. God has sealed them, and they will be protected until their ministry has been fulfilled.

Have you ever met a converted Jew? When a Jew comes to faith in Christ, you have never seen anyone with as much zeal for souls as a born-again Jew! I have several friends who are born-again Jews. I worked with one such gentleman. He was a man on fire for the Lord Jesus Christ. But his profession of faith cost him his entire family here on earth. When his family found out he had converted to Christianity, they visited him. There, in front of everyone, his father cut off a lock of his hair and burned it before him, signifying his son was now dead to him.

[3]In his commentary on the book of Revelation, John Walvoord noted, *"There are many precedents in Scripture for such a protection of God's own. When God sent the flood upon the earth, He separated Noah and his family from the rest of the human race, and the flood did not hurt them (cf. Gen. 7:1). When God destroyed Jericho, He protected Rahab and her household (cf. Josh. 6:22–23). Similarly, in the time of great tribulation, protection will be given to this group of 144,000 Israelites. The matter is so significant to God that the names of the tribes and the number to be saved from each are given in detail."*

He also continues his discussion that despite satanic persecution a godly remnant of Israel will be preserved to be on earth when Christ returns. The question has also been raised whether the "12,000" in each tribe means a literal 12,000. There seems to be an indication that more than 12,000 from each tribe will actually be saved. The point of this Scripture is that in any event 12,000 in each tribe are made secure. There will be other Israelites saved besides these 144,000, but many of these will die martyrs' deaths. The 144,000 are those who are delivered from their persecutors and brought safely through this terrible time of tribulation. In chapter 14 they are seen triumphant at the end of the tribulation when Christ returns.

For all its good intentions, the church has failed to reach the world. We have spent trillions of dollars; still, the world is filled with the unconverted and unreached. We live in a day of global communications, and still, we have not been able to take the Gospel to all the peoples of the earth. God help us; we won't even take the Gospel to the city where we live!

That will all change during the Tribulation! You might not imagine it, but the Tribulation will see the most extraordinary evangelistic effort the

---

[3] John Walvoord – The John Walvoord Prophecy Commentaries (Revelation) Moody Publishing

world has ever witnessed. These 144,000 redeemed Jewish preachers will take the Gospel to the whole world, and many will be saved. That excites me! I am glad the Lord is going to redeem millions during the Tribulation. Still, I want to see us do more to get the Gospel out in our day! We could do better, we should do better, and we must do better!

I won't pretend to have *all* the answers on the 144,000. We will study them in greater detail when we get to Chapter 14. I think now is a good time to praise God for His great plan to save many people during the most horrible time Earth will ever know.

So, here is the invitation. If you would like to praise the Lord for His grace and the seal, He has placed on you, please do that now. If you would like to ask Him to help you be a better witness for the glory of God, you come now. You don't need a preacher, priest, deacon, or elder to hear you. There is only one that you need to consult with. And that, my brothers, and sisters, is the Lord Jesus Christ! If you want to be saved so you can miss the Tribulation, you can do that now.

A MULTITUDE NO MAN COULD NUMBER

In the last chapter, we touched on the Tribulation and the Horsemen of the Apocalypse. We saw great horror befall our world as the wrath of God was loosed. In this chapter, I want to focus on the face of an angry yet forgiving God as he continues to offer redemption to those willing to accept his son. Let's read from the Word of God in **Revelation 7:9-17.**

Although I often use the NIV version for study, the text is taken from the King James version, as more people may be familiar with it. Regardless, yours should be similar. If it is not, we have a much larger problem!

> *7 [9] After this I beheld, and, lo, a great multitude, which no man could number, of all nations, and kindreds, and people, and tongues, stood before the throne, and before the Lamb, clothed with white robes, and palms in their hands;*
> *[10] And cried with a loud voice, saying, Salvation to our God which sitteth upon the throne, and unto the Lamb.*
> *[11] And all the angels stood round about the throne, and about the elders and the four beasts, and fell before the throne on their faces, and worshipped God,*
> *[12] Saying, Amen: Blessing, and glory, and wisdom, and thanksgiving, and honour, and power, and might, be unto our God for ever and ever. Amen.*
> *[13] And one of the elders answered, saying unto me, What are these which are arrayed in white robes? and whence came they?*
> *[14] And I said unto him, Sir, thou knowest. And he said to me, These are they which came out of great tribulation, and have washed their robes, and made them white in the blood of the Lamb.*

₁₅ Therefore are they before the throne of God, and serve him day and night in his temple: and he that sitteth on the throne shall dwell among them.
₁₆ They shall hunger no more, neither thirst any more; neither shall the sun light on them, nor any heat.
₁₇ For the Lamb which is in the midst of the throne shall feed them, and shall lead them unto living fountains of waters: and God shall wipe away all tears from their eyes.

As we continue through the Book of Revelation, we are in the middle of a parenthetical passage. Chapter seven is inserted into the narrative to allow us to glimpse God's grace at work during the most horrible time earth has ever known.

The seventh chapter of Revelation is the first "parenthetical passage" of the book. This first parenthetical passage is inserted here, between the sixth and seventh seals, and contains explanatory matter about things that will transpire during this time when the six seals will take place. This information was not contained when giving the six seals. The seventh chapter of Revelation is parenthetical. Instead of the natural order of events, the seventh seal does not follow the sixth seal immediately. Instead, an explanation of two distinct groups of redeemed people is given, breaking into the thought of the seals, and explaining certain things that are transpiring in and between the main order of events.

To understand the book of Revelation, one must be aware of seven parenthetical texts throughout the book of Revelation. Chapter seven is the first of these, coming between the sixth and the seventh seals, and reveals other things happening during this period. The two groups addressed here are the ministry of the 144,000 (Revelation 7:1-8) and the multitude saved during the Tribulation Period (Revelation 7:9-17).

In the first part of Chapter 7, we see the Lord redeeming 144,000 Jewish men. These men were sent out into the world to preach the Gospel of the Kingdom to all nations. In this passage, we will see the fruits of their preaching as a vast multitude is brought to faith in Jesus Christ and is delivered out of the Great Tribulation.

It comforts me to know that the Rapture of the church does not spell the end of people being saved. I praise the Lord that He intends to redeem a multitude that no man could number during the dark years of the Tribulation Period. This passage reveals the heart of our great and sovereign God! His heart of love continues to execute a plan to save sinners, and He will do just that during the Tribulation.

The Bible clearly shows that Jesus Christ came into this world to save sinners from their sins. **1 Timothy 1:15** states this clearly! *"This is a faithful saying, and worthy of all acceptations, that Christ Jesus came into the world to save sinners; of whom I am chief."*

It is also clear that God intends to save every person who will turn to Jesus by faith. Jesus said in **John 6:37**, *"All that the Father giveth me shall come to me; and him that cometh to me I will in no wise cast out."*

Here is God's promise to His elect, *"The Lord is not slack concerning his promise, as some men count slackness; but is longsuffering to us-ward, not willing that any should perish, but that all should come to repentance"* 2 Peter 3:9. That is the heartbeat of our sovereign God. It can be heard in the verses before us today.

Let's return to the tribulation period and rejoin John in his vision of that terrible time. In these verses, we will learn about a vast multitude of redeemed saints and get a glimpse into glory as the curtain is pulled back just a little.

Verses 9-12 describe this multitude. John's description reveals several things about these people. The first is their number. They are described as "a multitude which no man could number." They are a group of people so vast that John does not attempt to declare their number at all. What a wonderful image of the grace of our God!

On the Day of Pentecost, **Acts 2:41** depicts saving 3,000 souls. Sometime later, 5,000 were saved in one occasion, as depicted in Acts 4:4. We are also told in **Acts 2:47** that God *"added daily to the church such as should be saved."* I read that, and I am amazed at His saving power! But **Jonah 3:5-10** shows that about 1,000,000 were saved in Nineveh when the entire city repented and turned to faith in God. Praise God for His saving grace. The story of Israel's exodus from Egypt is even more impressive than that. Exodus 12 shows us that over 3,000,000 were saved by grace when they placed the blood on the doorposts of their houses by faith.

All these great demonstrations of God's powerful, saving grace pale compared to what He will do during the Tribulation Period! God will save a multitude that will number in the multiplied millions! Praise God for His grace!

The next thing we see are the nationalities of those who are saved! They come from "***all nations, and kindreds, people, and tongues.***" Here is a multitude that knows no racial, economic, social, or national distinctions. America certainly doesn't hold the only keys to salvation! The Gospel has been preached worldwide without respect to any group, and many are saved. They are Gentiles, and they have been saved by grace. In the first verses of this chapter, God dealt with Jews. Now, He extends His grace to the Gentile nations of the world.

I praise the Lord that the Gospel of Grace is a message that applies to all people everywhere. Mankind has prejudices, and we judge people by the color of their skin, their ethnic background, how they were raised, how much money they have, and many other foolish, ignorant standards. God, however, holds no such prejudices! He will save any soul that will come to Him by faith! I praise God that it is his way, or, like the old AC/DC song, it's a Highway to Hell!

This is a good time to voice a reminder! The Gospel message is neither Baptist, Methodist, Church of Christ, Catholic, or any other religious sect. I can tell you there will be people in heaven who worshipped in many different denominations and some who didn't worship in any! What matters will be those who have accepted Jesus Christ as their Lord and Savior and placed their faith in him alone for his saving power! I'm about to start preaching as I write this! I praise the Lord; the Gospel is for all! Any person who believes the Gospel anywhere in this world will be saved and go to Heaven.

Let's look at the nature of these people. Some people look at this multitude and see the church. <u>This multitude is not the church!</u> First, they are "standing". They are sitting when the church is shown in **Rev. 4:4** in Heaven. Second, as stated in verse 14, this crowd was saved "out of Great Tribulation." The church will be saved from that terrible time of wrath and judgment. Don't believe me? Look at **1 Thessalonians 1:10**, where the writer says, *"And to wait for his Son from heaven, whom he raised from the dead, even Jesus, which delivered us from the wrath to come."* While we are at it, let's look at **Romans 5:9** where it is written, *"Much more then, being now justified by his blood, we shall be saved from wrath through him."* And since we are already in the Book of Revelation, let's look at **Rev. 3:10** where John says, *"Because thou hast kept the word of my patience, I also will keep thee from the hour of temptation, which shall come upon all the world, to try them that dwell upon the earth."* While they are not the church, their appearance and condition in Heaven is clearly described.

First, we see that they are virtuous! We can see they are "clothed with white robes". This is always a picture of righteousness in the Bible. These people are saved by grace, and they have been rendered righteous. That is the promise of God to all who will come to Jesus Christ by faith. **1 John 1:7** says, *"But if we walk in the light, as he is in the light, we have fellowship one with another, and the blood of Jesus Christ his Son cleanseth us from all sin."* **Isa. 1:18** says, *"Come now, and let us reason together, saith the LORD: though your sins be as scarlet, they shall be as white as snow; though they be red like crimson, they shall be as wool."*

We need to remember and praise the name of the Lord that the blood of Jesus can reconcile us to God. When Jesus died, the wall of separation erected by sin was forever torn down, and now, we can be reconciled with God.

The second thing we see is they are victorious. These redeemed saints have palm branches in their hands. Palms are a symbol of victory. The crowds waved palm branches and placed them on the road as Jesus entered Jerusalem 2,000 years ago in **John 12:13**. These saints are celebrating the great victory that was given to them over sin, Satan, and the power of the Antichrist. They have overcome, and they enjoy the spoils of the victory they have been given.

Thirdly, let's look at what they shout! These saints lift their voices in an anthem of praise to their Redeemer for His redemption. They know they are in Heaven for one reason and one reason only. They are there because of the grace of God and the shed blood of the Lord Jesus Christ. They praise Him for His marvelous grace!

If there was ever a reason for praise, it is the grace of God and the sacrifice of Jesus for our sins! His salvation is the one reason for praise shared by all saints. Our circumstances may change, and we may walk through hard places in life, but if you are saved, your name is written down in the Lambs Book of Life, and it always will be. That is a reason for praise, shouting, singing, testimony, and all the glory we can render unto our great God. **Luke 10:20** demonstrates this when it says, *"Notwithstanding in this rejoice not, that the spirits are subject unto you; but rather rejoice, because your names are written in heaven."*

As we look at **verses 11-12**, we see them stimulate other voices of praise! When the angelic hosts around the throne of God witness the unbridled praise of this redeemed multitude, they join their voices with them in praise to God. The shouts of the multitude inspire the angels to praise the Lord too. Can you imagine the sound of millions, billions, and trillions of voices joining together in an anthem of praise?

Now, the angels lift their voices and cry, "Amen!" Thus, they add their agreement to the praises of the redeemed. They add a seven-fold statement of glory to God and praise Him for Who He is and what He does. They know what they have said is true, so they close their statement of praise with another "Amen!" Amen in Greek is written as Αμήν. The basic meaning of the Semitic root from which it is derived means "firm," "fixed," or "sure." The related Hebrew verb also means "reliable" and "trusted." The Greek Old Testament usually translates Amen as "so be it."

The angels cannot praise God for salvation, for they have never known the depths of sin. But these angels have seen the love of God in action as He went about saving lost humans. They marveled as they watched their Creator, the Lord Jesus, die on Calvary to save people who despised Him. They have witnessed the spontaneous outbursts of praise as sinners have been saved through the ages. Praising God for salvation is a human privilege. Angels are accorded the ability to rejoice for us! In **Luke 15:10**, Jesus said, *"I tell you, there is rejoicing in the presence of the angels of God over one sinner who repents."*

Verses 13-14 speak to the deliverance of this multitude. As John watches this powerful scene, one of the elders approaches him and asks John about the identity of this vast throng of people. John declares his ignorance of their identity and asks the elder to tell him who they are. The elder proceeds to do just that! John is told that these people "came out of great tribulation." These people have been living through the horrors of the Tribulations Period. But, even during that time of intense wrath and judgment, there is a ray of light as God's fantastic, boundless grace reaches down to touch a vast multitude of lost souls.

As we look at the method of their deliverance, we see these people were saved the same way they have always been and will always be. Their salvation is by grace through faith. **Ephesians 2:8-9** says clearly, *"For by grace are ye saved through faith; and that not of yourselves: it is the gift of God: ⁹ Not of works, lest any man should boast."*

We are told they *"washed their robes and made them white in the blood of the Lamb."* This simple statement reveals a profound truth. God only knows one method of salvation. Whether it was Adam and Eve in the Garden, Abel with his sacrifice, Abraham and his ram, or Israel and the sacrifices of the Tabernacle and the Temple, salvation in the Old Testament was through the blood of the Lamb. When they shed the blood of an innocent animal to atone for their sins, they were looking ahead to the day when God would send the perfect sacrifice that would take away sin forever. Those Old Testament saints were saved by looking forward to Calvary. When Jesus came and went to the cross, He accomplished what millions of animal sacrifices could not. When Jesus died, He obtained eternal salvation for all who will believe in Him!

Those of us on this side of the cross are saved by looking back to what Jesus did at the cross and realizing that His death and resurrection are all that is needed to our salvation. When we trust Him by faith, we are eternally saved. **Rom. 10:9-10** tells us, *"⁹ That if thou shalt confess with thy mouth the Lord Jesus, and shalt believe in thine heart that God hath raised him from the dead, thou shalt be saved. ¹⁰ For with the heart man believeth unto righteousness; and with the mouth confession is made unto salvation."*

Even amid the Great Tribulation, souls will be saved by the simple preaching of a simple Gospel. **1 Cor. 15:3-4** tells us, *"For I delivered unto you first of all that which I also received, how that Christ died for our sins* *according to the scriptures; And that he was buried, and that he rose again the third day according to the scriptures:"*

In verses 15-17, the Bible tells us they are destined to a heavenly presence. We are told in verse 15 that this multitude finds themselves at home in Heaven in the presence of Almighty God. Their days of suffering and sorrow have ended, and they have arrived in glory. They are no longer separated from the Lord by distance, sin, or time. They are home with Him, and they are there to stay!

We need to see where they are! Because they have been redeemed and cleansed, they are allowed to stand in the presence of God! This was unheard of in Bible times. In the Temple was the "Court of the Gentiles." This was the Temple's outer court, and non-Jews were not allowed to go any deeper into the Temple complex than this outer court. To do so brought a Gentile under the penalty of death.

When Jesus died, the veil in the Temple was ripped down the middle. **Matt. 27:51** says, "*[51] And, behold, the veil of the temple was rent in twain from the top to the bottom; and the earth did quake, and the rocks rent;*"

Look at this scripture carefully! The veil was not ripped from the bottom up but from the top down, as the mighty hands of God ripped the veil in an act that would forever end the Old Law. No longer would man have to go through a priest or someone to intercede on his/her behalf in order to come before the presence of the Lord. No more would the blood of bulls and goats be required to redeem sin. The blood of the *Lamb slain from the beginning of the world* had been offered as a sacrifice for the sin of **all mankind** from the beginning of time through the end of the age! The redeemed Gentiles are brought into the very presence of God. This signified the fact that all men had equal access to God.

As I preached in a live sermon, their present condition must make Satan livid with rage! Verse 14 tells us that they "came out of great tribulation." These people are in Heaven because they were martyred for their faith in Jesus and for their refusal to embrace the Antichrist. They are home, and judgment is being handed out on earth. The worst thing Satan could do to these people was to kill them, and it turned out to be the best thing that ever happened to them. They gave up the pain and sorrow of a world gone made for the safety and joy of an eternity in the presence of God!

The Bible says they will "serve Him day and night in His temple." This joyous, redeemed multitude is in the presence of God, and they are at the beck and call of God. They will spend eternity carrying out His will as they serve, worship, and bask in His presence.

Now, remember, these saints were saved out of the Tribulation Period. They had been saved but also suffered with everyone else on earth. Just because they turned to the Lord does not mean they were sheltered from the horrors of those days. Their faith in Jesus Christ might have made their lives even more miserable here. Remember, the book of Revelation is not in chronological order. We see people who have been martyred throughout the years of Tribulation. We are told several things about their past and what they can anticipate in Heaven.

They will hunger no more. Remember the famines we talked about in Rev. 6:5-6? We are also told that the Antichrist will require people to wear a mark on their bodies before they can buy or sell, **Rev. 13:16-18**. Because of their faith, they will refuse the mark and go hungry. The Bible also says that their refusal to wear the mark will be a death warrant to them, **Rev. 13:15**. But, we are told that in Heaven, the Lamb will feed them! There will be no more hunger in heaven. They are home, and they will be well cared for!

They will thirst no more. We are told that the earth's waters will turn to blood and be unfit to drink during the Tribulation, **Rev. 8:8**. As a result, the people of Earth will be thirsty. But, in Heaven, the Lamb leads them to fountains of living water. They are satisfied there.

They will suffer no more. The references to the sun and the heat remind us that the Tribulation Period will be a period of intense physical suffering, and the redeemed saints of God will not be immune from the effects of God's judgments upon nature. In Rev. 16:8-10, the sun's intensity will greatly increase, causing dehydrated men great pain and suffering. They will chew their tongues in their pain and agony. But, in Heaven, no things that hurt them on earth will be allowed to follow them there.

They will weep no more. Imagine all they have seen and suffered because of their faith! Their hearts have been broken, and their eyes wet with tears even as they gave their all for Jesus Christ. But the Lamb of God will wipe away the tears of their suffering and sorrow. He will comfort them and give them rest, peace, and blessings. These blessings can be ours as well!

I praise God for being a soul-saving God. I praise Him that He reaches down in grace to call lost sinners to Him that He might save them. It comforts my heart that He continues to do this even during the Tribulation Period. We ought to praise Him for His saving grace and power.

As I think about this multitude today, I pray none of my readers will ever be a part of that number. If you are saved, you will be swept up during the Rapture. If you are saved, you will see them one day and watch as they shout their praises unto God and the Lamb. Please remember eternity is only a heartbeat away.

I have had a couple of people ask me if I was truly going to close each chapter with an invitation. My answer is absolutely! There is no time to be saved like the present, and you don't need a church or a pastor to do so. So, here is the invitation!

If you are lost and would like to be save, come to Jesus today and let us show you how you can come to know Jesus. If you are saved but have issues between you and the Lord that need to be addressed, please make it right. If you want to thank Him for His grace and blessings, now is a good time! If you would like to pray for some lost people in your heart, let's do it! Whatever your needs are, remember Jesus is waiting.

HEAVEN FALLS SILIENT

We are now in **Revelation chapter 8**. In **Revelation 8:1-13** we continue to watch as the events of the Book of Revelation unfold. We have already witnessed the end of the church age, which will culminate in the Rapture of the church **(Rev. 4:1)**. We have watched as Heaven worships God and the Lamb for who they are, what they have done, and for what they will do, **(Rev. 4-5)**. We have seen the Lamb of God, the Lord Jesus, take the seven-sealed scroll from the hand of His Father. We have watched as He began breaking the seven seals **(Rev. 6)**. As He did, the earth was engulfed in one horror after another as the judgments of God began to fall on sinful men. We also studied the events of **(Rev. 7)**, where 144,000 Jewish evangelists are saved, sealed, and sent out to preach the Gospel of the Kingdom to all the world's nations **(Rev. 7:1-8)**. As they preached, a vast multitude was saved out of great tribulation, and their garments were washed in the blood of the Lamb. This redeemed multitude is pictured, healthy and whole, in Heaven in the presence of the Lamb and the Father **(Rev. 7:9-17)**.

That brings us to our text for this study. Let us read from the Word of God beginning in **Revelation Chapter 8, verses 1-13.**

> *8 When he opened the seventh seal, there was silence in heaven for about half an hour.*
> *² And I saw the seven angels who stand before God, and seven trumpets were given to them.*
> *³ Another angel, who had a golden censer, came and stood at the altar. He was given much incense to offer, with the prayers of all God's people, on the golden altar in front of the throne. ⁴ The smoke of the incense, together with the prayers of God's people, went up before God from the angel's hand. ⁵ Then the angel took the censer, filled it with fire from the altar, and hurled it on the*

earth; and there came peals of thunder, rumblings, flashes of lightning and an earthquake.
The Trumpets
⁶ Then the seven angels who had the seven trumpets prepared to sound them.
⁷ The first angel sounded his trumpet, and there came hail and fire mixed with blood, and it was hurled down on the earth. A third of the earth was burned up, a third of the trees were burned up, and all the green grass was burned up.
⁸ The second angel sounded his trumpet, and something like a huge mountain, all ablaze, was thrown into the sea. A third of the sea turned into blood, ⁹ a third of the living creatures in the sea died, and a third of the ships were destroyed.
¹⁰ The third angel sounded his trumpet, and a great star, blazing like a torch, fell from the sky on a third of the rivers and on the springs of water— ¹¹ the name of the star is Wormwood.[a] A third of the waters turned bitter, and many people died from the waters that had become bitter.
¹² The fourth angel sounded his trumpet, and a third of the sun was struck, a third of the moon, and a third of the stars, so that a third of them turned dark. A third of the day was without light, and also a third of the night.
¹³ As I watched, I heard an eagle that was flying in midair call out in a loud voice: "Woe! Woe! Woe to the inhabitants of the earth, because of the trumpet blasts about to be sounded by the other three angels!"

In **verse 1**, the Lord Jesus breaks the Seventh Seal, unleashing seven trumpet judgments upon the earth. If you think things have been horrible thus far, you are right, but the worst is yet to come.

In this chapter, we will watch as the first four trumpet judgments are sounded against the earth. We will see things go from bad to worse for those living on the earth during the Great Tribulation. Let's share the observations in this passage as we examine the subject *When Heaven Falls Silent*.

In **Verse 1**, John describes a scene that must be a first in Heaven. Absolute silence reigns there for one-half an hour. Chapters four, five, and seven describe Heaven as a place of worship, praise, joy, and song. Heaven is described as a place alive with noise. It is pictured as a place that throbs with the excitement of its inhabitants. Yet we are told there is silence in that land of praise for half an hour. The beast and elders are silent. The angels and the redeemed multitudes have neither no praise nor songs of joy to offer up. There are no divine pronouncements from the throne. Heaven sits in total silence.

Silence is a powerful thing. You can be about asleep in service, but let the preacher fall silent, and you will snap to attention. The silence at the beginning of a wedding enables you to know the time has come.

Silence can also be nerve-shattering! Have you ever been listening to the radio, and suddenly there is silence? You immediately wonder what has happened at the station, don't you? Imagine you have asked your girlfriend to marry you, and she sits silently for thirty minutes. Imagine you have been accused of a crime, and the jury has returned with your verdict. You are standing before the judge, waiting for him to read it to you, and for thirty minutes, he sits there in silence.

What we are seeing in this verse is the lull before the storm. The judgment of God is about to fall on the earth, and Heaven will have thirty minutes of silence before the judgments commence. **Habakkuk 2:20** says, **"But the LORD is in his holy temple: let all the earth keep silence before him."** Earth will not hear the Lord's voice, nor will they acknowledge Him at all. They rush on in their sins, living vain lives, all the while ignoring the God of Heaven. On the other hand, the inhabitants of Heaven understand what God is about to do and fall silent in awe at His presence and power.

Here on earth, people often ask for a moment of silence in the aftermath of tragic events. We saw that kind of thing after 9/11. We do it after the event because we cannot know when tragedy will strike. On the other hand, Heaven calls for a moment of silence before the event. Heaven knows tragedy is about to strike, and Heaven falls silent in the face of impending judgment.

In verses 2-5, we see preparations before the altar depicted. Seven angels are pictured standing before God, ready to do His bidding. These angels present a good lesson for us. We should also stand ready to do our Lord's bidding. In a day when people are concerned about education, wealth, health, and a host of other things they think they need to serve God, the most outstanding ability is still available. The Lord is looking for people with a heart like Isaiah's. He is looking for people who will say, *"Here am I"* when He asks, *"Whom shall we send?"* (**Isa. 6:1-8**).

These seven angels are given seven trumpets. These seven trumpets are going to be used to send judgments upon the earth. Trumpets, as you know, figured heavily in the lives of the ancient Jews. **Numbers 10:1-12** tells us that two silver trumpets were to be used to notify the people of Israel that certain events were about to occur. A certain blast was used to assemble all the people; another was used to assemble just the heads of the tribes. A particular sound was used to tell the people when it was time to break camp and march; another alerted them when there was a war. There was a specific sound that was to be made for each event. That is why Paul said, *"For if the trumpet give an uncertain sound, who shall prepare himself to the battle?"* (**1 Cor. 14:8**) So, trumpets were very important to the people of Israel.

Think with me for a minute about an event involving trumpets in ancient Israel. You will find the text in **Joshua 6:1-21**. The Israelites marched around Jericho once daily for six days and then seven times on the seventh day. As they marched, they sounded their trumpets. You know what happened! On the seventh day, after the seventh lap, they blew their trumpets and shouted, and the walls of Jericho fell flat.

There is a day during the Tribulation when Heaven will sound its trumpets against rebellious earth, and the walls of rebellion erected against holy God by sinful man will fall before His unstoppable wrath. These trumpets are war trumpets, and they are used to sound the attack. When God attacks the earth in His wrath, no one can repel His advance.

Verses 3-4 tell us another angel takes a censer filled with incense. He takes the incense and offers it along with the prayers of the saints on the altar before God. The smoke of the incense and the prayers of the saints ascend together into the very presence of God. These are mysterious verses, but they have some lessons to teach us today.

God keeps the prayers of the saints. As our prayers leave our hearts and lips to ascend to the throne of grace, they are not sent out to disappear forever. These verses show us that God holds onto our prayers and keeps them in His presence. Some prayers cannot be answered when we pray them; the time must be correct! However, they will be answered in His time, as we see in these verses.

Then, we see God answer the prayers of the saints. I am convinced that we are seeing the prayers of the saints under the altar. I am also convinced that the prayers of God's people down through the ages are also being answered. For two thousand years, God's people have prayed, *"**Our Father which art in heaven, Hallowed be thy name. Thy kingdom come. Thy will be done in earth, as it is in heaven.**"* Those prayers are about to be answered. For thousands of years, the people of God have asked Him to demonstrate His power, avenge His name, and get glory over sin and sinners. Those prayers are about to be answered. They have been kept and mingled with the fire of the finished work of Christ from the altar. They ascend before God, and they will be answered!

It is also important to note the prayers of the saints have power with God. Here are prayers that have been heard, preserved, and answered in God's time. **Eph. 5:2** says that Christ's finished redemptive work is a *"**sweet-smelling savour**"* in the nostrils of God. When we pray in Jesus' name, our prayers mingle with His finished work and rise before God as a sweet-smelling offering. It is an offering that He accepts and blesses for His glory! Our prayers ascend to God based on the shed blood of the Lord Jesus Christ, and God hears us when we pray.

There is power in the prayers of the saints of God! Think about it! We have an Advocate in Heaven **(1 John 2:1)**. An Advocate is a lawyer. We have one pleading our cause in Heaven. But wait, we have an Advocate in our hearts. **John 14:6** uses the word *"**Comforter**"* to refer to the Holy Ghost. It is the same word translated *"**Advocate**"* in **1 John 2:1**. We have one member of the Godhead pleading our cause in Heaven. We have one member of the Godhead pleading God's cause in our hearts. That is why you and I have power in our prayers!

Our praying may seem weak and ineffective at times, but by the time our prayers arrive in glory, they are not in the same form as when they left our feeble lips. The Spirit of God takes them and offers them to the Lord Jesus, who takes them and offers them to God. When He hears our prayers, they are a powerful force He uses for His glory!

The most influential people in this world are not the political movers and shakers. The most influential people are not kings, queens, dictators, presidents, and generals. The most influential people are not the celebrities and the wealthy. The most influential people in this world are widows, women, men, children, the poverty-stricken, and others who believe in the God of Heaven and call out to Him by faith. As you pray, your prayers are mingled with the finished work of Jesus, and you have power with God! There is more power in your prayers than you could have ever imagined!

In **Verse 5**, the angel takes the censer, fills it with fire from the altar, and casts it into the earth. When he does, there are sounds from the planet. These sounds are the premonitions of the ordeal coming upon the earth. Did you notice that the same fire that causes the incense and prayers to rise up also causes the judgments to come down? Men have rejected God's love, grace, and the gift of His Son, and nothing is left for them but the undiluted wrath and judgment of an offended God. That is what we are about to see as these trumpets are sounded and judgment falls upon the earth.

Verses 6-13 show us the great suffering on the earth. Verse 6 tells us that the angels take their places and prepare to sound their trumpets. As they do, we are about to see one horror after another visited upon the earth and its inhabitants.

Verse 7 depicts the trumpet of devastation. The first trumpet brings hail and fire mingled with blood. This may describe hail falling from the skies, mingling with lava from volcanic eruptions. The blood might be that of men and animals killed in the cataclysm, or it could refer to contaminated water droplets that appear as blood. Whatever the nature of this judgment, this storm of wrath falls upon the earth and burns up one-third of all the trees and all the grass. As a result of this judgment, oxygen levels will plummet, and the quality of breathable air will suffer greatly.

The word *"trees"* speaks of *"fruit trees."* Wheat, used to produce bread, is a type of grass. The grass is used for grazing livestock. So, this judgment will have a tremendous impact on worldwide food supplies. Here we are in great geological, ecological, and economic disaster.

In **verses 8-9**, we hear the trumpet of destruction. When the second trumpet sounds, a fiery mountain is seen falling into the sea. One-third of the sea is contaminated, one-third of all marine life dies, and one-third of all human ships are destroyed.

This could describe a meteor falling out of space and hitting the oceans. If that were to happen, it could easily destroy one-third of all life in the sea. This would contaminate the oceans with the dead, rotting bodies of marine life. It would also trigger massive tidal waves that would sink many ships. Their rusting hulks will choke shipping lanes and hinder the movements of men and materials. Mankind is very dependent upon the resources he retrieves from the sea. Man will suffer from hunger and economic disaster when the oceans are taken away as a source of life and livelihood.

Verses 7 and 8 both mention blood. Blood will fall from the skies, and the seas will be turned to blood.

Verses 10-11 show another trumpet is sounding. This is the trumpet of death. Another object falls from Heaven. It may be a comet since it is described as having a tail. It falls upon the fountains of fresh waters and causes them to become poisoned. The word "***wormwood***" translates the Greek word "***apsinthos***". It means "***bitterness***". It refers to a plant whose leaves are used to manufacture a certain drink called "***absinthe***". This alcoholic beverage is so toxic that it is banned in many countries. One-third of the sweet, fresh waters of the earth are poisoned, and many die from drinking these tainted waters.

In the town center of Chornobyl, there is the Wormwood Star Memorial, which depicts an angel blowing a trumpet, recalling the biblical prophecy. There is currently no star or comet that bears the name Wormwood.

However, in *Wormwood Forest*, Mary Mycio, a journalist with an ethnic Ukrainian background, provides the reader with a vivid impression of what the exclusion zone around the Chernobyl plant is really like. She first visited the zone ten years after the accident and describes the many people who assisted her on her visits, the local people she met, and the various bureaucratic niceties involved in administering and visiting the zone.

The book starts by correcting a mistaken impression that Chernobyl takes its name from the Ukrainian word for wormwood, a medicinal herb. *Chornobyl* is actually mugwort, *Artemisia vulgaris*, not wormwood, which is *A. absinthium*. It is odd, then, that the book is titled *Wormwood Forest* and has an associated quote on the cover: "And the name of the star is called wormwood; and the third part of the waters became wormwood; and many men died of the waters because they were made bitter." You can see the name wormwood remains a topic of conversation and fear in human society.

Yet Revelation is not the only place Wormwood is mentioned in the Bible. Consider these verses:

Proverbs 5:3-5
For the lips of a strange woman drop as an honeycomb, And her mouth is smoother than oil: But her end is bitter as wormwood, sharp as a two edged sword. Her feet go down to death; Her steps take hold on hell.

Revelation 8:11
And the name of the star is called Wormwood: and the third part of the waters became wormwood; and many men died of the waters, because they were made bitter.

Jeremiah 9:15
Therefore thus saith the LORD of hosts, the God of Israel; Behold, I will feed them, even this people, with wormwood, and give them water of gall to drink.

Proverbs 5:4
But her end is bitter as wormwood, sharp as a two-edged sword.

Lamentations 3:19
Remembering mine affliction and my misery, the wormwood and the gall.

In these verses, it is obvious Wormwood refers to the result of the tragedy, not the object thereof. Do we know of an asteroid or comet of sufficient size to cause this catastrophe, whose orbital pattern already brings it close to the Earth? The answer is yes. What I am about to share with you now is NOT from the Word of God and is purely based on analysis and scientific data.

In 2004, NASA identified a gigantic NEO (near-Earth object) or asteroid named Apophis. This asteroid has several startling statistics: It is currently 1200 feet across (the width of four football fields), weighs 20 million metric tons, and travels at 28,000 mph. Consumer-grade telescopes should be able to see it in about 4-5 years. After that, it will be visible to the naked eye.

NASA's website states they expect a "near miss" of Apophis on April 13, 2029, with an asteroid remaining 18,000 miles away. Unofficially, NASA feels the asteroid's gravitational field is so massive that it could neither miss Earth nor be destroyed or mitigated. The impact of something that large would unleash a blast, the equivalent of a billion tons of TNT (greater than 65,000 bombs the size of those dropped on Hiroshima and Nagasaki during WWII. To keep from alarming the public, space agencies are working behind the scenes to learn more and possibly mitigate an unhappy incident by this or any other spatial body. Former President Trump's Space Agency is just one such example.

Don't leave this chapter section with an alarm that says Mike Letterman is calling for the end of the world by **this** heavenly body! I am merely pointing out that these objects certainly exist, and our sovereign God can choose to use them for this purpose or, with a single thought, send us all to hell with a thunderclap.

In **Verse 12,** we hear another trumpet. This is the trumpet of darkness. When the fourth trumpet sounds, God reduces the power of the sun, moon, and stars by one-third. They are dimmed, and when they shine, they are not as bright as they used to be.

Based on the events that have unfolded before the fourth trumpet, there are many logical scientific reasons why this could be. This could result from all the ash and debris from the earlier judgments. This could also be the supernatural hand of God. However, the results are the same. The earth is plunged into darkness as the sun, moon, and stars refuse to give their light. This will affect growing seasons, weather patterns, plant life, temperatures on the earth, and mankind's physical and emotional health. This trumpet will take a tremendous toll on humanity.

Since the beginning of time, man has taken God for granted. Man has ignored Him, blasphemed Him, and lived as though He did not exist. Man has also taken God's creation for granted. There have always been plenty of trees and green grass. There has always been plenty of oxygen to breath. The sea has always been there, and it has always yielded its bounty to man as he has traveled and fished its waters. There has always been plenty of fresh water to drink. Just go to the faucet or the water fountain and turn it on. The sun, moon, and stars have always been in their place in the sky, and they have always given their light. During the Tribulation, God will take away what man has always taken for granted. Man will be judged for his refusal to bow before God and to acknowledge His Lordship.

Finally, in **verse 13,** we see the testimony and announcement of impending doom for the late great planet Earth. This chapter closes with an angel flying through Heaven, pronouncing further woes upon the earth. At this point, things are bad on the earth. However, they will become much more terrible. The worst part of the Tribulation still lies ahead.

We look at these things and ask, *"How could this ever happen?"* It will happen, just as God says it will. I want to share a couple of verses as I prepare to close this chapter.

The first is **Ezekiel 38:22-23,** *"And I will plead against him with pestilence and with blood; and I will rain upon him, and upon his bands, and upon the many people that are with him, an overflowing rain, and great hailstones, fire, and brimstone. Thus will I magnify myself, and sanctify myself; and I will be known in the eyes of many nations, and they shall know that I am the LORD."*

God will prove His glory on the day of His judgment. He will do the things we have read in these verses to show man who God is and the all-encompassing might of his power.

Another passage is **Matthew 24:29,** where Jesus says, *"Immediately after the tribulation of those days shall the sun be darkened, and the moon shall not give her light, and the stars shall fall from heaven, and the powers of the heavens shall be shaken:"* Jesus is describing the very events depicted in this chapter today.

Notice that last phrase: *"**and the powers of the heavens shall be shaken.**"* I want you to pay close attention here. Some readers will say, "Mike has been playing in the Greek again!" Yes, I have! Greek is a mighty and expressive language!

The word *"**powers**"* comes from the word *"**dunamis**"*, which gives us the word *"**dynamite.**"* It means *"**inherit, explosive power.**"* The word *"**heaven**"* comes from the word *"**uranos**"*, which gives us the word *"**uranium**"*. The word *"**shaken**"* means "to be set off balance." Now, without trying to change what the Scripture says, but looking at it this way, it reads: *"**And the powers of uranium shall be set off balance.**"*

When God created the universe, He built within the tiniest part of this universe, the atom and the subatomic particles that make up the atom, with the very power to destroy this universe. When man learned to *"**split the atom,**"* he unleashed the most potent and destructive force. Mankind possesses the power to destroy the world literally. Could it be that God will use a nuclear explosion to accomplish some of these things? I do not know, but I do know that He has built the potential into every atom in this universe. Everything around you, from the air you breathe to the chairs you sit in, can become an instrument of destruction.

We could elaborate more on this topic. But I believe you get the point! I could say more, but the bottom line is this: Judgment is coming upon this earth and upon all those who refuse the accept Jesus as their Savior. The best thing you can do today is be saved by His grace and be ready to meet Him when He comes so you can avoid the coming tragedies. Are you saved?

WHEN HELL COMES CALLING

There can be little doubt that the Book of Revelation contains some of the most frightening images in the entire Bible. This passage may be the most terrifying of them all.

Our text for this chapter is taken from Revelation 9, verses 1-12.

> *9 And the fifth angel sounded, and I saw a star fall from heaven unto the earth: and to him was given the key of the bottomless pit.*
> *² And he opened the bottomless pit; and there arose a smoke out of the pit, as the smoke of a great furnace; and the sun and the air were darkened by reason of the smoke of the pit.*
> *³ And there came out of the smoke locusts upon the earth: and unto them was given power, as the scorpions of the earth have power.*
> *⁴ And it was commanded them that they should not hurt the grass of the earth, neither any green thing, neither any tree; but only those men which have not the seal of God in their foreheads.*
> *⁵ And to them it was given that they should not kill them, but that they should be tormented five months: and their torment was as the torment of a scorpion, when he striketh a man.*
> *⁶ And in those days shall men seek death, and shall not find it; and shall desire to die, and death shall flee from them.*
> *⁷ And the shapes of the locusts were like unto horses prepared unto battle; and on their heads were as it were crowns like gold, and their faces were as the faces of men.*
> *⁸ And they had hair as the hair of women, and their teeth were as the teeth of lions.*
> *⁹ And they had breastplates, as it were breastplates of iron; and the sound of their wings was as the sound of chariots of many horses running to battle.*

> *¹⁰ And they had tails like unto scorpions, and there were stings in their tails: and their power was to hurt men five months.*
> *¹¹ And they had a king over them, which is the angel of the bottomless pit, whose name in the Hebrew tongue is Abaddon, but in the Greek tongue hath his name Apollyon.*
> *¹² One woe is past; and, behold, there come two woes more hereafter.*

We are amid the seven trumpet judgments. The first four trumpets have been sounded, and they brought forth horrible scenes of death and destruction. The earth's environment has been shattered, and mankind is writhing under the awful judgments of a holy God. Chapter 8 closes with an angel flying through Heaven pronouncing three *"woes"* upon the *"inhabiters of the earth"*. This angel knows that the plagues unleashed by the sounding of the last three trumpets will be far more horrible than anything we have witnessed.

Why does the Lord give us these graphic descriptions of what the world will face during the Tribulation? Why write about such tragedy, death, and suffering? There are three excellent reasons why these things are dealt with in the book of Revelation.

These things are mentioned so the church will know what we have been saved from. Knowing that God will deliver His people from this kind of judgment is exciting. He extends this glimpse of the future as a warning to those who have not trusted Jesus as their Savior. He wants them to know what they will face if they continue in their sin and in their rejection. They are given so that those who know the truth might be motivated to share the Gospel with the lost.

As we consider the judgment associated with the fifth trumpet, I would like to share some of the awful realities presented in these verses. There is a word here for you, whether you are saved or lost.

We are living in a day when the subject of Hell is viewed with much skepticism. People don't believe in a literal place of torment. Many preachers and church members have begun to reject the notion of Hell as it is presented in the Bible. People joke about Hell and use the word as a byword in everyday language. But the fact is, Hell is a real place! Those of you who were with us when we started the radio and Internet streaming ministry series The Final Countdown can recall the sermon I preached on Hell. Real people are going to endure real torments for a real eternity in a real place called Hell. They can attempt to deny it if they wish, but Hell is still real. In these verses, Hell visits Earth. I want to take these verses and highlight the terrible realities that will be visited upon the earth in the last days. In this chapter, we will focus on *When Hell Comes Calling!*

In **verse 1,** the fifth angel sounds his trumpet, we are introduced to a horrible personality. We are seeing the Devil in this verse. Look at how he is described! He is called a *"star"*. Some commentators attempt to spiritualize this passage and link this being with the star of **Rev. 8:10-11**. That could be true. I think the word *star* as it is used here has more than one meaning, in that the star of **Rev. 8:10-11** is a comet while this star is also a literal person.

When we think of stars, we often think of celebrities; of those who are famous in this world. There is a sense in which this person is famous. He is known in three worlds. He is known in Heaven; he is known on earth, and he is known under the earth. He is a famous personality. Of course, the Devil has a name. His name is *"Lucifer" (Isa. 14:12.) The name "Lucifer" means "Brilliant star; Light-bearer or Shining one."* So, we are introduced to Lucifer, a famous personality. This source of pain for mankind is a fallen personality. The word *"fall"* is a perfect tense verb. That means it refers to something that occurred in the past and still has present results. In other words, the sense of that word is *"fallen."* We are dealing with a fallen personality.

Satan's fall took place sometime in the past (**Luke 10:18**). As you know, Satan or Lucifer was a highly exalted archangel, but he was not content to be what the Lord created him to be. He wanted to be God (**Isa. 14:12-17; Eze. 28:11-19**). Pride was found in Lucifer, and he was cast out of Heaven. He still has access to the presence of God, where he accuses the brethren (**Job 1:6-12; 2:1-7**). He is the *"prince of the power of the air"* (**Eph. 2:2**). But there will come a day when Satan will be eternally cast down to the earth (**Rev. 12:10**). So, here we see Satan, cast out of Heaven, and forced to confine his activities to the earth. The thing that brought Satan down is the same thing that causes mankind his worst problems: *Pride*! Pride will cause you to think you are good enough without God. It will cause you to refuse to bow. It will cause you to walk in your self-righteousness. It will take you to Hell. God says if you humble yourself under His mighty hand, He will lift you up (**1 Pet. 5:6**). However, if you exalt yourself, He will bring you down (**Luke 14:11**). As the writer of Proverbs puts it, *"Pride goeth before destruction, and an haughty spirit before a fall,"* (**Pro. 16:18**).

There are differences between *"pride"* and being *"proud"* of something, perhaps your work. The late Rev. Billy Graham noted this in some of his writings. There's a difference between someone taking pride in their work and someone being prideful. Being proud of a good day's work differs from being proud at the expense of another. Do you see the difference? Christians fail to understand this difference and, in doing so, often do not share one of God's greatest gifts with others. Themselves! They are afraid of sharing their life experiences to the point where they think someone would think they are being prideful. Instead, they need to feel it is OK to share their experiences with others, as long as it is not at that other individual's expense! In almost every instance in the Bible, pride is associated with failure, not success.

We hear much about the inferiority complex, but the superiority complex of pride is seldom spoken of. Pride keeps thousands away from Christ as they ponder what their friends will think if they live a life surrendered to God. Jesus said, "Whoever exalts himself will be humbled, and he who humbles himself will be exalted" (Matthew 23:12). The entrance to the kingdom of Heaven is gained through coming to Christ with a humble spirit, not a spirit of pride.

We then see this individual has a fearsome personality! This famous, fallen figure is given a key to the bottomless pit. He is given the authority to unlock a terrible prison and unleash a horrific plague upon the world. We were told in **Rev. 1:18** that Jesus has the keys to "death and of Hell." For a short time, the power over a host of demonic spirits imprisoned in Hell is given to Satan.

Speaking of the devil, allow me to make a few statements about him. First, Satan is a real personality. He exists in this universe, and his power is genuine. He is not a myth; there is a genuine Devil. Second, Satan has never been in Hell. He is not there today, and he never wants to go there. He will be sent there one day as stated in **Rev. 20:10**. When he goes, he will go as a victim and not as a ruler. He hates the thought of Hell, but he will be punished there throughout eternity!

Third, Satan is one of the great mysteries of the Bible. Why would God allow a being like him to have the power that he does? Satan does have power! That is why we are told to be aware of him and of what he is doing. **1 Pet. 5:8** tells us so!. He has more power than you or I have, but praise the Lord, God is far more powerful than Satan will ever be!

Verse 2 tells us about this horrible place. In this verse, Satan takes the key he has been given, and he uses it to open the door to Hell. This verse tells us just how close men are to Hell. One turn of the key and Hell is unleashed upon the earth. This verse has some things to say about that place called Hell. Let's look at these!

First, it is called a "***bottomless pit***". The word "***bottomless***" gives us our word "***abyss***". It refers to a very deep chasm. The word means "***well***". When Satan turns his key and opens the pit, he opens the shaft that leads into Hell. Science denies it; lost men deny it; human reason denies it; but there is a place called Hell. The souls of lost people suffer in the fires of Hell. It is clear from the verses in this chapter that certain demons are being held in Hell, awaiting their liberty (**2 Pet. 2:4; Jude 6**).

We are also told this is a dark place. We are told that smoke ascends out of this pit and the smoke is so great that it obliterates the sun's light. Hell is a place of fire (**Luke 16:19-31; Rev. 14:10-11; 2 Thes. 1:8-9**). Yet, it is a place of darkness, anguish, and torment (**Matt. 8:12**). It is a place that no one should ever want to go.

Men joke about Hell and try to pass it off as silly superstition, but Hell is real, and wise people make their preparations to avoid its flames. You may not believe it, but a good, gracious God will allow you to go to Hell. My advice to you is that you should flee the wrath to come. Run to Jesus and be saved! Hell is disturbing to me simply because it exists. I don't like to think about it, but it is a real place where people will go unless they are saved. So, as disturbing as it is, we must take the time to consider it. Allow me to share a few features of Hell that make it truly disturbing.

Hell is a demonic place. Throughout the New Testament, Hell is associated with demonic activity. **Luke 8:31** teaches us the truth that the demons fear being sent to the abyss. **Rev. 11:7** tells us the Beast, the Antichrist, will ascend out of this place. As I have already mentioned, fallen angels are bound there and Satan himself will spend eternity in Hell.

In **verses 3-12,** we see a horrible plague. A demonic plague spews out onto the earth when the abyss is opened. The demons *"reserved unto judgment"* (**2 Pet. 2:4**) are released to carry out their infernal mission. Imagine a world in which every prison door was suddenly opened. Murders, rapists, serial killers, and the criminally insane are all allowed to walk free. Can you imagine the chaos, the pain, and the suffering that would occur? Well, the prison doors of the earth will not be opened, but Hell's prison will be opened and emptied, and a lost world will be thrown into a time of terrible judgment!

They are described as locusts. But these are no insects. The description probably comes from the greatness of their numbers. One locust swarm reported in 1889 covered over 2,000 square miles. The image here is of an innumerable host of demons being allowed to ascend out of Hell onto the earth. There are a couple of reasons why I say that these are not real locusts. **Verse 4** tells us they do not harm plant life but torment humans. Verse 11 tells us they have a king. **Pro. 30:25** tells us that locusts in the insect world have no king.

Verses 3-4 tell us about their power! These demons are described as locusts, but unlike locusts, they will not harm the vegetation. A literal locust swarm will leave a green landscape looking like a desert in a very short period. Locusts devour the leaf, the grain, and the stalk. These locusts do not come for the plant life but for human life. They will have the power to sting like a scorpion. Scorpion stings are known to be very painful. They cause swelling and numbness, but they are rarely fatal in humans.

So, these demonic beings are allowed out of Hell, they have the power to cause great pain to people. But their targets are limited. They will only sting those who are unsaved. The 144,000 and other believers are protected from the attacks of this great horde of Hell.

Verses 5-6 speak to the pain they produce. When this attack comes, people will not be killed, but they will be tormented for five months. Five months, May to September, is the typical lifespan of a locust. These hellish locusts will torment men for five months. The pain inflicted upon men will be unimaginable. Every moment of every day, that demon will be there, tormenting, stinging, causing pain and suffering. There will be no escape!

Men will seek every way they can to escape the torment of these demons, but nothing will help them. No pills, no potions, no modern medicine will work. Alcohol and drugs will not deaden the pain. For five long months, they will suffer, and they will find no relief from their suffering.

In our day, people flee death. They do everything they can to stave off his coming. Doctors are consulted, pills are consumed, and everything that can be done is done to extend life for a moment more. But in that day, men will pursue death to be free from their pain. People will leap from buildings, crushing their bodies upon the ground, and still not be able to die. People will drink deadly poisons and ravage their vital organs and not be able to escape. Others will place guns in their temples and attempt to kill themselves, but they will only succeed in adding more misery to their torment.

People may try to kill their loved ones to help them escape, but to no avail. For five months there will be no funerals on earth. Death will take a holiday while men endure the pain and suffering inflicted on them by this demonic invasion.

Some may say, *"Brother Mike, I don't think it will happen like that."* Read it again! *"**During those days people will seek death but will not find it; they will long to die, but death will elude them.**"*. It breaks my heart to have to tell you these things, but they are real. They are true and they will be your future if you refuse to come to Jesus for salvation!

Verses 7-11 give us an extraordinary visual. Beginning in verse 6, these demons are described for us. Let's take a few minutes to consider John's vivid description of this demonic army.

Verse 7 tells us of *horses prepared to battle* – They resemble mighty war horses, prepared for battle, straining at the bit. They have golden crowns on their heads. They come to the earth as conquerors. No medicine or act of science can conquer them. For five long, awful months, these demons reign on the earth. It also speaks to *faces like those of men*. This speaks of their intelligence. The human face is so expressive. It reveals the emotions buried beneath the surface. These beings are intelligent.

Verse 8 tells us they have *hair like a woman*. They are attractive to people. They may have some seductive charm by which they lure their victims to them. People have always been attracted to the occult. Just look at the popularity of so-called psychics, the current fascination with angels, etc. They also have *teeth like a lion*. Their bite is infectious and painful. A lion's bite never really heals. There is so much infection and bacteria in the bite of a lion that the wound will rarely heal completely.

Verse 9 depicts *breastplates of iron*. They are invulnerable to attack and insensitive to humans' sufferings. Men will try to kill these demons, but that will be impossible. Men will scream in their pain and will beg for mercy, but their pleas will not touch the hearts of their tormenters. It is also noted they have *wings that sound like chariots*. This implies swiftness. They will be able to surround and capture their prey with ease. Men will attempt to run, but there can be no escape.

Verse 10 speaks of the *stings in their tails.* We have already touched on their capability to inflict pain. It is mentioned here to emphasize the fact that the pain and torment of men is their sole objective.

Verse 11 tells us *they have a king over them*. They will be organized and united in their attacks upon humanity. The fact that this king's name is given in Hebrew and Greek shows us that all unbelievers, both Jew and Gentile, will be targeted by this demonic invasion.

I want you to think for a moment. What would it be like to awaken one morning to find this creature waiting for you? That day will come for multiplied millions of lost people. People hear talk about demons, and they laugh it off and say, "*Oh my! No one believes in demons anymore!*" Oh really? It would seem from reading this passage that God does! Just because you can't see them does not mean they are not real.

When the bubonic plague was ravaging Europe during the Middle Ages, men tried every way they could to cure the disease. They came to believe that the plague was caused by clean, fresh air, so they plugged up their chimneys, burned disgusting things in their fireplaces, sat in smoke-filled houses, believing they would be all right. Whole cities were clothed in foul-smelling, putrid smoke. They would fire their cannons regularly to blow away the fresh air. If you had walked into one of those towns and told the people that the plague was caused by an invisible organism transmitted by tiny fleas, they would have laughed you out of town. We now know that what they couldn't see was killing them. Modern man has adopted the same attitude regarding the spiritual realm. He can't see demons, so they must not be real. Well, they are! Jesus believed in them and even confronted them in the Gospels. Paul had a run-in or two with demons in Acts. They are real!

You do not have to be here for the day when Hell comes calling. If you come to Jesus, He will save your soul and take you to a beautiful place called Heaven. If you are saved, you will miss the violence and torment of the Tribulation. You can miss out on this terrible time if you will come to Jesus Christ. There is a way out! Don't wait until **Hell Comes Calling** to cry out for mercy. Cry out to God today and be saved by His grace! Where will you spend eternity?

A WORLD AT WAR

The images depicted in **Revelation 9:13-21** make it one of the most disturbing passages in the entire Bible. In **verses 1-12**, we studied a description of a swarm of demons. These demons came to the earth to torment all those who refused to bow to God. They tormented men for five long months and brought terrible suffering to the unsaved. The only grace in those verses is the fact that those who know the Lord Jesus as their Savior will be spared from that attack. It is also a blessing to know that those saved will miss that terrible time because they are safe, at home in Heaven, with the Lord Jesus.

As we continue to look at the events of **chapter 9**, we come to the sixth trumpet judgment. When that trumpet sounds, a voice is heard from between the golden altar's horns. The mention of this altar reminds us of the golden incense altar in the Tabernacle and the temple. The golden altar was where incense was burned as an offering to God. It was the place of prayer, the place of intercession. It was a place of mercy where prayers could be offered to the Lord.

In these verses, the place of mercy has become a place of judgment. When people reject God's grace, mercy, and love, they are left with nothing but His wrath and judgment. That is what we are going to see in these verses. The world has rejected grace, and they are given judgment.

Let's take some time today to examine the events of the latter part of **Revelation 9**. We are given a picture here of *The World at War*. Let's look at God's Word.

> *13 And the sixth angel sounded, and I heard a voice from the four horns of the golden altar which is before God,*
> *14 Saying to the sixth angel which had the trumpet, Loose the four angels which are bound in the great river Euphrates.*
> *15 And the four angels were loosed, which were prepared for an hour, and a day, and a month, and a year, for to slay the third*

part of men.
¹⁶ And the number of the army of the horsemen were two hundred thousand thousand: and I heard the number of them.
¹⁷ And thus I saw the horses in the vision, and them that sat on them, having breastplates of fire, and of jacinth, and brimstone: and the heads of the horses were as the heads of lions; and out of their mouths issued fire and smoke and brimstone.
¹⁸ By these three was the third part of men killed, by the fire, and by the smoke, and by the brimstone, which issued out of their mouths.
¹⁹ For their power is in their mouth, and in their tails: for their tails were like unto serpents, and had heads, and with them they do hurt.
²⁰ And the rest of the men which were not killed by these plagues yet repented not of the works of their hands, that they should not worship devils, and idols of gold, and silver, and brass, and stone, and of wood: which neither can see, nor hear, nor walk:
²¹ Neither repented they of their murders, nor of their sorceries, nor of their fornication, nor of their thefts.

Verse 14-15 shows us this is a time of great demonic activity. The voice from the altar commands the release of four fallen angels kept chained in the Euphrates River. We do not know why these angels were chained to begin with. We do not know how long they have been chained. But we know that when they are let loose on the world, terrible death and destruction follow with them. We are not given much information about these angels, but a few truths are mentioned here that need to be addressed. We see in **verse 14,** that a specific place is mentioned. We are told that they are bound in the *"River Euphrates."*

River Euphrates Modern Day Turkey

This river is one of the most prominent in the Word of God. It was here that God planted the Garden of Eden in **Gen. 2:14**. It was here that God made mankind. The Euphrates River has been the scene of many of the firsts of humanity. The first sin, the first apostasy, the first murder, and the first rebellion against the Word of God all occurred here.

The ancient city of Babylon sprang to life along the banks of this river. Babylon was the birthplace of false religion, demon worship, and idolatry. Many of the false religions practiced in our world today can trace their origins to Babylon. This area was the home of Nimrod (**Gen. 10:8-10**). He was the father of many vile, ungodly worship practices, some of which still exist to this day!

Along the banks of this great river, it was here that all the world's great cultural, religious, and political systems came to life. This river was said to be the eastern boundary of the land promised to Abraham (**Gen. 15:18**). This river forms the dividing line between the Middle East and the Far East. The world's attention is focused on this area today, and it will continue to be the focus of the world's attention until Jesus comes in glory.

Verse 15 tells us of a specific plan. These angels have been kept bound until a specific time. God will use them for His purposes as He judges the earth. The words, *"were prepared for an hour, and a day, and a month, and a year,"* tell us that God has a plan! As we read this book, things may appear spinning out of control. But the opposite is true! God controls and works out His will according to a highly detailed, specific timetable. He knows what He is doing and can be trusted to do it right.

A specific purpose is also mentioned. This verse is very graphic. It tells us that these demonic spirits are released for the sole purpose of destroying one-third of humanity. Consider these facts. Rev. 6:8 says that 25% of the earth's population is killed there. **Rev. 8:11** says that many will die from drinking poisoned waters. If the population of the earth is about 6 billion when the Tribulation begins, it will have been cut in half by the time the sixth trumpet judgment is carried out, and another one-third of humanity is slaughtered. Imagine, in the space of a few short years, 50%, one out of every two people living on the earth are dead and gone! In the United States, it would be the equivalent of 150 million people dead in a very short period. Yes, according to **Rev. 9:5-6**, the dead will take a five-month holiday, but they will come back with a vengeance, and billions will die at the hands of these four fallen angels!

People read this, and they look at it with doubt. They make fun of the notion of fallen angels, bound in a river, released on the earth, bringing with them untold death and suffering. Men may deny the truth of these verses, but that does not diminish their reality.

Angels have power, and fallen angels have power as well. Daniel found this out when he prayed to the Lord, and the answer to his prayer was delayed three weeks by demonic activity (**Dan. 10:12-13**).

We cannot see it, but there is a struggle around us right now (**Eph. 6:12**). Angels and demons are at war. One day, the reality of the spiritual battle will be made real to humanity. Four demons will be released on this earth, and one-third of the remaining human population will die!

Verses 16-19 speak of a time of great destruction. These four demons will be released with the mission of killing one-third of humanity. They will use their power to energize a vast human army. They will use this demonically inspired force to accomplish their mission. Let's talk about this army.

We are told this army will number *"two hundred thousand thousand."* A little math reveals that we are talking about an army of 200,000,000 men! We are talking about an army of immense proportions! Someone has calculated that an army that large could line up 1 mile wide and 87 miles long in a formation! A few generations ago, an army of that size was almost incomprehensible. Today, it is not just a possibility but a stark reality.

Communist China has had the ability since 1964 to raise a fighting force of over 200,000,000 men. In the year 2,000, China had 363,050,980 available men between 15 and 49. Of that number, some 199,178,361 men were fit for military service. Each year, another 10,839,039 men reach fighting age in China. Today, China sports a military might of about 2.8 millio0n, twice that of the United States.[4]

Verses 17-19 tell us of the symbolism of this army. As we read this description of this vast army, one of the questions that arises is whether this army is human or demonic. I believe that we are looking at a human army that is demonically energized. They are men, but they are men who march under the banner of Hell. They are humans, but they are humans under the control and direction of Satan and His demons. Let's look at what John tells us about this army.

Something that strikes me is the language used to describe these soldiers. *It is the language of symbolism, and it is language that is descriptive of Hell.* The men have fire, jacinth, brimstone, or sulfur breastplates. These are the colors: red, blue, and yellow. These are all the colors of fire. These are colors associated with the torments of Hell itself. Their horses breathe fire, smoke, and brimstone. Again, these suggest images of Hell and its torments. Hell will be a place of smoke, of fire, and

---

[4] Courtesy Brookings Commentary

of brimstone. These soldiers come with the colors of Hell, the smell of Hell, the weapons of Hell, and the energy of Hell. It is a picture of an army controlled by Hell.

People always want to know what we Christians believe about Hell. Do we believe that Hell is real or just a symbol? I always tell people that they had better hope it is real. A symbol is always a weak attempt to describe something very real. If the language in the Bible regarding Hell is symbolic, then Hell is far worse than anything we have ever heard or read.

There is also language used to describe indescribable things. John is trying to use First-Century language to describe a Twenty-First-Century army. As we look at John's descriptions of these men, their horses, and their methods of killing, it seems that he is trying to describe a scene for which he does not have the correct vocabulary.

John indicates their **faces are like lions**. This may indicate that their horses, or whatever vehicles they ride, are fierce looking. **Men are killed by the smoke, fire, and brimstone that issue from the mouths of these beasts.** Could this describe tanks, rockets, machine guns, flame throwers, lasers? **These beasts have power in their heads and tails to kill and do damage**. This suggests images of helicopters, missiles, warheads, etc.

Imagine a man from the 1600's plucked out of his time and placed in our day. Now, imagine that same man being taken back to his time. Now, imagine him trying to describe what he saw in our day to people in his day using the vocabulary he possessed.

Regardless of how you interpret these words, one thing is clear. It will be a terrible time of destruction, death, and demonic activity. I praise the Lord for the fact that I will not be here when these events come to pass!)

Verses 20-21 tell us this will be a time of depraved activity. We are told very clearly that these demons unleash a vast army upon the earth. One-third of all the people living on the earth will be killed. You would think that death and destruction on that scale would cause mankind to look within his heart, acknowledge his sins and turn in repentance toward God.

Those who survive the carnage continue in their sins, refusing to repent. These verses are a clear view of the condition of the human heart. We can long to find good in man if we wish, but man is totally depraved. He is a hopeless sinner; apart from the Lord Jesus Christ's atoning work, man has no good (**Rom. 3:10-23**). Every human carry within his heart the seeds of evil, and he or she can commit any sin that can be imagined. Lest we think better of ourselves than we should, the same capacity to plumb the depths of evil also dwells in our hearts!

In **verse 20** we see that man is depraved in his worship. Given all the sin and chaos during the Tribulation, one might think it would be a time empty of religious activity. As we will learn from this verse and future studies, the Tribulation will be a time marked by intense religious activity. But, as you know, no religion can save. It takes faith in the shed blood of Jesus to accomplish that!

Man is a religious creature. Regardless of where you go, you will find people engaged in worship. From the darkest jungles of Africa and South America to the highest mountains in Asia, to the great cities of Europe and America, you will find people engaged in worship. Every culture, whether primitive or advanced, has some involvement with worship. Even the atheist worships. He merely directs his worship toward himself.

Religion in the Tribulation Period will be marked by the worship of demons and by the worship of material things. Men will be caught up in the worship of the occult. There is an increase in our day in the interest in the occult. Movies, music, and other popular media provide an opportunity for many to learn more about the devil, demons, and Satanism. Witchcraft is becoming more popular than ever, and the number of practicing witches is increasing astonishingly. All of this is leading toward the day when mankind will worship demons.

You see, involvement with the occult begins with *entertainment*. People learn about it and begin to dabble in it. Then, it moves into the arena of *enlightenment*. People then begin to seek answers and help for their problems in the world of the occult. It then moves into the area of *enslavement*. People get trapped in the system and are unable to get free. America and the rest of the world are headed in that direction today! If you reject God and His Son Jesus, then you have nothing left but Satan!

Man will also worship the gods of his creation. He will worship *"idols of gold, and silver, and brass, and stone, and of wood: which neither can see, nor hear, nor walk."* This may mean that man will make gods to bow down to and worship. Or it could mean that he will worship the material possessions of life. Man will worship his money, car, home, and possessions. Even though he will give these things his love, adoration, and worship, they are not gods at all. They cannot see, hear, or move to help him. His worship of these things will not benefit him at all!

I would ask every reader to look at the God he or she worships. Look at that person or thing that has your love, adoration, and worship. Can your God hear you when you pray? Can your God see you when you have a need? Can your God move to do something about your problem? If not, then you need a God Who can! Many worship gods like those of ancient Israel (**Psa. 115:1-8; Jer. 10:3-6**).

Verse 21 tells us that man is depraved in his works. There will likely be a significant increase in wickedness in that day. John uses four words to describe the moral condition of the sinners living during the Tribulation. Let's consider those four words briefly.

John speaks of **murders.** It is hard to imagine a civilization being more murderous than our own. Hardly a day goes by without us hearing about several murders here in America. In large cities or small towns, no place is immune from the blight of murder. People kill others out of hatred or lust every day.

Some hitmen will kill someone they do not even know if the money is right. They don't kill for hate. They kill for profit. Then there are serial killers. These are people who roam the country killing total strangers for their perverted reasons. They kill for thrills.

Why are things this way? We have taught a generation that man descended from apes. We have taught a generation that there is no God to be accountable. We have taught a generation that every person can determine what is right and wrong for himself. Our children are raised on a steady diet of godless humanism, and they have no thought for the rights and property of others. Just look at how rude and violent people have become!

This verse teaches us that murders will mark the Tribulation. The violence of mankind will increase after the removal of the church.

John speaks of **Sorceries**. The word "*sorceries*" comes from the word "*pharmakeia*". You recognize that word. We get the modern word "*pharmacy*" from it. There are two possible interpretations for using this word in this verse. First, as we have already seen, the Tribulation will see a marked increase in satanic worship. Second, there will also be a rise in drug abuse. We are seeing this take place right before our eyes. The marijuana of the 1960s and 70s has been replaced with the crack and meth of this generation. Hardly a week passes without our hearing of a drug bust or a drug-related arrest. Our world is busy seeking an escape hatch from its problems using mind-altering drugs. This trend will increase as we move through these last days. It will reach pandemic proportions during the Tribulation. It is even possible that the government will resort to drugs to control an increasingly violent population.

John speaks of Fornication – This is translated from the Greek word *"porneia"*. It gives us our modern word *"pornography"*. It is a word that was used in that day to refer to every kind of illicit, sexual sin. It covers ever type of sexual activity that mankind can be engaged in. Our country has already seen the *"free love"* movement and the *"love ins"* of the hippies. We have been through the *"sexual revolution"*. We have witnessed the day when things that were not even discussed in public were as common on our television screens as a Coca-Cola commercial. Cable, satellite, and the Internet pipe endless streams of pornographic fare into our homes, and network television is just as bad. Children who are allowed to watch television without adult supervision know more about sex by the age of seven that most of us knew when we got married! Our society is saturated by sex. Man has taken a beautiful gift from God and perverted it.

Sexual perversion will increase as we move into the last days. Other parts of the world face even more perversions than we are in the United States. As time goes on, this will increase worldwide, and the United States will not be exempt.

John speaks of **thefts**. The personal rights and property of others will have no meaning at all. We are already seeing this trend in our society, as a segment of our population believes that it is their right to take what they want when they want from whomever they can get it from. This attitude will become increasingly evident in the last days and will reach terrible proportions during the Tribulation. As food, water, medicine, clothing, and shelter become increasingly scarce, men will take what they want.

The Bible paints a bleak picture of the events of the Tribulation Period. There will be death and violence on an unprecedented level throughout the world. Amid it all, men will continue to harden their hearts to the Gospel of Christ and will continue their headlong plunge into the fires of Hell.

That is why we should do everything we can to reach them with the Gospel. No sacrifice is too great, no distance too vast, no expense too steep and no effort is wasted in reaching humanity for Jesus.

As I close this chapter, I will leave you with this invitation. This could be your future if you have never been saved. Come to Jesus and be saved. Then you can miss the Tribulation and make Heaven your home. Second, if you are saved, but you haven't been living it like you should, this is the day to get things settled between you and the Lord.

THE BEGINNING OF THE END

Revelation 10:1-11 takes us into another one of the parenthetical passages in Revelation. Remember, we encountered one of these between the sixth and the seventh seals. Now, we encounter one between the sixth and the seventh trumpets. There are several reasons why the Lord gives us these pauses in the action. One reason is to give the reader a break. We have been studying terrible scenes of tragedy and death. He gives us these pauses to regroup and gather our emotions. These pauses allow the Lord to give us words of encouragement and comfort.

Let's read from the Word of God.

> *10 And I saw another mighty angel come down from heaven, clothed with a cloud: and a rainbow was upon his head, and his face was as it were the sun, and his feet as pillars of fire:*
> *² And he had in his hand a little book open: and he set his right foot upon the sea, and his left foot on the earth,*
> *³ And cried with a loud voice, as when a lion roareth: and when he had cried, seven thunders uttered their voices.*
> *⁴ And when the seven thunders had uttered their voices, I was about to write: and I heard a voice from heaven saying unto me, Seal up those things which the seven thunders uttered, and write them not.*
> *⁵ And the angel which I saw stand upon the sea and upon the earth lifted up his hand to heaven,*
> *⁶ And sware by him that liveth for ever and ever, who created heaven, and the things that therein are, and the earth, and the things that therein are, and the sea, and the things which are therein, that there should be time no longer:*
> *⁷ But in the days of the voice of the seventh angel, when he shall begin to sound, the mystery of God should be finished, as he hath declared to his servants the prophets.*

⁸ And the voice which I heard from heaven spake unto me again, and said, Go and take the little book which is open in the hand of the angel which standeth upon the sea and upon the earth.
⁹ And I went unto the angel, and said unto him, Give me the little book. And he said unto me, Take it, and eat it up; and it shall make thy belly bitter, but it shall be in thy mouth sweet as honey.
¹⁰ And I took the little book out of the angel's hand, and ate it up; and it was in my mouth sweet as honey: and as soon as I had eaten it, my belly was bitter.
¹¹ And he said unto me, Thou must prophesy again before many peoples, and nations, and tongues, and kings.

As you read about the horrors of the Tribulation Period, you might conclude that sin and Satan are in control. But God steps in to remind us that He is still the Sovereign God of the universe! God wants us to know that regardless of how dark the hour becomes and despite what the devil and his crowd might do, God is still on His throne and in control of everything!

These pauses also focus our attention on the blessed Lamb of God. Amid His wrath, we desperately need to be reminded of His great power.

You see, there is one fundamental problem with the world today. The world leaves Jesus out of its calculations and plans. In ancient times, astronomers like Aristotle and Ptolemy believed that the Earth was the center of the universe. It wasn't until Nicholas Copernicus and Johannes Kepler discovered that the sun was the center of the solar system and all other things revolved around it that everything fell into place and began to make sense.

This world has removed Jesus, the Son, from the picture and replaced Him with the United Nations and other faulty man-made institutions. The result has been chaos. When Jesus is restored as the focal point of mankind's attention, all things will make sense and fall into place. That is what God is up to here. (That will work in an individual's life as well!)

This passage introduces the middle of the tribulation period. It also serves to place Jesus back on center stage.

In **verses 1-3,** John sees a *"mighty angel"* descending from Heaven. We are not given the identity of this angel. Some people believe it could be

Gabriel the archangel. Others vote for Michael. We do not know. However, I will suggest that this angel is none other than the Lord Jesus Christ. I will give you several reasons in a moment. Hold on! Before you read more into this sentence, I am not saying Jesus us an angel!

As you may remember, Jesus frequently showed up in the Old Testament. These pre-Bethlehem appearances are called *"Theophanies or Christophanies."* Theophany (Ancient Greek: (ἡ) θεοφάνεια lit. 'appearance of a deity') is an encounter with a deity in which it manifests in an observable and tangible form. A **Christophany** is an appearance or non-physical manifestation of Christ. Traditionally, the term refers to visions of Christ after his ascension, such as the bright light of the conversion of Paul the Apostle.

Jesus appeared to Abraham at his tent door. Jesus appeared the Samson's mother and father. Jesus appeared to Joshua outside Jericho. Jesus met with Shadrach, Meshach, and Abednego in the furnace. Jesus helped Daniel in the Lion's den. If He could show up, then there is no reason to believe He could not do the same thing in these verses. As these verses are studied, all the evidence points to the fact that this is none other than Jesus Christ Himself. Let's examine the evidence together.

Verse 1 tells of his dwelling place. This angel comes down from the very place where Jesus Christ dwells. **John 3:13**, *"**And no man hath ascended up to heaven, but he that came down from heaven, even the Son of man which is in heaven.**"* Jesus Christ is in Heaven today, seated at the Father's Right hand, making intercession for you and me **(Heb. 1:3; 10:12)**.

The rest of verse 1 and the first part of verse 2 give us a description. Several key descriptive phrases are used to illustrate this angel's appearance. We see that he is **clothed with a cloud**! The cloud is garment of deity, **Psa. 104:3**, *"**Who layeth the beams of his chambers in the waters: who maketh the clouds his chariot: who walketh upon the wings of the wind**"*!

In the Old Testament, during the wilderness wanderings, the Lord Himself led His people with a glory cloud through the trackless desert, **Ex. 16**. He was with them to guide and guard them then. Here, in the darkest days the earth will ever see, He is still with His people to protect them and lead them. Dark clouds covered Sinai when Moses received the Law, **Ex. 19**. God clothed Himself in a glory cloud when He met Moses on the mountain, **Ex. 24, 34**. When Jesus ascended to Heaven, a cloud received Him (**Acts 1:9**). When He returns, He will do so on the clouds (**1 Thes. 4:16-17; Rev. 1:7**). He is clothed with a cloud!

The Word tells us he has a **rainbow upon his head**. The rainbow is a symbol of the mercy and faithfulness of God. It first appeared in **Gen. 9** after the flood to guarantee the Lord's promise that He would never destroy the earth with water again. It is a symbol of His faithfulness. It also appears in **Rev. 4**, where an emerald rainbow surrounds the throne of God. Here, it is a symbol of His mercy. So, the Lord comes as the faithful One and as the merciful One. It is a blessing to know that even in wrath, the Lord remembers mercy (**Hab. 3:2**).

Our text goes on to tell us his **face shines like the sun**! This describes His glory! When Jesus walked the dusty roads of this world, He appeared to be an ordinary man. He was so ordinary that He did not stand out as anyone special by His appearance alone (**Isa. 53:2-3**). He concealed His heavenly fame within His earthly frame (**Phil. 2:5-8**). However, there was one occasion when His glory came out (**Matt. 17:1-8**). When Saul of Tarsus met Him on the road to Damascus, Jesus was brighter than the noonday sun (**Acts 9**). Men love darkness, but when the Light shines on their sins, they are brought to their knees before the glorious Lamb of God.

John tells us his **feet are like pillars of fire**. This is a picture of His judgment. When Jesus comes, He is not coming as the Savior. He is coming back as the Sovereign Lord of the universe. He is coming to execute judgment on all those who have rejected Him!

The word "*pillars*" also brings images of firmness, stability, and strength to mind. We are looking at a God Who is unwavering and unbendable. He is going to judge this world, the sinners in the world, and Satan himself, and no being or anything in creation will be able to prevent Him from doing what He intends to do!

Verses 2 and 3 also tell us of his dominion. Here is a beautiful picture of our Lord. He is standing with one foot on the land, one foot on the sea and He has a little book in His hand. This is a picture of His dominion over the entire world.

In ancient time, when a person was going to take dominion over a place or a person, he put his foot on it. When God gave Canaan to Israel, He said, *"Every place that the sole of your foot shall tread upon, that have I given unto you, as I said unto Moses"* (**Joshua 1:3**). When one king would conquer another king, he would place his foot on the defeated king's neck as a symbol of total domination.

We are also told that He *"cried with a loud voice, as when a lion roareth"*. It is said that the roaring of a lion can strike fear into the bravest heart. An adult male lion's roar can be heard as far as five miles away. Lions usually roar just after sunset. They do so to proclaim a place as their territory. That is what we are seeing in these verses. The Lord is staking His claim, and He is saying, "I am the Lion of the Tribe of Judah. This world is my world. Keep your hands off what belongs to me!"

That is what we see here. We see the victorious Jesus laying claim to the planet Earth. He holds in His hand the book, which is the title deed to the planet. He stands with one foot on the dry land and another on the sea. Jesus has come to take control of this world. He has come to take what is his.

Let the devil do what he will. Our Lord reigns today, and He will forever. This truth will become increasingly clearer as the end draws near.

Verses 3-7 continue to describe the things John saw and heard. It tells us John heard mysterious voices. It is here that John hears seven thunders speaking. The text indicates they spoke a language John could understand, and he got ready to write down what they were saying. But the Lord stopped him and told John to seal up the things he heard the thunders say.

So, what did they say? I do not know! Neither does anyone else! Why write about it if we are not told what they say? God has some things that He wants to keep concealed for now. Paul writes of a time when he was caught up into the third Heaven. He was taken into the very presence of God, and He was not allowed to write about it, **2 Cor. 12:4**.

Perhaps God puts this to teach us a precious lesson. Maybe he wants us to know that some things in life will remain a mystery! Look at **Deut. 29:29**. That verse says, *"The secret things belong unto the LORD our God: but those things which are revealed belong unto us and to our children forever, that we may do all the words of this law."*

There are thousands of questions in life for which you and I do not have answers. Why do good people suffer? Why do babies get sick and die? Why is there so much evil in our world? Why is living holy so hard? We will never have the answers to these and ten thousand other questions this side of Heaven. The best thing we can do is to leave the mysteries with the Lord and trust Him to do right (**Gen. 18:25; Rom. 8:28; 2 Cor 4:17**).

We are currently looking at life from a precarious and one-sided position. One day, we can see things from the other side. It will make sense then! Paul says, ***"For now we see through a glass, darkly; but then face to face: now I know in part; but then shall I know even as also I am known"*** (**1 Cor. 13:12**).

In **verse 5**, we see there are voices of manifestation. While the voices of the thunders remain a mystery, the next voice John hears brings a crystal-clear message. The person John saw lifted His holy hands and made a tremendous promise. He tells John that the waiting days are finished. God is preparing to consummate His work and complete His Word. God is preparing to end His work of judgment and redemption.

Allow me to remind you that God does not operate like we do. His timetable is vastly different from ours. We see things differently and think we are in a period of delay. We think things are moving so slowly. We think God will never fulfill all the promises He has made. Well, we are wrong! God wears a different kind of timepiece than we do (**2 Pet. 3:8**). a dear preacher friend of mine gave one of the best examples. He always makes the statement that God lives outside of time and space!

You see, it appears that sin and Satan are winning the battle. The truth is far different.

I was "born and raised" in East Tennessee, as we say. Oh yes, it's true. I am sure you might hear it in my voice if you could hear me. I have been blessed with a lifelong thirst for knowledge and, as a result, earned a Ph.D. and a couple of master's degrees, and I am working on another one. I was partially educated in London. But you don't hear a British accent. Unless I soften it, you will hear my native East Tennessee accent, which I am proud of. Anyway, we didn't have Xbox, PlayStation, or cell phones. We played outside! We thought we had all the time in the world. In truth, we only had from daylight until dusk. When the sun's red and gold rays began to show toward sunset, we knew our time was getting short.

Our lives are like that. We start in the daybreak of life, and as we move through our lives, we eventually arrive at the sunset of life. Looking backwards, we often realize we wasted the greatest gift God has to offer, outside of his son, Jesus. We wasted time. God does not waste time!

Here we see God has called in the close of the day come up and there'll be no more delay. Look at **Heb. 10:37**, *"For yet a little while, and he that shall come will come, and will not tarry."*

I like that! According to God's calendar, Jesus has only been gone two days. Soon, God will turn the page, tell Gabriel to blow his trumpet, and Jesus will return for His church. Then, God will judge the earth, sin, and the devil and usher in eternity.

In **verses 8-11** John is told to take the little book out of the hand of the Angel. He is told to eat it, but he is warned that the book will be sweet in his mouth and bitter in his stomach. John does as he is told and finds that the words of the Angel are true. The book was sweet as honey to his taste, but it was bitter in his belly. Then John is told to take the message he has written and share it with others who need to hear it.

This is a strange little section of Scripture. However, it teaches a couple of lessons about the Word of God that we need to understand.

The Bible is spiritual food. Jesus said, *"But he answered and said, It is written, Man shall not live by bread alone, but by every word that proceedeth out of the mouth of God,"* (**Matthew 4:4**). Jeremiah said, *"Thy words were found, and I did eat them; and thy word was unto me the joy and rejoicing of mine heart: for I am called by thy name, O LORD God of hosts,"* (**Jer. 15:16**). Job said, *"I have esteemed the words of his mouth more than my necessary food,"* (**Job 23:12**). Peter said, *"As newborn babes, desire the sincere milk of the word, that ye may grow thereby,"* (**1 Pet. 1:22**)

There is something special about this Book! It is food for the hungry soul. It is a balm for the hurting soul. It is our meat for the growing soul. If we are to be all that God wants us to be, then we are to get into the book and feed. We are to drink deeply of its words so that our souls can grow strong in the things of the Lord. We must get into the Bible for ourselves every day!

When John swallowed the Book, he found it was both a blessing and a burden. It was sweet and bitter at the same time.

The sweetness of this Book can be found in its passages about the grace, love, and mercy of our God. It is very sweet when we read of Jesus dying for our sins and rising from the dead read of Heaven; it is so lovely. It is also so sweet when we read that He will meet our needs, never leave us, and come to take us home someday! When the sinner reads that Jesus will save him if he only comes to Jesus by faith, that is sweeter than words describe. This is a book filled with sweetness!

But it is also a Book filled with bitterness. This Book tells us about a Hell that awaits all the lost. The Spirit of God uses this book to convict the hearts of saints and sinners alike of sin. This Book tells of judgment, wrath, and damnation. It is a bitter book, too.

Sometimes, I read my Bible, and I am both thrilled and blessed. There are other times when I read it, and I am brought to tears over something it has revealed in my life. It is a bittersweet Book!

Be that as it may, when we take the whole Book, the bitter and the sweet, the blessings and the burdens, we can say that it fits together so well. It reveals our problems, but it always points us to the right solution. Praise the Lord for the Word of God!

The Word of God is to be shared with others! John was told to share the message of the Book with others. The same burden has been placed on our shoulders today. We are to take this Book with both its blessings and its burdens, and we are to share its message with a lost and dying world (**Matt. 28:19-20; Mark 16:15**). God did not give us His Word for our benefit only; He gave us His Word to share with the world. We are to go forth with the Word of God in our hearts and on our lips and tell a lost world that ***"Jesus Saved and Jesus Saves"***!

When we leave this chapter behind, we will enter a time of tragedy like we have never seen before. Thank God that He has given us this fresh glimpse of His Son, reminded us that He is in control, and reminded us of the importance of His Word. Do you need to come home to the Father? Think about it. Where will you spend eternity?

THE TRIBULATION TEMPLE

We are still in the midst of a parenthetical passage that began in **chapter 10**. We in a pause in the actions and activities of the Tribulation Period judgments. As we come to **Revelation 11**, we have arrived at one of the most difficult passages in the book of Revelation. It is hard to understand. However, keeping two thoughts in mind will help us study these verses.

Let's read from the Word of God!

11 I was given a reed like a measuring rod and was told, "Go and measure the temple of God and the altar, with its worshipers. ² But exclude the outer court; do not measure it, because it has been given to the Gentiles. They will trample on the holy city for 42 months.

Remember what I told you in the section on how to study the bible? One of the objects to closely watch is where you are. Here are some points to remember.

We are on Jewish ground. The images and terminology are Jewish in nature. These verses deal with the future of the people of Israel. We are dealing with future events. Some theologians take these verses and try to make them fit the past. Some even try to make them fit into the present. My studies demonstrate that they will only fit into the future.

In this chapter, we study a prophecy concerning the future Temple in Jerusalem. I want to take some time in this chapter and consider these matters in detail. So, with that in mind, let's examine John's words concerning the future Temple. I want you to see that this prophecy contains some very specific visions of the future of the Jewish people.

Verse one shows us a vision of promise. When John mentions the Temple, he refers to a place dedicated to Jewish worship. The Jews have been without a Temple for nearly 2,000 years. This verse makes it clear a new temple will be built in Jerusalem. Let's examine some facts related to the Temple.

For over 500 years, from Moses to David, the people of Israel worshiped God at the Tabernacle. It was there that sacrifices were carried out. There, the priests made intercession for the sins of the people. It was there that Israel sought their God.

Before David died, he wanted to build a permanent house of God, a Temple, where God's presence could dwell **(2 Sam. 7:1-4)**. God, however, refused to allow David to build the Temple because he was a man of war **(1 Chron. 28:3)**. The privilege of building the Temple fell to David's son, Solomon **(2 Sam. 7:12-13)**. David was not allowed to build the Temple, but he began accumulating the building materials necessary for its construction **(1 Chron. 22:1-5; 13-16)**. Before David died, he charged Solomon to build the Temple **(1 Chron. 22:6-19)**.

Solomon built the Temple as David, **(1 Kings 6:1)** commanded him. It took seven years to complete the building, **1 Kings 6:38**. (There is that number seven again!) It was dedicated to the Lord with a lavish sacrifice when it was finished. **1 Kings 8:63** says that twenty-two thousand oxen and one hundred twenty thousand sheep were offered to the Lord at the Temple dedication. At this dedication, when the Ark of the Covenant was brought from the Tabernacle into the Temple, God demonstrated His approval of this house of worship by filling it with His Shekinah glory **(2 Chron. 7:1-3)**. The word Shekinah refers to God's presence or dwelling.

This magnificent Temple cost an enormous amount of money to build. If that Temple were built in our day, its cost would approach 500 billion dollars!

This Temple building dominated the Jerusalem skyline until it was destroyed by the Babylonian King Nebuchadnezzar in 538 BC. The Jews were taken into captivity in Babylon at this time. Some were allowed to return to Jerusalem, and in 490 BC, the Temple was rebuilt by Zerubbabel. However, this temple was not as elaborate or beautiful as the first one.

The prophet Haggai writes, *"Who is left among you that saw this house in her first glory? and how do ye see it now? is it not in your eyes in comparison of it as nothing?"* **Hag. 2:3**. **Ezra 3:12** adds this insight regarding the rebuilt Temple, *"But many of the priests and Levites and* *chief of the fathers, who were ancient men, that had seen the first house, when the foundation of this house was laid before their eyes, wept with a loud voice; and many shouted aloud for joy."*

This Temple was also destroyed. In 168 BC, Antiochus Epiphanes desecrated the Temple by slaughtering a sow on the altar and demanding that he be worshiped as a god. He dismantled the Temple. To gain the support of the Jews, Herod the Great rebuilt this Temple around 6 BC. Herod's Temple took some 46 years to build, **John 2:20**, and it was far grander than the second Temple has been. It would have been Herod's Temple, where the Lord Jesus worshiped and preached.

This Temple was also slated for destruction. In **Matthew 24:1-2**, Jesus prophesied that the Temple would be destroyed. This took place in 70AD when Titus, the Roman general, besieged Jerusalem. During that siege, which lasted from 66 AD to 70 AD, some one million Jews were slain. It is said that Titus crucified so many Jewish men during the siege that he ran out of wood to make new crosses. The roads were lined with crosses occupied by the rotting remains of the Roman victims.

When Jerusalem fell in 70 AD, the city was destroyed. The Temple was demolished. All that remains of the ancient Temple is the Western Wailing Wall. Orthodox Jews go there to pray every day. They believe that all prayers ascend to Heaven through Jerusalem. So, they write their prayers on paper and stuff them in the wall's cracks. Jews from around the world can E-mail their prayers to Jerusalem. These prayers are printed and taken to the Wailing Wall. Currently, the Jews have no Temple, but that will change soon.

It might interest you to know there are preparations for a new temple today! When John mentions a Temple in **verse 1**, he lets us in on the truth that a new Temple must be built in Jerusalem. It might surprise you that some people are already preparing for such an event. Let's take a quick look at what the Jews are doing to get ready.

[5]According to Chaim Richman, the director of the Temple Institute in Jerusalem, a "Temple in waiting" has essentially already been created.

---

[5] Courtesy *Jewish Voice (www.jewishvoice.org)*

The Temple Institute is actively engaged in the research and preparation of the resumption of service in the Holy Temple to the extent of preparing operational blueprints for the construction of the Temple according to the most modern standards," Richman told CBN NEWS' Chris Mitchell.

Indeed, the Institute has already created over 60 sacred Temple vessels that will be needed for worship in the coming rebuilt Temple. The High Priest's breastplate containing the 12 precious stones of the tribes of Israel, and the musical instruments of the Levitical choir are also ready. In addition, the Institute has prepared the priestly garments. These garments will adorn a new generation of Levitical Priests (Kohanim) already in training. It is now possible that the Temple can be rebuilt since the Jews have returned to their land.

In keeping with the tradition established by Chief Rabbi Kook to view with expectation God's speedy fulfillment of His prophecies regarding the Temple, the Temple Institute along with the Third Temple Academy has begun such preparations for the Third Temple.

In 2009, a field school was built in Mizpe Yericho to prepare Kohanim (priests) and Levites for service in the Third Temple. In 2010, uncut stones were collected from the **Dead Sea** to construct the Temple altar. Such pristine stones are believed to fulfill the injunction that such building material be free from contact with metal tools. (DEUTERONOMY 27:5)

The Third Temple Academy in Mitzpe Yericho is about a 20-minute drive from Jerusalem on the road that leads to Jericho and the Jordan Valley. By building a replica of the Temple, the school has given the priestly students a hands-on experience of Temple sacrificial worship.

In August 2013, an evening was set aside for the grand opening of the school with a semi-dress rehearsal covering the complete daily service. Participants, some dressed in full priestly adornments, carried out the service step by step as prescribed through the Torah (Five Books of Moses), the Mishnah (rabbinical interpretations of the Torah) and other rabbinical writings.

In the picturesque Samarian hills near Shiloh, a lamb was inspected, and its blood was passed from one Kohanim to another in silver vessels called mizrak. On the second day of Pesach this year, yet another great stride was taken in bringing back the service of the Holy Temple—a practice run for the bringing of the omer (barley offering) to the Temple, as mandated in Leviticus 23:10.

In the Third Temple, a small amount of omer will be offered on the altar, and the Kohanim serving in the Temple will eat the rest. The omer marks the beginning of the countdown to Shavuot (Feast of Weeks or Pentecost).

Although the Temple vessels have been created and the priests are in training, some severe issues must be resolved before constructing a new Temple. One key element missing now is the finding of a ritually pure red heifer, which is necessary to fulfill the command to use a red heifer to purify the altar. **(Numbers 19)**. Such specimens must be without blemish and not even two of their hairs may vary in color. Previous red heifers have been disqualified, including a New Jersey red heifer that became ineligible this year when it gave birth to a black calf. Pregnancy and the subsequent birth disqualify the cow.

Rather than wait for one to appear randomly in a flock somewhere on earth, the Temple Institute has begun a special red heifer breeding program that includes implanting frozen Red Angus embryos into domestic Israeli cattle. A crowdfunding campaign is underway to help fund it.

A group called "The Temple Mount Faithful," led by Gershon Salomon, has prepared the cornerstones for a new Temple, using diamond rather than steel cutting tools, to conform with the Bible injunction that no metal tool be used in the construction of the Temple—a tower of peace. The six-ton stones have been consecrated with water drawn from the Biblical pool of Siloam. For the last several years, Salomon and his followers have attempted to place these cornerstones on the Temple Mount but each time they are stopped by authorities. The end-time Temple should be built on the same location as the First and the Second Temple."

But of course, that is the crux of the problem.

The Dome of the Rock is where the First and Second Temples were located on the Temple Mount. *(Photo by by Rogerio Bromfman).* What is Judaism's most holy site is Islam's third holiest site, following Mecca and Medina in Saudi Arabia. A Hadith (sayings about Mohammed) describes Mohammed as having embarked in a dream to meet with the other prophets of the Bible at what is defined as "the farthest mosque." This is interpreted to mean Jerusalem and, by interpretation, the Temple Mount. According to Islam, he was reportedly taken up into the second heaven, where he spoke with the angel Gabriel, Isa (Jesus), and Yahya (John the Baptist). Next, it says he went to the third heaven, where he met Joseph, and on to the fourth, fifth, sixth, and seventh, having met such luminaries as Aaron, Moses, Abraham, and God Himself.

At present, the Temple Mount (which in Arabic is referred to as Haram al-Sharif or the "Noble Sanctuary") is home to both the gold-covered Dome of the Rock, which supposedly encloses the rock from which Mohammed is believed to have ascended to heaven, and the Mosque of Omar or Al-Aqsa Mosque. The Muslim claim of ownership of the Temple Mount site seems to make any Jewish attempt to build a Third Temple futile.

Why would Temple's vessels be created and Temple priests be trained in the face of such obstacles? The prophets Daniel and Ezekiel and the apostle Paul make it quite clear that another Temple will be built, so preparing a modern-day priesthood is an act of anticipation and faith. Verses that describe the End-Time Temple prepare us for this eventuality.

Daniel 9:27 explains that a covenant of one "seven" (seven years) will be made between a man of desolation and the people—a peace treaty allowing the Jewish People to resume sacrifices and offerings. But at the three-and-a-half-year mark, everything will change.

"He will make a firm covenant with the many for one week [seven years], but in the middle of the week he will put a stop to sacrifice and grain offering." **(Daniel 9:27)**

To put an end to offerings presumes a Temple is in place. But still, how could anyone convince the Muslim Waqf to build a Temple on the site where Muslims deny all Jewish rights or claims? The apostle Paul gives us a clue when he wrote to the Thessalonians. He says,*" **Don't let anyone deceive you in any way, for that day [the Day of the Lord] will not come until the rebellion occurs and the man of lawlessness is revealed, the man doomed to destruction. He will oppose and will exalt himself over everything that is called God or is worshiped, so that he sets himself up in God's temple, proclaiming himself to be God."* **(2 Thes. 2:3–4)**

One problem that has always stood between the Jews and a new Temple is the Mosque of Omar, or the Dome of the Rock. It was completed in 691 AD. Inside the dome is a great rock. Muslims believe that that Mohammad ascended into Heaven from this rock, conferred with Moses, and returned to earth with the prayers that all Muslims are supposed to pray. For many centuries, it was believed that the Dome of the Rock was built on the site of the original Temple. It was believed that the Dome of the Rock would have to be demolished before a new Temple could be rebuilt. **However, recent excavations revealed that the ancient Temple was about 100 meters (about 109 yards) north of the Dome of the Rock site. If the measurements are correct, a new Temple could be built without disturbing the Muslim holy place.**

The problems in the Middle East today are not political problems; they are religious problems. Every group involved in the turmoil in the Israel wants control of the ancient city of Jerusalem. It is the most contested ground in the world. For the Jews, their struggle is one of survival. For the Arabs and Muslims, their goal is the annihilation of Israel. It will all be settled one day!

All the Jews need are the ashes of the Red Heifer so they can consecrate a priest. They are doing their best to breed an acceptable animal as we speak. They are also trying to find the Ark of the Covenant. They may succeed someday! At any rate, much more could be said about Jewish preparations for rebuilding the Temple.

The message delivered by this promise of a new Temple in Jerusalem is that God is not through with the Jewish people. They are still His chosen people, and God plan for them. He has already returned them to their homeland. On May 14, 1948, a nation that had been extinct for nearly 1,900 years was raised from the ashes. Israel became a nation and was restored to her former lands. The Jews began to return to Israel. Our generation has seen God's hand of protection upon the people of Israel during the wars they fought and won against overwhelming odds. God isn't through yet! He will continue to use them and will save a remnant of the Jewish people in the end. The promise of a new Temple is simply God's way of saying, *"I am not finished with Israel!"*

In **verse 1,** John gives us a vision of preservation. John is told to take a reed and measure the Temple, the altar, and the worshipers. This reed refers to a plant that grows in the Jordan Valley. These reeds grow to a height of 15 to 20 feet. They are hollow and lightweight, yet they are exceedingly strong. They are used for walking sticks, as in **Eze. 29:6**. They are cut down, sharpened, and used as writing tools. They were also used in ancient times as measuring sticks. A *"rod"* is about six cubits, or nine feet. John is told to take the measuring rod and measure the Temple. This is symbolic of two things.)

The first is a symbol of full preservation. The act of measuring speaks of possession. God is claiming the Temple, the altar, and the worshipers as His Own. This is just another reminder that God is not through with the Jewish people!

The second is a symbol of faithful preservation. God will keep every promise He has ever made to Israel. He has set them aside for a time because of their unbelief. In the end, however, Israel will be saved! God will continue to work in and through Israel until a remnant is saved.

Some in our day are attempting to replace Israel with the church. They claim that Israel has been forever set aside and the church has inherited the promises God made to Israel. My dear reader, we do not want the promises God made to Israel! Our promises as the church are far superior to those given to Abraham and his descendants. There is a difference between Israel and the church, which must always be considered when studying the Bible.

In **verse 2,** we see another promise. This is a promise of punishment. While this measuring of the Temple is in one sense a blessing for the nation of Israel, it also brings to mind images of judgment. The rod is mentioned four times in the book of Revelation. One is in these verses. The three other times are in connection with the Lord Jesus, and they tell us that He will rule this world with a *"rod of iron"* (**Rev. 2:27; 12:5; 19:15**). So, while there is a vision of Promise and Preservation, there is also a vision of Punishment.

The realities of this punishment are very real! John is told not to measure the outer court of the Temple. It is to be given to the Gentiles and they will occupy the city for three and one-half years. These are the days of the second half of the Tribulation Period. This verse brings out some thoughts that need to be considered.

The Temple will be rebuilt sometime during the early days of the Tribulation. Undoubtedly, one of the first accomplishments of the Antichrist was to arrange a peace treaty between Israel and her enemies. He will do what no other diplomat has ever been able to do. Today, diplomats and world leaders are trying to secure peace in Jerusalem. They will all fail! The Antichrist will bring a temporary, pseudo peace. When Jesus Christ, the Prince of Peace comes, He will bring permanent peace to Israel.

This peace treaty will give the Jews the right to build their new house of worship. The Jews will rebuild their Temple and begin their sacrificial worship system. Once again, the Jews will slaughter animals in their attempt to keep the Law of God.

Things will go well for a while, but the Antichrist will enter the Holy of Holies in the Temple somewhere around the mid-point of the Tribulation and enthrone himself as god (**Matt. 24:15; 2 Thes. 2:3-4**). This event will mark the beginning of the most intense time of persecution Israel will have ever experienced (**Matt. 24:16-22**). The Jews will lose their Temple and they will be driven from their lands. They will be hunted down and killed by the forces of the Antichrist and by the rest of their enemies.

Israel will be shown in the most vivid manner possible that animal sacrifice cannot take away sin and bring peace with God. God will allow them to build their Temple, and He will allow them to sacrifice again. However, their new Temple is nothing more than a further rejection of their Messiah, the Lord Jesus Christ. Their sacrifices repudiate the Gospel and reject the cross and the blood of Jesus. The blood of Jesus Christ did what the blood of animals has never been able to do or will ever be able to do and their refusal to accept the preaching of the cross by the 144,000 Jewish preachers will not go unpunished.

Because they have rejected the Gospel, the Jews must pay a price. They will be persecuted and pursued by their enemies. This process will serve to purify the Jewish nation and prepare them for the return of the Lord Jesus. When He comes, the remnant of the Jewish nation that is left will turn to Him and receive them as their Messiah (**Zech. 12:10-13:1; 8-9**).

Some ministers are teaching that Jews are saved by a different method than other people. In truth, there is one plan of salvation for all people and His name is Jesus Christ (**Acts 4:12; John 14:6**). The Jews have rejected Jesus, and they will be punished as a result. Those who believe will be saved (**John 1:11-12**).

I hope you can see from these verses that God still has a plan for Israel and for the future. I also hope you can see from current events that everything is lining up to ensure that God's plans will be brought to pass. Israel is preparing to build their Temple. They are looking for their Messiah to come and save them. He is coming! But I would like to be able to tell them that He has already been here. He has shed His blood. He has paid for sin and will save all who call on Him by faith.

People need to make their preparations to leave this world. Listen to what Jesus said, in **Luke 21:28-31**.

> *28 And when these things begin to come to pass, then look up, and lift up your heads; for your redemption draweth nigh.*
> *29 And he spake to them a parable; Behold the fig tree, and all the trees;*
> *30 When they now shoot forth, ye see and know of your own selves that summer is now nigh at hand.*
> *31 So likewise ye, when ye see these things come to pass, know ye that the kingdom of God is nigh at hand.*

STANDING ON THE EDGE OF ETERNITY

Revelation 11:15-19 brings us to the halfway point of the book of Revelation. It also brings us to the end of a very long section that began in Revelation 10:1. In this passage, the seventh trumpet, announced in **Revelation 10:7**, is about to sound. When it is sounded, this trumpet will unleash God's final acts of judgments upon the earth.
Let's see what God's word has to say from this text.

> *[15] And the seventh angel sounded; and there were great voices in heaven, saying, The kingdoms of this world are become the kingdoms of our Lord, and of his Christ; and he shall reign for ever and ever.*
> *[16] And the four and twenty elders, which sat before God on their seats, fell upon their faces, and worshipped God,*
> *[17] Saying, We give thee thanks, O LORD God Almighty, which art, and wast, and art to come; because thou hast taken to thee thy great power, and hast reigned.*
> *[18] And the nations were angry, and thy wrath is come, and the time of the dead, that they should be judged, and that thou shouldest give reward unto thy servants the prophets, and to the saints, and them that fear thy name, small and great; and shouldest destroy them which destroy the earth.*
> *[19] And the temple of God was opened in heaven, and there was seen in his temple the ark of his testament: and there were lightnings, and voices, and thunderings, and an earthquake, and great hail.*

The seventh trumpet will bring about a devastating wave of judgment. It will fulfill the ancient prophecies of Joel 2:1-2, **"Blow ye the** *trumpet in Zion, and sound an alarm in my holy mountain: let all the inhabitants of the land tremble: for the day of the LORD cometh, for it is nigh at hand; (2) A day of darkness and of gloominess, a day of clouds and of thick darkness, as the morning spread upon the mountains: a great people and a strong; there hath not been ever the like, neither shall be any more after it, even to the years of many generations."*

When it is sounds, the seven bowl judgments are revealed. These bowls contain the final, awesome, awful judgments of God, **Rev. 15:1**. The sound of the seventh trumpet alerts the world that King Jesus is about to reclaim everything that belongs to Him.

I want to stop here and point out that the Old Testament is still valid in many ways. No, we are not under its law, as some theologians would have you believe. It points the way—the way to Jesus and all the way to the end of time!

Now, the seventh trumpet is sounded here in Rev. 11:1, but the events it brings to pass are not recorded until we get to Rev 15. Chapters 12-14 retell the Tribulation story from a different perspective. In Rev. 6-11, the focus has been on the Lord Jesus. We have learned about the process He uses to take possession of this earth. Rev. 12-14 takes the focus off the Lord and places in on the Antichrist. We have been observing the Tribulation from God's perspective. For the next few chapters, we will observe that awful period from Satan's perspective.

This passage takes us forward in time to the very edge of eternity. We are transported to the end of the age to a time when Jesus took possession of the world and judged sin and sinners. As we look ahead to that blessed day, we find Heaven in a state of rejoicing.

Today, we want to investigate these verses and, by virtue, into Heaven itself. In doing so, we are allowed to witness Heaven's reaction to the reign of the Lord Jesus. I want to show you the great *reasons* why we see worship, praise, and excitement in Heaven as time ends. The words "great voices" translate the Greek words *"mega"* and *"phonay"*. We get the word *"megaphone"* from these words. It refers to shouting and loud speech. This is a picture of loud, vigorous praise in glory in verses 15-16!

In **verses 16-17** we see rejoicing over a mighty ruler! Heaven rejoices because God and His Son Jesus have taken possession of a world that was lost to sin and Satan thousands of years ago! In verse 15, we see the scope of his kingdom as in the verbiage "kingdoms of this world." In the Greek, the word *"kingdoms"* that is used here is derived from the Greek word Βασίλειο. In this text it is singular. There are many rulers, leaders, kings and presidents in this world, but there is but one true kingdom. Men think they rul. In reality, Satan rules this world today. Satan is called *"the god of this world"* in 2 Cor. 4:4. The Lord Jesus called him *"the prince of this world"* three times in John's Gospel, John 12:31; 14:30; 16:11.

The truth of Satan's rule can be seen in the hatred that is being leveled against Jesus Christ and His Gospel in this world. People have no reason to hate Jesus. They do so because they are led to by the devil! He is the ruler of this world today. I praise the Lord that His kingdom is to be short-lived. Jesus Christ will come in glory and power and assume His rightful place as King, Lord and God of this world! There is just one rightful King and one day, the whole world will bow at His feet and worship Him!

Verse 15 also tells us the term or span of his kingdom. The text says, *"He shall reign forever and ever."* Jesus will not be like a human ruler. All human rulers eventually reach the end of their reign. They die or are deposed and replaced by another. Not Jesus! He will reign eternally, **"Thy kingdom is an everlasting kingdom, and thy dominion endureth throughout all generations,"** Psalm 145:13.

Verse 17 tells us of the strength of His kingdom. God is called *"Almighty"*, **"Thou hast taken to thee Thy great power, and Thou hast reigned."** Every human kingdom fails because it is built on the limited power of men. Saddam Hussein ruled by the power of fear, but he was overthrown. Kim Jung and Vladimir Putin rule by intimidation and brutality. **They will be defeated!** God's kingdom is established on one who holds all power, **Matt. 28:18.** Any enemy will never overcome him, for He has placed all His foes under His feet, **Heb. 2:8.** He will never be deposed by any rival, for He has no rivals, **Psa. 86:10.**

We also see the stability of his kingdom in the part of the passage that says **"Which art, and wast and art to come"** – God's kingdom is an everlasting kingdom! He has always reigned! It may look like Satan has his hands on the thermostat of this world today. It may look like he is in control. Even Satan is the servant of Almighty God and he operates within a limited sphere of activity. He does only that which God allows him to do. His activity is limited by the providence, sovereignty, purposes and power of God. Remember mighty Satan had to get permission to attack Job. Satan is a finite, limited, created being. He must always yield to the one who has reigned and will always reign!

We also see the surety of His kingdom. The koine Greek verb phrase **"are become"** is in the **"proleptic aorist"** tense. This tense describes future events that are so certain they can be spoken of as they had already happened. This tense is used in Isa. **53:3-9**. Though he ministered 700 years before Jesus, he writes of the sufferings of Jesus as though they had already happened! People can believe what they wish. One day the kingdom of this world will be given over to the Lord Jesus. He will rule and reign on the throne of this earth forever. Praise God! No wonder Heaven rejoices.

This brings us to **verse 18,** where there is rejoicing over a reward! Soon, the sinners will be rewarded. Did I say that? Oh yes! This world hates Jesus and demonstrates that hatred against Him when He comes to reign. This verse looks ahead to that day when the world's armies will gather to fight against the Lord Jesus Christ at His coming. We see this in Revelation 16:14. The hatred of the world is clear to see in our day. Everywhere you look, this world is trying to eradicate the name of Jesus and anything to do with Him from the public arena. They will not bow to Him! But **Psalm 2:4-9** tells us that God will have the final say.

In the end, lost sinners will be rewarded for their rejection of Jesus by having to face Him in judgment, **Rev. 20:11-15, v. 18**. God will have the final word, and all lost sinners will receive the due reward of their sins, **Rom. 6:23**. What a tragedy, since they could be saved if they would only come to Him!

We may wonder about Heaven's saints rejoicing over sinners' punishment. It does upset us when we see things like this. After all, we do not want to see anyone go to Hell. We want to see people saved. When we arrive in Heaven, we will possess a mind like that of the Lord Jesus. We will think like He thinks, and we will agree with His plan to judge all those who reject Him! When He pronounces their sentence, we will say *"Amen!"*

But we also see another reward. The saints will be rewarded. While the lost sinners will face the Lord in judgment, faithful believers will be honored for their devotion to Him. He will reward His servants (*"prophets"*). The Lord will reward those who have faithfully preached His Word one day. He will also reward His saints (*"them that fear thy name, great and small"*). One day, every act of devotion to Jesus will be rewarded by Him. Nothing was so small that He missed it. He saw every sacrifice, every labor of love, every gift, every deed, which was done in His Name, and He will reward all those who faithfully serve Him! Even something so small as a cup of cold water or coffee given in His name will be rewarded someday, Mark 9:41.)

Verse 19 is out of place in this chapter. It just doesn't seem to fit in with the scene of rejoicing in Heaven. But this verse is important. The mention of the Temple places us back on Jewish ground. You see, the church does not have a Temple, we are the Temple! This verse contains two great realities I want to touch on for a moment.

The first is the reality of access. The open Temple and the Ark's vision remind us that in Heaven, we will have access to the Lord. We will see Him and be able to worship Him. There will be no veil to separate us from Him. There will be no flesh to separate us from Him. There will be nothing to keep us away from Him on that day! We will have free, unfettered access to the God of glory, **Rev. 22:3-4**!

The second is the reality of affirmation! The mention of the Ark places us squarely on Jewish ground. You see, for the Jew, the Ark of the Covenant represented the presence of God, the communion of God and the redemption of God. Here, the Jews are reminded that God is not finished with them. He will complete His plan for Israel, and He will keep His covenants with the seed of Abraham!

Take note for a little theology lesson here. In the Bible, there are five different names for the Ark of the Covenant. These five names reveal what God is doing in these verses.

1. The Ark of the Covenant – **Num. 10:33** – The ancient Ark contained the Law. In these verses we see a world that has transgressed God's Law. The world has angered the Lord and He has come down to judge them!
2. The Ark of the Testimony – **Ex. 25:22** – The Ark testified to God's holiness and man's sinfulness. God is still holy and man is still a sinner. As a sinner, man will be judged by a holy God.

3. The Ark of God – **1 Sam. 3:3** – The Ark was the only visible throne of God on the earth. This vision of the Ark reminds everyone that God is still on His throne!
4. The Ark of Strength – **Psa. 132:8** – It was called this because of the miracles and great works associated with it. We are reminded here that God is still Almighty God and He still reigns in power.
5. The Holy Ark – 2 **Chron. 35:3** – It was called the Holy Ark because it is where God dwelt! This vision of the Ark reminds us that God is still alive and well!

Verse 19 closes with premonitions of impending disasters. More horrors, worse horrors, than those we have seen thus far, are on the horizon. We are at the halfway point of the book and of the Tribulation. We have seen things from God's perspective. Now, we will see things from Satan's perspective.

These verses have taken us to the very edge of eternity. The question that must be faced today is this: Which group mentioned in verse 18 are you a part of?

Are you a part of that group that will be doomed and damned to Hell? Are you lost today? If you are, you need to know that the wrath of God already abides on your life, John 3:36; 3:18; Rom. 1:18. You also need to know that you do not have to stay in that condition for another minute! If you come to Jesus, He will save you by His grace! Come now if He is calling you to come to Him.

If you are part of that group that will be rewarded and rejoice in that day, praise the Lord! You ought to bow before Him and tell Him how thankful you are that He has saved you.

If you are lost today, you may be here for the Tribulation, and you may not. But think about this. You are one heartbeat away from eternity. Have you ever thought about that? All that has to happen for your heart to stop, and the moment it stops, and your spirit will leave your body, you will be in eternity.

There is a tree in a faraway country with at least one bullet hole in it. It was here that one of my brothers-in-arms was shot and killed. The bullet was from an AK-47 7.62 x .39 rifle. Those of you who know ballistics and firearms know that round only too well. The bullet tore clear through my friend's torso. He died for his country in a country that doesn't like Americans. I feel confident the tree is still standing. It was a very old and large tree fed by the rainforest and jungle surrounding it. This tree identifies the place where my brother stepped from time into eternity.

For everyone, somewhere on this earth, there is a mark. It may be on a deathbed in a hospital somewhere. It may be on an interstate highway where an accident will occur. Your time will stop at some point, and your eternity will begin. So, in the final countdown, where will you spend eternity?

TWO WITNESSES

With Revelation 11:1-14, we are still in parenthetical Scripture. God is describing a break in the action of the Tribulation as He takes care of some heavenly business. As I previously mentioned, this is one of the most difficult passages in the Revelation to interpret.

There are two facts to keep in mind as we study these verses. We are still on Jewish ground, and we are dealing with events related to the future!

Let's read from God's Word.

11 And there was given me a reed like unto a rod: and the angel stood, saying, Rise, and measure the temple of God, and the altar, and them that worship therein.

² But the court which is without the temple leave out, and measure it not; for it is given unto the Gentiles: and the holy city shall they tread under foot forty and two months.

³ And I will give power unto my two witnesses, and they shall prophesy a thousand two hundred and threescore days, clothed in sackcloth.

⁴ These are the two olive trees, and the two candlesticks standing before the God of the earth.

⁵ And if any man will hurt them, fire proceedeth out of their mouth, and devoureth their enemies: and if any man will hurt them, he must in this manner be killed.

⁶ These have power to shut heaven, that it rain not in the days of their prophecy: and have power over waters to turn them to blood, and to smite the earth with all plagues, as often as they will.

⁷ And when they shall have finished their testimony, the beast that ascendeth out of the bottomless pit shall make war against them, and shall overcome them, and kill them.

⁸ And their dead bodies shall lie in the street of the great city, which spiritually is called Sodom and Egypt, where also our Lord was crucified.

⁹ And they of the people and kindreds and tongues and nations shall see their dead bodies three days and an half, and shall not suffer their dead bodies to be put in graves.

¹⁰ And they that dwell upon the earth shall rejoice over them, and make merry, and shall send gifts one to another; because these two prophets tormented them that dwelt on the earth.

¹¹ And after three days and an half the spirit of life from God entered into them, and they stood upon their feet; and great fear fell upon them which saw them.

¹² And they heard a great voice from heaven saying unto them, Come up hither. And they ascended up to heaven in a cloud; and their enemies beheld them.

¹³ And the same hour was there a great earthquake, and the tenth part of the city fell, and in the earthquake were slain of men seven thousand: and the remnant were affrighted, and gave glory to the God of heaven.

¹⁴ The second woe is past; and, behold, the third woe cometh quickly.

In **verses 1-2** we discovered that a new Jewish temple will be built in Jerusalem. The Jews will consecrate a priesthood, and they will offer animal sacrifices as prescribed in the Law of Moses. They will worship God under the old covenant, not recognizing the fact that Jesus shed His precious blood to save the souls of humanity.

The following vision we are given is of two special witnesses. God sends two ambassadors from Heaven to preach His Gospel message to the people in Jerusalem. We want to consider these men and their ministry in this chapter. I would like to share this passage's insights concerning these *Two Witnesses.*

In **verses 3-7** we see the ministry of the two witnesses. Verses 3-4 tell us how the ministry is designed. These two men are raised up for a special purpose. These two verses tell us much about these men and what they are sent to do.

1. **They are called witnesses** – This word translates the word that gives us our English word *"Martyr"*. The word originally referred to someone who gave testimony about something, a witness. However, as so many Christians began to give their lives for the cause of Christ, the word came to be associated with those who gave their lives for their faith. These two men have come to witness to God's truth and, as we shall see, they will give their lives for Him too.
2. **They are sent as a team** – God always has His witnesses! In the days before the flood, God had His Noah. In the dark days of idolatry in Israel, the prophet Elijah complained to the Lord that he was all alone in the fight against sin. God told Elijah that there were over 7,000 who had not bowed their knee to Baal. (**1 Kings 19:14**). God has always had His witness teams: Moses and Aaron, Joshua and Caleb, and Paul and Silas. God sends two witnesses because He wants the truth to be established. The Law stipulated that all matters had to be established by the word of two witnesses. (**Deut. 19:15; Matt. 18:16**).
3. **They are sent to prophesy**. What will be the content of their message? No one knows for sure, but I think they will stand outside the newly completed Temple and preach Jesus to the Jews in Jerusalem. They will discuss how Jesus Christ has fulfilled prophecy. They will tell of His death, His resurrection, and His return. They will prove from the Word of God that the Temple and its worship are vain. They will preach the Gospel of grace and salvation through Jesus Christ. They will tell the people that the Antichrist will desecrate the Temple. These men will be hated by Jew and Gentile because of the message they will preach.
4. **They will be clothed in sackcloth** – Sackcloth is a symbol of mourning. These men will not come with a message a peace, comfort, and hope. They will bring a message of condemnation and judgment to a wayward people.
5. **Their ministry will last for three and one-half years** – While we cannot be too sure of when their ministry will begin, we can safely

say that they will commence their preaching sometime after the Temple is built there in Jerusalem.
6. **They are described as *"olive trees"* and *"candlesticks."*** *This is symbolic of God's hand on their ministry. The olive tree is the source of olive oil. In the Bible, it is often a type of the Holy Spirit.* The Spirit of God anoints these men for their particular ministry. The *"olive tree"* speaks of their **function**. The *"candlestick"* speaks of their ***function***. They will bring the light of God's message to a darkened world.

In **verse 5,** we see these two men being extremely unpopular because of the message they have been sent to deliver. As a result, many will try to kill them. But these men are under divine protection. They will kill everyone who tries to kill them. They will have the power to destroy their attackers with fire from their mouths.

In verse **6**, we see these two men will be able to use miraculous signs to prove the authenticity of their message. They will be able to shut up the heavens as Elijah did. They can turn water to blood and call down plagues from Heaven as Moses did. They will have immense power at their disposal and be able to use it whenever they wish.

Many modern preachers claim to be able to perform miracles. The only problem is that most are liars! Many are charlatans and scammers who only care about getting their hands on the money of people who fall for their lies. These two witnesses are not scammers and have been sent by God to show they are who they are and to preach God's message! Before we move deeper in this passage, let's take a minute to talk about who these men might be. First, let me say that no one knows for sure. The Bible does not identify them, and no one can say with absolute certainty just who they are.

There are a couple of guesses, and I will share those with you, as well as why certain men are mentioned. Before I proceed, I am now in the realm of conjecture. There is **no clear biblical record to which I can say conclusively.** Based on my theological study and commentaries from several learned men of theology, I can point out possibilities. Here we go!

They could be **Moses and Elijah**. According to **Mal. 4:5**, Elijah will return before Jesus comes. John the Baptist fulfilled this prophecy according to Jesus. (**Matt. 11:14; 17:10-13**). However, Malachi says that Elijah would come *"Behold, I will send you Elijah the prophet before the coming of the great and dreadful day of the LORD: And he shall turn the heart of the fathers to the children, and the heart of the children to their fathers, lest I come and smite the earth with a curse,"* **Malachi 4:5-6**.

Also, consider that one of the miracles the two witnesses will perform will be stopping the rain. This was one of Elijah's miracles in **1 Kings 17:1**.

As for Moses, he is mentioned in **Malachi 4:4** just before Elijah is mentioned in **verse 5**. The miracles performed by the two witnesses are reminiscent of those performed by Moses in Exodus. Moses and Elijah appeared with Jesus on the Mount of Transfiguration.

One of my seminary professors believes it will be Enoch with either Moses or Elijah. Enoch was a preacher of righteousness as indicated in **Jude 1:14**. And, Enoch never tasted of death, **Gen. 5:24**.

We won't know who they are until they come. All that we need to know is that God always has His witnesses! Let's move out of the realm of Biblical Detective and return to stated facts.

Verses 7-10 tell us of the massacre of the two witnesses. As pointed out in **verse 7**, when they have finished their appointed ministry, the Antichrist will be allowed to kill them. Until that moment, they are protected by the hand of God and cannot be killed. We are told they are killed by *"the beast that ascendeth out of the bottomless pit."* This is a reference to the Antichrist. He is called *"the beast"* 38 times in the Revelation. He ascends out of Hell itself, letting us know that he is demonically charged and controlled. He will make war against the witnesses, and he will be allowed to overcome them and kill them. We will learn more about him in the coming chapters.

There is a blessed jewel here for every saint of God. Death is not in the hands of a man or of a devil. Death is in the hands of God Almighty. He decides when people leave this world, and you cannot die until He says it is time. So many people live their lives in fear of death. They fail to grasp the truth that death is powerless against them until God severs the golden cord of life and allows death to claim the soul. There is, therefore, no need to fear men, armies, or devils. You will not die until He says it is time, and you will not live a second longer when He says it is time to go! (**Isa. 54:17**).

I participated in various military and intelligence operations to defend our great nation when I was young. I saw a lot of action. I carried a bullet frag in my right thigh until it finally worked its way out. I still carry Type-2 Malaria, which hit me very hard in November of 2020. I was a *guest* of some very unsavory individuals for a week until I was able to take advantage of a particular situation and with another member of my team, make good our escape. I used to say that I cheated death. In fact, I didn't cheat at all. I was very young, and it took me time to realize God protected me because, like Israel, he wasn't finished with me yet!

Verses 8-10 tell us of the reaction to the deaths of the two witnesses. The bodies of these men will be left in the very streets where they were killed. They will lay there in Jerusalem, and no one will remove their bodies or attempt to bury them. **Verse 9** tells us that all the people of the earth will see this sight. **Verse 10** tells us that the world's people will rejoice because these two men are dead.

For three and one-half years, these men have preached the Gospel and caused plagues to be poured out on men. Now they are dead, and the world celebrates. They act as if it were Christmas. They celebrate, they party, and they exchange gifts because these men are dead. Why do they do this? It is likely the preaching of these two witnesses drove them crazy. We are talking about a world that rejected Jesus Christ and His blood. They have turned a deaf ear to Bible preaching. They have given their allegiance to the devil, and they do not want to hear about God. These men have been preaching the truth and their message of judgment and condemnation got under people's skin. Now they are dead, and the world throws a party! This is the only scene of joy on the earth during the Tribulation. And there are happy because God's men are dead, and God's message is silent. What a tragedy!

Just for the record, the world will rejoice when preaching is finally silenced. Now, they love the preaching of this crowd that exalts the flesh. They like that feel-good preaching that tells people they are okay. This world hates preaching that exalts Christ and demands holiness. This world hates preaching that stands on the Bible. This world hates preaching that magnifies Jesus as the only way to reach God. They will rejoice when it is gone. Then, they can settle in, listen to the prophets of love and acceptance that flood the airwaves with feel-good preaching, and be happy as they plunge headlong into Hell.

In **Verse 11** a miracle occurs. The bodies of these men are allowed to lie in the streets of Jerusalem for three and one-half days. The world has watched as their bodies turn blue, pass through the various stages of rigor mortis, and begin to bloat. Then, a strange thing happens! Those bodies begin to stir! The two witnesses stand, and the world trembles in fear. Why does the world react in fear? The fact that these men are alive again after being dead for three days proves that they are the real deal. People know that they are men of God and that the message they have been preaching is valid. Perhaps they understand that this is the work of God. Maybe they have a brief moment when they know they are headed for judgment! Then in **Verse 12** we see another miracle. We see the miracle of their ascension.

While the world watches, the Lord God will reenact the Rapture (Rev. 4:1), and the two witnesses will rise into Heaven. The world will see what it missed when Jesus came. Maybe they will comprehend in that moment what happened when millions of people disappeared in the church's rapture.

The world will be given a clear testimony of the power of God Almighty! Satan, Antichrist and lost man will be reminded that God is in control of the world and all that happens in it. They will be helpless to stop this resurrection and rapture of the two witnesses.

Then in **Verses 13-14**, we see another miracle as they are avenged! Before the world can catch its breath, a great earthquake will hit Jerusalem. God will judge the city that has denied Him and His son, Jesus. A tenth part of the city will crumble to the ground, and seven thousand people will die. We are told that *"**the remnant were affrighted, and gave glory to the God of heaven**"*. This probably refers to a remnant of the Jews. They see these events, repent their sins and call on Christ for salvation. God will use even these events to bring glory to His name! There is a key point here, and I have said it before. Despite all the tragedy that is striking this world, with its putrid stench of sin, God is still in the business of saving souls.

In **verse 14**, we are told, *"**The second woe is past; and, behold, the third woe cometh quickly**."* More horrors are on the way! The worst is yet to come, and we will investigate far more horrible things in the coming chapters.

Let me close this chapter with this thought. We think our world is in bad shape, and it is! We talk about the wickedness of men, the hardness of human hearts, and the evil that flourishes around us. But think about this: We live in a world that the redeemed people of God inhabit. The Bible is here and preached around the world. The Holy Spirit is here suppressing evil and hindering its spread worldwide. In the Tribulation Period, the church is gone, so no one is praying for the world. The Bible will probably be taken out of circulation. You can almost guarantee it won't be preached in power and authority. The Spirit of God will leave when the church leaves. A world like that will grow eviler than you and I can comprehend. I am glad I am saved and will not be here for those awful days.

What about you? Are you saved? Are you trusting Jesus as your personal Savior today? If not, you can be! If you have strayed away from Him, you can come home today.

THE WOMAN AND THE DRAGON

This chapter and **Revelation 12:1-6** moves us into the second half of the book of Revelation. This second portion opens with a fantastic vision of some great wonders in the heavens.

Let me remind you that the book of Revelation is not written chronologically. **Chapters 4-9** take us through the end of the Tribulation Period. **Chapters 10-11** are passages that stand as a parenthesis in the action. They reveal some of the *"behind the scenes"* activities of the Lord. Chapter 11 took us to the very edge of eternity. It closes with the Lord Jesus claiming His rightful dominion over this universe and shows us how the inhabitants of that glorious land praise their King. Chapters 12-19 take us back through the Tribulation once again.

While **chapters 4-9** deal with the timeline or the plan of the Tribulation, **chapters 12-19** deal with the characters, or the people of the Tribulation. We are introduced to some of the individuals who will dominate during that period.

So, we will tread once again on ground we have already visited. One writer said, *"In Revelation 4-9 we see the events of the Tribulation through a telescope; in Revelation 12-19 we see things through a microscope."* In other words, we are about to get a more detailed look at the events of this period.

What is said in **chapter 12** is essential to a proper understanding of what is to follow in the rest of the book. If we misinterpret things here, we will be off the rest of the way through Revelation.

Let's read from God's word!

12 And there appeared a great wonder in heaven; a woman clothed with the sun, and the moon under her feet, and upon her

head a crown of twelve stars:
² And she being with child cried, travailing in birth, and pained to be delivered.
³ And there appeared another wonder in heaven; and behold a great red dragon, having seven heads and ten horns, and seven crowns upon his heads.
⁴ And his tail drew the third part of the stars of heaven, and did cast them to the earth: and the dragon stood before the woman which was ready to be delivered, for to devour her child as soon as it was born.
⁵ And she brought forth a man child, who was to rule all nations with a rod of iron: and her child was caught up unto God, and to his throne.
⁶ And the woman fled into the wilderness, where she hath a place prepared of God, that they should feed her there a thousand two hundred and threescore days.

So, let's dig into these six important verses. The primary characters of this passage are a woman and a red dragon. Let's see what we can learn about them today.

Verses 1-2 show us a lot about the woman's personality. The identity of this woman has been the subject of debate and false doctrine for centuries. Let me share a few of those with you. Some Roman Catholics believe that this woman is Mary. There are several reasons why this cannot be true. Mary never ascended in Heaven. Mary gave birth on earth and not in Heaven. Mary cannot be wedged into **verse 6**.

Let's move on. Some believe the woman is the church. However, it was Christ, the man-child that gave birth to the church and not the other way around. So, who is this mysterious woman? The clues in the text tell us all we need to know about her identity.

Verse 1 describes the woman in detail. The woman is *"clothed with the sun," which speaks of heavenly glory. The "Moon" is "under her feet," which speaks of dominion and power. She wears "a crown," which* speaks of royalty. The *"twelve stars"* speak of the twelve tribes of Israel.

From my study and research, I see that this woman is none other than the nation of Israel. I think this is seen quickly by a couple of Old Testament passages. The first tells of a dream that Joseph had thousands of years ago, **Gen. 37:9-11 says,** *"⁹And he dreamed yet another dream, and told it his brethren, and said, Behold, I have dreamed a dream more; and, behold, the sun and the moon and the eleven stars made obeisance to me.¹⁰ And he told it to his father, and to his brethren: and his father rebuked him, and said unto him, What is this dream that thou hast dreamed? Shall I and thy mother and thy brethren indeed come to bow down ourselves to thee to the earth?¹¹ And his brethren envied him; but his father observed the saying.*

Jacob's reaction to Joseph's dream makes it obvious that the sun, moon, and stars represent the nation of Israel. The second passage is Gen. 15:5. There, the seed of Abraham is compared to "stars."

This verse reminds us of what we already know to be true. **God is not finished with Israel!** He chose them out of the nations of the earth for His purposes and He has not written them off forever. They will once again be clothed with glory and have dominion over the earth.

Verse 2 speaks to the destiny of this woman. She is in the throes of childbirth, in great pain and anguish as she tries to bring her child into the world. In verse 5, we are told that her son is to the world's ruler. This is a reference to the Messiah, **the Lord Jesus Christ.** We will say more about Him in a moment. For now, our focus is on the woman.

This picture of Israel in childbirth reminds us that it was the nation of Israel that God used to bring His Saviour into the world. Jesus Christ is a Jew. In **Matthew 1:11** He is called both *"the Son of David"* and the *"Son of Abraham"*. When God gave the great prophecy of **Gen. 3:15**, He said, *"And I will put enmity between thee and the woman, and between thy seed and her seed; it shall bruise thy head, and thou shalt bruise his heel."* The woman is Israel, and the seed of the woman is the Lord Jesus. Remember JESUS is the other Adam!

Again, **Romans 9:4-5** says, *"Who are Israelites; to whom pertaineth the adoption, and the glory, and the covenants, and the giving of the law, and the service of God, and the promises; (5) Whose are the fathers, and of whom as concerning the flesh Christ came, who is over all, God blessed for ever. Amen."*

So, it was the nation of Israel that God chose to be the womb through which He sent His Son into the world. Did you notice that this woman was in travail? She is in labour, and she brings forth this Son with pain and suffering. This calls to mind all the pains and persecutions suffered by Israel as Satan tried his best to attack and circumvent the plan of God. In fact, when Jesus was born, the nation of Israel was writhing under the iron heel of the Roman Empire. So, this expectant woman is Israel who brought the Messiah into the world. She paid a price for that privilege. That was her destiny!

In **verses 3-4** we see the woman has a persecutor! The next vision is of a *"great red dragon"* who has *"seven heads and ten horns and seven crowns on his heads."* Let's take this description of the dragon and break it down symbol by symbol!

First, the dragon is red which is the colour of war and bloodshed. It suggests the red horse of **Rev. 6:4**. This dragon is a killer. He brings death, war, and bloodshed with him when he comes. Secondly, it describes a *dragon.* A dragon is a winged serpent. There is no such thing left in our natural world. This is a picture of the devil. In fact, we are very safe in identifying the dragon and the devil because of what **Rev. 12:9** says.

Thirdly, it has *Seven heads*. This speaks of vast intelligence. We are dealing with a brilliant and wise creature. Fourthly, the dragon has *ten horns*. Horns are a symbol of power. Satan is not all-powerful, but his power is vast. The number ten may refer to a ten-nation kingdom that will figure greatly during the last days.

This brings us to number five. This being has **seven crowns** – Crowns are a symbol of authority. Satan is still *"the god of this world"*, 2 **Cor. 4:4**.

In **verse 4** we see the reference to the *"stars of heaven"* being *"cast down to the earth"* by the tail of the dragon. This refers to the fall of Satan. He has not always been an evil creature. In the beginning, he was a ranking angel in Heaven, **Eze. 28:12-15**. Verse 15 says, *"[15] Thou wast perfect in thy ways from the day that thou wast created, till iniquity was found in thee."*

Pride was found in Lucifer's heart, and he tried to take God's throne and overthrow the Lord, **Isa. 14:12-14**. Lucifer sinned and became Satan. He was cast out of Heaven, **Isa. 14:15; Eze. 28:16-18**. When Lucifer fell, he drew one-third of the angels of Heaven into his rebellion. They were cast out of Heaven as well. We call these fallen angels, demons. They are part of Satan's kingdom and do his bidding, **Eph. 6:12**.

The dragon has an evil plan! Satan is pictured as standing before Israel waiting for the birth of her child. He intends to destroy the seed of the woman as soon as He is born. Satan has worked from the beginning of time to prevent the birth of the promised seed of the woman. Satan moved Cain to kill Abel, thinking he could stop God's plan. He did not know that God would send Seth. He tried to corrupt the human bloodline by having the godly line of Seth intermarrying with the evil line of Cain. He did not know about Noah and the Ark. He aroused Esau to anger so that Jacob might be killed. He did not know God would help Jacob escape. He tried to kill off the Jews in Egypt by having Pharaoh slay all the little boys. He did not know that God would save a little boy named Moses who would lead the people out of Egypt. He tried to lead Israel away into idolatry thinking God would destroy the nation. He did not see God sending them into captivity, where He would forever rid them of their idols.

He failed in every attempt to stop the birth of Christ. And, when the time came for Jesus to enter the world, Satan did everything in his power to slay the Christ child when He was an infant. He even moved Herod to destroy all the babies in Bethlehem under the age of two, **Matt. 2:16-18**.

Verse 5 speaks of the seed of the woman, who is called a "man child." The seed of the woman came into the world like every other baby. He came from the womb of His mother, but this child was unlike any other child that had ever been born or would ever be born. The seed of this woman was born without a human father, **Matt. 1:20**. His mother was a virgin, **Isa. 7:14**; **Luke 1:34**. And He was and is God in human flesh, **John 1:1; 14; Phil 2:5-8**! The Seed of the Woman is none other than the Lord Jesus Christ.

The child has destiny like no other! He is *"to rule the nations with a rod of iron"*. This man-child would come into the world, and He would one day rule the world. We see this prophecy fulfilled in **Rev. 19:15**. He will rule for several reasons. First, He will rule because He created this universe and it is His, **Col. 1:16-17**. Second, He will rule because He purchased this world with His blood when He died in the cross, **Rev. 5:9**. Third, He will rule because He alone is worthy to rule and reign, **Rev. 4:11**.

The man-child is pictured being caught up to God and to the throne of God. Here is the good news of the Gospel contained in this verse. Jesus Christ died for our sins on the cross. But He did not stay dead! He arose from the dead three days later, **Rev. 1:18**. After He arose from the dead, He ascended back to Heaven, **Acts 1:9-11**. He sat down at His Father's right hand in Heaven, **Heb. 1:3; 10:12**. He will not stay there forever! He is returning for His bride very soon, **1 Thes. 4:16-18**. Then, He will come to defeat His enemies and assume His rightful place as *"King of Kings and Lord of Lords."* Sorry, I had to pause to deliver a hearty Amen!

Verse 6 tells us how this woman is protected. The woman flees from the dragon and goes into the wilderness to hide. We are reminded here that Satan hates the nation of Israel. He has tried to defeat her and destroy her since she first appeared. I have already touched on this. No other nation on the face of the earth has suffered as much as Israel. No other race has been persecuted as much as the Jews.

The history of the Old Testament is filled with story after story of nations coming against Israel to destroy it. The pages of history are filled with hatred, persecution, racism, and murder, all aimed at the Jew. Just a generation ago, a man named Adolph Hitler did his best to destroy the Jews in what he called *"The Final Solution"*. He did not destroy them, but he did manage to murder over 6 million in the death camps of Nazi Germany. Josef Stalin killed millions in the gulags of the Soviet Union.

The Jew has suffered, but the Jew has survived! They have survived because of the providence of God. He is not through with Israel. Ill. **Jer. 31:35-36**! The only way to get rid of the Jew is to drag the sun, moon, and stars from their places in Heaven!

The hatred against the Jews is growing stronger in our day as the Muslim nations of the Middle East cry for the destruction of Israel. As of the writing of this book, Hamas attacked Israel and now Israel is fighting back, invoking their right to survive and defend itself. This hatred will continue to grow into the Tribulation Period. During that Time, the Antichrist will bring persecution upon the nation of Israel and the Jewish people like nothing they have ever experienced. When that persecution arises, Israel will seek refuge. This was prophesied by the Lord Jesus in **Matt. 24:15-22**. Yet, they will survive that too, for God has a plan for them!

Satan hates Israel for two reasons. He hates Israel because she is a constant reminder to him that his power is limited. He attempts to destroy Israel, and time and again, she is delivered by the power of God. Satan hates that! He also hates her because she constantly reminds him of the glory he used to wear. (The glory of Heaven rests on Israel just as it used to rest upon him.)

Israel will be delivered! Israel will find refuge in the wilderness. Some believe this will be in the ancient Edomite city of Petra. The city is surrounded by towering hills of rust-colored sandstone, which gave it some natural protection against invaders. The entrance into Petra is through the Siq, a ravine enclosed by immense walls that reach hundreds of feet at places. Its layout makes for a good place to hide and seek shelter.

In the 1920's, there was a man in United States, known as W. E. Blackstone. This man was so certain that Petra would be the secret hideout of Jews during the tribulation that he invested $8,000.00 to place boxes of Bibles in all the caves in Petra so that the Jews would have some interesting reading when they were hiding from the ravages of war.

We do not know if this be the place, they will seek shelter or not, but there will be a place prepared for them by God that will give them protection from the anti-Christ and his armies, all energized by Satan and his hatred for Christ and the people from whom He came.

We are told that the people of Israel will be taken care of in this wilderness refuge. We do not know who the *"they"* are who will feed the Jews, but we do know that for the last half of the Tribulation Period, 1,260 days, Israel will be cared for. Despite the sin, the hatred and the evil of those days, God will see to the needs of His people. He will either use friendly nations or supernatural means, but when the Tribulation ends, and Jesus returns, there will be a remnant of the nation of Israel left. These faithful Jews will embrace the Lord Jesus and worship Him as their Messiah.

One thing I want you to remember! Jews are waiting for the coming of the Messiah. According to the Jewish Talmud, Jews are obligated not only to believe in the Messiah, but to yearn for his arrival. Many traditional Jews recite a creed that concludes with this statement: ***"I believe with perfect faith in the advent of the messiah, and though he may tarry, I will await his arrival every day."***

During the Jewish Passover Seder, the Passover meal, there is the tradition of opening the door for Elijah, who will precede the coming of the Messiah. They don't understand that Messiah has already come, and His name is Jesus. The nation of Israel gave birth to their long-awaited Messiah, yet they failed to recognize Him. John said in **John 1:10-11**, *"He was in the world, and he made the world, and the world knew him not. [11] He came unto his own, and his own received him not."*

The Messiah died on Calvary's cross, was buried, and rose from the dead on the third day and was caught up to heaven where He awaits the hour when He will come back to rule and reign upon the earth.

These verses emphasize this truth: God has a plan for the ages, and that plan will be worked out in His way in His time.

Are you part of God's plan? Have you trusted Jesus as your Savior? Has the blood of the crucified and risen Lord washed away your sins? Are you saved? Are you living for Him as you should? Are you thankful that He saved your soul?

You might want to talk to Him about your relationship with Him. I am going to do something a little different at the end of this chapter. I want to end it with a prayer.

I ask you to pray with me. *Dear God, the architect of the universe, our gracious Lord, we come to you today in solemn prayer. God, you are truly amazing! Even in these horrible times in Revelation, you are still in the business of saving souls and offering forgiveness. Lord, if there be anyone today that has accepted you but not living a Christian life, Father, I ask that you speak to their heart and chasten them to return to you. Father, we know the angels in heaven rejoice over one soul that returns to you. How great is your name! Father, if anyone has not accepted Jesus Christ as their Lord and Savior, we ask that you speak to their heart, Oh Lord! We know nothing is free.*

Lord, you offer us salvation through the precious blood of our Lord Jesus Christ. Christ paid the price for our sins, from the first sin of man down through the ages to the end as we know it. God, please, Lord, lead them to you now. Make a way for them. Remove all obstacles from their path. Show them that there is nothing that can separate us from your love. The only thing that separates us from salvation, God, is our own stubborn behavior. Lord bless us today. For this prayer, Oh God, we pray in the precious name of your son Jesus Christ. Amen.

THE WAR IN HEAVEN

Revelation 12 is a chapter wrapped in conflict and **verses 7-17** describe a great war in heaven. In our last study we witnessed war between the nation of Israel, symbolized by a pregnant woman, and Satan, symbolized by a great red dragon. As we read our text, you may have noticed that these verses continue to represent the image of conflict. Verse 7 is quite a shock to the senses. Let's read from the Word of God!

> *⁷And there was war in heaven: Michael and his angels fought against the dragon; and the dragon fought and his angels,*
> *⁸And prevailed not; neither was their place found any more in heaven.*
> *⁹And the great dragon was cast out, that old serpent, called the Devil, and Satan, which deceiveth the whole world: he was cast out into the earth, and his angels were cast out with him.*
> *¹⁰And I heard a loud voice saying in heaven, Now is come salvation, and strength, and the kingdom of our God, and the power of his Christ: for the accuser of our brethren is cast down, which accused them before our God day and night.*
> *¹¹And they overcame him by the blood of the Lamb, and by the word of their testimony; and they loved not their lives unto the death.*
> *¹²Therefore rejoice, ye heavens, and ye that dwell in them. Woe to the inhabiters of the earth and of the sea! for the devil is come down unto you, having great wrath, because he knoweth that he hath but a short time.*
> *¹³And when the dragon saw that he was cast unto the earth, he persecuted the woman which brought forth the man child.*
> *¹⁴And to the woman were given two wings of a great eagle, that she might fly into the wilderness, into her place, where she is nourished for a time, and times, and half a time, from the face of*

the serpent.

¹⁵ And the serpent cast out of his mouth water as a flood after the woman, that he might cause her to be carried away of the flood.

¹⁶ And the earth helped the woman, and the earth opened her mouth, and swallowed up the flood which the dragon cast out of his mouth.

¹⁷ And the dragon was wroth with the woman, and went to make war with the remnant of her seed, which keep the commandments of God, and have the testimony of Jesus Christ.

When we read of war in Heaven, we are taken by surprise. We do not think of Heaven as a place where wars are fought. If the Bible announced a war on earth, we would not be shocked. Our world has a long history of bloody warfare.

According to one statistician, in the 5,560 years of recorded human history, there have been some 14,565 wars. Many of history's wars were conflicts between two nations or two factions within a country. However, World War II took war to new and devastating heights. By the time the war reached its zenith, only twelve nations were not involved in the conflict on at least some level. In 2024 at least thirty-nine armed conflicts are being fought on the soil of thirty-five different nations.[1] Our world is a world of warfare!

Yet, when we read of warfare in Heaven, we are taken aback. This war will settle a conflict that has been raging since before there was a world. As we discovered in the preceding chapters, Lucifer, who seems to have been the chief among God's angels, sinned against God. He led one-third of the angels of Heaven away from God in this rebellion, and he and they were removed from God's presence. Lucifer became Satan, and he has done everything in his power to disrupt the eternal plan of God to redeem His elect people and His ruined creation. Since that time, as we will discover, Satan has had limited access to Heaven. This chapter tells us about the final battle in this age-old war. Satan, the great dragon, is forever cast out of Heaven in this battle.

While some details here are confusing, these verses are a blessing to the children of God. They tell us of a day when Satan will finally and eternally be cast out of Heaven. Let's look at these verses and examine a few more of the participants of the Tribulation Period.

Let's examine this evil dragon! There are several passages about the devil, his origin, and his activities. (**Isa. 14:12-20, Eze. 28:12-19, 1 Pet. 5:8**). This passage reveals the devil far more clearly than any other passage in the Bible. So, let's learn a little more about the dragon.

Verse 9 tells us his name! A quick look at the names given to this creature reveals more about him than he wants people to know. First, he is described as a dragon. A dragon is a winged creature that resembles a serpent with four legs. Dragons are usually associated with fierceness, brutality, violence, and destruction. Superstitious people in the Dark Ages lived in fear of fire-breathing dragons.

This image is fitting for Satan. He is a violent character bent on the total and complete destruction of God and His creation. He is responsible for countless deaths and wars.

Secondly, he is described as a serpent. This immediately calls us back to the first appearance of Satan in the Bible. (**Gen. 3:1**). In that passage, Satan appears to Eve in the form of a serpent and entices her to sin. The image of a serpent is an image of something evil, contemptible, detestable, deceitful, and sly. What a perfect depiction of the devil! He spends his time attempting to deceive everyone he encounters.

Thirdly, he is described as the **Devil**. The word devil comes from the word "*diabolos*". It refers to one who is a "*slanderer, a false accuser*". It pictures him as a creature who stands before God, accusing the saints of God. This is just what the Bible says he does in **Job 1-2**. When we fail, he accuses us before the throne of God. He slanders our name, and he slanders our Saviour, too.

Fourthly, we know his name is Satan. This word means "*adversary*' or "*one who stands opposed*". This is what Satan is all about. He opposes everything that has to do with God. He opposes everything God is trying to do. He opposes the people of God, the House of God, the Word of God, and the plan of God. He stands in open opposition to everything that is decent, holy, and right. He is the adversary!

Verses 9-10 tell us about the nature of this great evil! This passage reveals Satan through his names and his nature, including the two most common activities of the devil.

Verse 9 shows him revealed by his earthly deceptions. We are told that it is he *"which deceiveth the whole earth"*. The word *"deceiveth"* means *"to seduce, to lead astray, to lead out of the right way*. That is Satan's mission! When he appeared before the Lord in **Job 1:7; 2:2**, he was asked about his activities. He replied that he had come *"from going to and fro in the earth and walking up and down in it."* He was on the prowl for souls to deceive. That is what Peter says about him in **1 Pet. 1:5**. The word *"seeking"* in that verse means *"to crave, to reason, to plot.* Satan is always plotting someone's fall. He craves the souls of men. He reasons out ways to turn people away from God and Christ. Do not underestimate him. He is very good at what he does! He can come into our midst and not even be recognized. (**2 Cor. 11:13-14**). Satan is a deceiver, and he always has been. When he came to Eve in Eden, he was called *"subtil"*. That word means *"crafty and shrewd"*. Satan deceived Eve, and he has been deceiving people ever since. He will continue to weave his web of lies and half-truths until he is cast into the Lake of Fire.

Verse 10 shows him revealed by some heavenly declarations. Satan is described by the host of Heaven as *"the accuser of our brethren is cast down, which accused them before our God day and night.* The word *"accuser"* means *"to make an accusation." It speaks of "a plaintiff who brings up another person on charges."* That is Satan's business!

Job 1:6 and **2:1** show us that Satan still has some limited access to the throne of God. When he appears there, he does so to condemn the saints of God. He did this to Job and Joshua. (**Zech. 3:1**). He stands before God and points out our sins and failures. He does not have to lie about us, because we have enough failure and sin in our lives that he has a ready supply of accusations to make. Yet, when he opens his mouth and declares his case, the saints of God have a Man on the inside! We have an attorney and advocate in Heaven. (**1 John 2:1, Rom. 8:34, Heb. 7:25**). The word *"Advocate"* in **1 John 2:2** means *"one who pleads another's cause before a judge"*. Jesus Christ, our Advocate, stands up to declare us just and justified. He pleads our case by showing His hands and feet the nail prints. He pleads the blood He shed on the cross as the perfect, eternal payment for all our sins.

Verses 7-9 show us the fate of this dragon! We do not know who initiates this war in Heaven, but we know who wins it. The angelic hosts of Heaven are led in this conflict by an angel named Michael. His name means *"Who is like God?"* He is a special angel. He is called an *"archangel'* in **Jude 1:9**. In **Daniel 10:13** he is called *"one of the chief princes."* In **Daniel 12:1** he is called *"the great prince."* Michael opposes the onslaught of Satan and his demonic army. He leads the heavenly angels in permanently ousting Satan and His demons from Heaven. **Verse 8** tells us *"neither was their place found anymore in heaven"*. And **verse 9** tells us that he and his angels were *"cast out into the earth"*. The words *"cast out'* mean *"to let go of a thing without caring where it falls."* Satan is forever driven from Heaven!

Verses 10-11 further exemplify his defeat at the hands of holy witnesses. When Satan is cast out of Heaven, the glory spills out of the cup and overflows the saucer. Heaven explodes in praise and thanksgiving. The tormentor, the accuser of the brethren, the archenemy of God, and the most feared and hated being in the universe has been forever expelled from Heaven! So, the citizens of Heaven praise God and the Lamb for their power and glory in overcoming the devil!

Then, praise is rendered on behalf of the Tribulation saints who were martyred for their faith. While Michael was able to expel him from Heaven, these Christian martyrs also overcame him! They used three weapons to defeat the devil!

First, they used the Blood of the Lamb! They did not fall for Satan's lies that religion or their works would be good enough. They did not fall for the lie that **they** were good enough. When they saw their condition, they turned to Jesus by faith and were washed in the blood of the Lamb. Once they were hidden behind the fortress of the blood of Jesus, they were safe from all attacks by Satan against their souls. He might kill their bodies, but he could not touch their souls! They had been redeemed, and they obtained eternal victory!

Second, they used the word of their testimony. They would not renounce their faith in Jesus. The word **"testimony"** means **"report"**. They made good on their claim as redeemed followers of Jesus, and they never backed down from that claim. Their steadfastness helped them achieve victory over Satan. He may have killed their bodies, but they overcame his evil with their testimonies fresh on their lips! His defeat was sealed with every death.

Finally, they used their great love for Jesus! Even when they were threatened with death, they would not back down. They loved their Redeemer more than they loved their own lives. They would rather die for Jesus, who died for them than deny Him. They stood their ground and courageously faced a martyr's death, knowing that when life left the body here, it would continue forever in His blessed presence!

We can see from the text that Satan does not take like being cast out of Heaven! He turns his wrath to the only place he can still operate. He turns his wrath on planet earth!

Verse 12 tells us of Satan's wrath! He pronounces a divine woe upon the "*the inhabiters of the earth*" because they are about to feel the unfiltered fury of an angry Devil. He knows that he only has a limited time before the eternal plan of the Lord is finished and he is facing certain judgment. Since he cannot vent his anger toward Heaven and God, he turns his hatred earthward and attacks the people living upon the earth. Verses 13-17 tell us the focus of the Dragon's attack! The primary object of Satan's wrath becomes the chosen people of God, the nation of Israel. As we saw in **verses 1-6**, Satan hates Israel and does everything in his power to destroy that nation. These verses give us a few more details of that terrible time.

We are told that Satan "*persecuted'* the woman. The word "*persecuted'* means "*to chase or to pursue.*" It refers to a hostile pursuit. Satan goes after Israel with a vengeance and pursues them with an agenda bent on violent destruction!

But we are told again that they are divinely protected. The image of the eagle's wings symbolizes God's protection of His chosen people. We see this in **Ex. 19:4**, "*Ye have seen what I did unto the Egyptians, and how I bare you on eagles' wings, and brought you unto myself.*" God brings Israel into a place of safety that He has prepared for them. He will feed and care for them there for three and one-half years. Satan will be prevented from destroying the nation of Israel!

Verse 15 depicts the attacks of Satan being like a great flood of water. He will try everything at his disposal to destroy Israel. But even the earth gets involved. We are told in **verse 16** that "the earth opened her mouth *and swallowed up the flood*". This may mean that some friendly nations of the earth, Gentile people, will reach out to Israel, take them in, and give to their needs during those dark days. Or it may mean that the earth will absorb the blows Satan intended for Israel. Whatever these images mean, one thing is clear. God has a plan for Israel, and Satan will not thwart that plan! God is sovereign, and He will do as He has said He will do concerning all things, especially the nation of Israel!

Verse 17 teaches us that there will be a faithful remnant of Israel during the dark days of the Tribulation. There will be a multitude of Jews saved through the preaching of the 144,000 Jewish evangelists and the two witnesses who will preach in Jerusalem. These redeemed Jews will embrace the Messiah and return to the Word of God. They will be persecuted for their faith, but a remnant will be saved. **(Matt. 24:1-22)**. God will have the final say.

As I have studied and preached on the information behind these chapters, I have seen, studied, and preached some horrible things. Yet, even in this dark, mysterious book, we can find a cause for rejoicing. In this passage, we learn that the devil, that evil being who has fought against God, His plan, and His people for thousands of years, will be defeated. We learn that the one who has accused us when we fail and has condemned us by name in Heaven will one day be cast out of that city. We will learn later that his path will end in the flame of the Lake of Fire.

THE BEAST FROM OUT OF THE SEA

Revelation 13:1-10 ushers in the Beast from the Sea. The beast from the sea is Satan's agent on earth. The beast also had seven heads since Satan was pictured as a seven-headed dragon. The beast is the counterpart to the Lamb. The beast and the Lamb are said to have been slaughtered yet returned to life, but there the similarities cease. The beast is a mockery of the Lamb. Whereas the Lamb was slain, the beast only appears to die and return to life. Whereas the Lamb conquers by faithful suffering, the beast conquers by violent warfare. Whereas the Lamb redeems people of every tribe and nation, the beast oppresses people of every tribe and nation (**Revelation 5:5-1,13:6-7**). Readers living in New Testament times would have understood that the Lamb was a present reality for them. Similarly, they would have understood that the beast's power was a present reality for them and that this meant they were called to resist it.

The beast represents an oppressive power that has operated at many times and places.

Let's read from God's Word!

13 And I stood upon the sand of the sea, and saw a beast rise up out of the sea, having seven heads and ten horns, and upon his horns ten crowns, and upon his heads the name of blasphemy.
² And the beast which I saw was like unto a leopard, and his feet were as the feet of a bear, and his mouth as the mouth of a lion: and the dragon gave him his power, and his seat, and great authority.
³ And I saw one of his heads as it were wounded to death; and his deadly wound was healed: and all the world wondered after the beast.

> *⁴ And they worshipped the dragon which gave power unto the beast: and they worshipped the beast, saying, Who is like unto the beast? who is able to make war with him?*
> *⁵ And there was given unto him a mouth speaking great things and blasphemies; and power was given unto him to continue forty and two months.*
> *⁶ And he opened his mouth in blasphemy against God, to blaspheme his name, and his tabernacle, and them that dwell in heaven.*
> *⁷ And it was given unto him to make war with the saints, and to overcome them: and power was given him over all kindreds, and tongues, and nations.*
> *⁸ And all that dwell upon the earth shall worship him, whose names are not written in the book of life of the Lamb slain from the foundation of the world.*
> *⁹ If any man have an ear, let him hear.*
> *¹⁰ He that leadeth into captivity shall go into captivity: he that killeth with the sword must be killed with the sword. Here is the patience and the faith of the saints.*

In our previous study we met the Antichrist. We tried to consider what the Bible says about this coming world ruler who is called the "**Man of Sin**"; the "Son of Perdition". The Antichrist gives us an opportunity to see how Satan operates. The devil is an imitator. He takes what God does and he tries to duplicate it.

You see, Jesus, the real Christ, is a revelation of God the Father. In **John 1**, three verses are worthy of note, **John 1:1, 14, 18**. These verses teach us the truth that living, breathing revelation of God the Father. The **verse 18**, the word "*declared'* translates the Greek word that gives us our English word "*exegesis*". The word means "*to narrate, to explain, to lead out, to draw out*". It speaks of "*an explanation, or a narration*".

In preaching, we use exegesis to "*lead out and explain*" the truths contained in the text. When Jesus came, He came to "*explain, to lead out, to narrate*" God. In other words, Jesus Christ was and is God in the flesh. He was able to say, "*I and my Father are one,*" **John 10:30**. He was also able to say, *"he that hath seen me hath seen the Father,"* **John 14:9**. Jesus is God incarnate; He is God in the flesh.

In the Antichrist, Satan attempts to duplicate this relationship between Jesus Christ and God the Father. The Antichrist will be a living, breathing revelation of the devil. He will be the devil incarnate; he will be the devil in the flesh.

We know that our God is a triune Being. He is one God who manifests Himself in three Persons: Father, Son, and Holy Ghost. All three are One God, yet each is a Person. They come together to make up the Holy Trinity.

In **Revelation 12-13**, we are introduced to the Satanic Trinity. Satan imitates God the Father. The Antichrist imitates God the Son. The False Prophet, whom we will meet in our subsequent study, imitates God the Holy Spirit.

Let's give our attention once again to this man who will be known as the Antichrist. These verses give us essential details concerning his mission, methods, and miracles. Consider these first ten verses of **Revelation 13**, and let's study *The Beast from Out of The Sea*.

Verses 1-2 tell us how he originates. As John stands on a seashore, a mysterious *"beast" rises from* the sea. This is symbolic language. The *"sea"* in the Bible represents the masses of humanity. This individual will come from among men. In other words, while he may possess power that surpasses all the other great rulers of me, he will be nothing more than a man!

Satan will empower the Antichrist, and he will wield tremendous power and authority. But, unlike Jesus Christ, he will have a human mother and father. He will not be a Godman like Jesus. He will be a man who receives his kingdom and power from Satan.

Where will he come from, and what will his nationality be? No one knows! According to the Bible, he would lead a ten-nation confederacy that resembled the revived Roman Empire. Therefore, he may be European by birth. Of course, **Daniel 11:37** tells us that he *"will not regard the God of his fathers."* This verse leads many to speculate that he will be Jewish by birth. The fact is no one knows.

Verses 1-2 also give us a little insight into this man called Antichrist. The symbolic language tells us something about his character and the nature of the kingdom he will rule.

1. **Seven Heads** – The explanation is given in **Rev. 17:9,** *"The seven heads are seven mountains, on which the woman sitteth."* **Revelation 17** is a passage about *"The Great Harlot'*, or the apostate church that will dominate world religion during the Tribulation Period. We are told that the *"Harlot'* sits on *"seven hills"*. There is only one city in the world built on seven hills. That is the city of Rome.
2. **Ten Horns—Horns are a symbol of power and authority.** Again, **Rev. 17:12** explains these horns. We are told that the ten horns are "ten kings."
3. **Ten Crowns** – These ten kings have great authority and power. The Antichrist will arise from among this confederation of ten powerful kings.
4. **The Names of Blasphemy** – These world leaders will stand in open defiance of all that is holy or that has to do with God.

Many believe that what we see here is a revival of the ancient Roman Empire. The Roman Empire was never really defeated. It just dissolved into separate kingdoms. There have been many attempts to revive it down through the centuries. Charlemagne, Napoleon, and Hitler tried, but they all failed. The Roman Empire will be revived again, and the Antichrist will dominate this confederation of nations.

We are already seeing this process come to pass in the European Union. This union is comprised of twenty-seven European nations with more who are candidates for admission. The land area occupied by these nations covers much of the land area occupied by the old Roman Empire. We will see this body produce the Antichrist and provide the ten kings who will rule the world at the beginning of the Tribulation Period.

To understand the description given of this beast in these verses, you have to go back to **Daniel 7:3-8**. In Daniel's vision, he describes the great world empires that will follow one after another until the end of the world.

Daniel speaks of a *"lion"* in **verse 4**. This beast pictures the Babylonian Empire. Like a lion, ancient Babylon was powerful, fearsome and had a ravenous appetite for domination. The *"bear"* in **verse 5** speaks of the Medo-Persian Empire. Like a bear it possessed incredible power to crush its enemies. The **"leopard"** in **verse 6** speaks of the Greek Empire. It is called a leopard because the Greeks quickly dominated the world. The fourth beast in **verse 7** is the Roman Empire. With teeth of iron, they dominated the ancient world.

The Bible teaches us that the Antichrist will possess the power and the personality of all these ancient empires. He will combine all their strengths and possess none of their weaknesses.

1. **Body Like a Leopard** – His rise to power will be swift.
2. **Feet Like a Bear** – He will crush his opponents.
3. **Mouth Like a Lion** – Like a lion, he will devour all who dare stand in his way.
4. **Called A Beast** – The word *"beast'* refers to *"a wild animal."* It is used as a metaphor for a man who is "brutal, savage, and ferocious." Like a wild animal, Antichrist will attack the kingdoms of the world and he will destroy all who get in his path. He will be a fearsome, powerful man.

We are told that the Antichrist rules the world, but not by his own power. He is Satan's Superman. The Dark Prince energizes him. We are told that Satan gives him three things. 1. His Power – This word refers to *"strength, power, and ability. 2. His Seat – This is his "throne." He rules because Satan has given him dominion. 3. Great Authority – This word refers to the "ability to do as one pleases."* The Antichrist will do as he pleases on this earth for a time, and no one will be able to stop him.

The Antichrist will accept the offer Jesus refused in **Matthew 4**. When Jesus was on the Mount of Temptation Satan offered Jesus all the kingdoms of the world if Jesus would bow down and worship the devil. **(Matt. 4:8-9)**. Jesus refused Satan's ridiculous offer. It appears, however, that the Antichrist will accept, and Antichrist will rule the world. Satan will control this future world ruler.

There is an interesting parallel that I want to point out today. The human heart was made to be occupied. When you are lost, the heart is occupied and controlled by Satan, **Eph. 2:1-3**. When a person is saved, the Holy Spirit resides in your heart and assumes control of your life. If you have never received Jesus as your Savior, then Satan is your lord and your master, **John 8:44**.

Verses 3-4 point out the Antichrist's amazing achievements. Verse 3 tells us he will receive the world's wonder! At some point during the Antichrist's reign, he will die. It may be an assassination or some other form of upheaval, but he will be killed. As the world watches and mourns the death of this very popular man, a miraculous thing happens: This dead man comes back from the dead. He experiences a resurrection.

Remember, I told you that Satan is an imitator. In this verse, we are told that Satan seeks to duplicate the resurrection. God's Son died on the cross and rose from the dead, and the world, for the most part, ignores Him. This man will die and rise again, and the world will wonder after him. He has the world right where he wants it, eating out of the palm of his hand.

In **Verse 4**, we see that he receives the world's worship. Whether the resurrection is real or just a bit of satanic sleight of hand, we do not know. Yet, the citizens of the world will be taken in. They will be so caught up in the power, glory, and wonder of the Antichrist that they will give him their worship! The world will bow before this hellish king and give him what they have steadfastly refused to give God.

Just as God receives the worship of man through His Son the Lord Jesus Christ, Satan will receive the worship of men through the Antichrist. He will be getting what he has always wanted. Men will worship the Beast and the Devil. What a tragedy! While Heaven rejoices over the fact that Satan has been cast out of Heaven, **Rev. 12:10**, the *"earth dwellers"* give their worship to the devil.

It is here the world will declare the Antichrist to be undefeatable. What they fail to understand is that there will come a day when the Antichrist will be defeated and cast into Hell. **(Rev. 19:20; 20:10).** Jesus Christ can beat the devil's superman with no problem. But may I also point out the truth that God's people living during the Tribulation can also defeat him? **(Rev. 12:11)**. Satan has power, and the Antichrist will have power. But they will face Jesus, who has **ALL POWER! (Matt. 28:18)**. He will defeat, destroy, and judge them!

Verses 5-8 tell us the Antichrist will use his newfound power over men to further Satan's agenda. These verses tell us what kind of man the Antichrist will be. The Antichrist will be a man of great oratorical ability and will use this ability to defy God. He will be able to move the masses with the power of his tongue. If you have ever seen films of Adolph Hitler, you have seen a man who understood the power of the tongue. His words stirred up a nation and convinced them that they could rule the world. He convinced the German people that they were superior to all others. Hitler's words brought about unbelievable suffering and innumerable deaths. Hitler once said, ***"You say something long enough and loud enough, and people will eventually believe you."***

When the Antichrist comes, his power with words will make Hitler seem like a babbling idiot! He will galvanize the world's nations with the power of his words. He will speak ***great things*** and they will believe him. He will speak blasphemes against the God of Heaven, and they will worship him. He will use his words to attack everything related to God, and the world will hang on to every word. He will do everything in his power to turn humanity against God. He will even declare himself to be God!

In **Verse 7**, we see the Antichrist will make it his mission to seek out and destroy anyone who still worships God. There will be people saved during the Tribulation. These people will become the focus of the Antichrist's intense hatred of God. He will not be able to defeat the 144,000 Jewish preachers as they travel the world preaching the Gospel of the Kingdom. He will not be able to defeat the two witnesses who stand in Jerusalem and preach the Gospel of the Kingdom. He will not be able to stop them until their time is finished, and then he will be allowed to kill them too. But anyone else on this earth who refuses to bow to him in worship will be put to a martyr's death!

In Verse 7, we also see he will dominate the nations of this world! The Antichrist will rule the world! Every nation will come under his power and domination. He will be the ultimate world ruler. He will be the king of the world!

In **Verse 8**, we see that he will deceive the masses! **Verse 8** is crystal clear! Every person who is not saved by god's grace will eventually bow in worship of Satan and his Superman.

Notice that these worshipers are called *"**all that dwell upon the earth**"*. The word *"**dwell**"* means *"**to settle down.**"* This phrase refers to people who have chosen to make this world their home. They have decided that they aren't interested in Heaven or in anything God can offer them. They have staked all their hopes and their futures in this world. God abandons them to their choice! They want the world, and He lets them have it, with all the consequences of such a decision.

These "***earth dwellers***" have refused God and His Messiah and they have chosen Satan and his false messiah. God gives them over to their perverse thinking and lets them have the world and the god they have chosen. **(2 Thes. 2:11-12)**.

The final two verses of our text have a special message for us today. **Verse 9** says, "***If any man have an ear, let him hear***". Do you recognize that statement? We have seen a statement like it several times before. If you read these verses you will find that they say, "***He that hath an ear, let him hear what the Spirit saith unto the churches***". Do you see what is missing? Two things are missing here. This is the "***Spirit***" and the "***churches.***" Both the Spirit and the church were removed from the world at the Rapture. The **age of grace has ended**, and the world is in the grip of the Great Tribulation. When God speaks here, He does not warn His people; He warns the earth dwellers, but it is too late for them to repent. They are locked into their choice, and they will worship the Beast, and they will die and go to Hell!

Verse 10 drives this point home. The whole point of **verse 10** is that people reap what they sow. **(Gal. 6:7)**. If you live for the devil, you will reap the devil. If you reject Jesus, you will be rejected by Jesus. The time to make a choice is today! There will come a day when it will be too late.

When will that day be? No one knows but God! It could be today, tonight, or tomorrow. There will come a day when God stops calling you and abandon you to your choice. If you are not saved, you need to come to Jesus today.

If you are saved, **verse 10** offers hope. The "patience and faith of the saints" is the knowledge that Satan and Antichrist will be defeated in the end. On that day, God and righteousness will reign. The Final Countdown has begun! Where will you spend eternity?

THE BEAST FROM THE EARTH

For the past few chapters, we have been treading on some very unholy ground. We have spent a lot of time talking examining the devil and the Tribulation period. While we continue our studies, I want you to remember Satan is an imitator. He hasn't had an original thought in over six thousand years. **Revelation 13:11-15** shows this in detail.

As we all know, there is a Holy Trinity. The Holy Trinity is comprised of God the Father, God the Son, and God the Holy Spirit. These three individuals make up the Godhead. Satan has a trinity too. His trinity, however, is anything but holy.

The unholy trinity is composed of Satan, the Antichrist, and the False Prophet. Each member of the Holy Trinity has a specific purpose.

God the Father receives the worship of His people through His Son the Lord Jesus Chr, the Lord Jesus Christ. The Holy Spirit facilitates this holy worship. He stirs up the believer's heart to worship God.

Remember, Satan is an imitator. His trinity functions exactly the same way. In Satan's unholy trinity, Satan receives the worship through the person of the Antichrist and the False Prophet facilitates this worship.

We have already considered the first two members of the unholy trinity. We have looked extensively at Satan and at the Antichrist. In this chapter we will look at these verses and get a glimpse of the False Prophet. He is the person who will guide the world's religion during the Tribulation Period. Let's look into these verses together and notice the insights the Bible gives us concerning *The Beast From The Earth*.

Let's read from God's Word.

> *[11] And I beheld another beast coming up out of the earth; and he had two horns like a lamb, and he spake as a dragon.*
> *[12] And he exerciseth all the power of the first beast before him, and causeth the earth and them which dwell therein to worship the first beast, whose deadly wound was healed.*

¹³ And he doeth great wonders, so that he maketh fire come down from heaven on the earth in the sight of men,
¹⁴ And deceiveth them that dwell on the earth by the means of those miracles which he had power to do in the sight of the beast; saying to them that dwell on the earth, that they should make an image to the beast, which had the wound by a sword, and did live.
¹⁵ And he had power to give life unto the image of the beast, that the image of the beast should both speak, and cause that as many as would not worship the image of the beast should be killed.

Verse 11 tells us of the personality of this beast. This second beast is a man just as the first beast was. The word *another* translates the Greek word *allos*. It means *another of the same kind and quality*. The figure described here is a man. This is also proven by his fate as we see in **Rev. 19:20**.

This beast has horns, which are a symbol of power. He has *"two horns"*. Two is a number that symbolized *"testimony"*. While the first beast had power because of the territory he ruled, this beast will have power because of the testimony he gives.

The first beast had *"ten horns,"* but this beast had *"two horns."* The first beast had *"ten crowns,"* but this beast had no crowns. The first beast is described in terrifying language as a leopard, a lion, and a bear. This beast is called *"a lamb."* The first beast comes as a powerful world ruler. This beast appears as a mean gentleman of faith.

This individual will appear on the world stage as a gentle, meek, loving and kind religious leader. He will have charisma and a gentle nature. He will possess the religious power of the Pope. While the Antichrist will rule the world with brute force; this man will attract the world through his pleasant personality and pleasing words. This man is not as he appears. He has all the outward appearances and trappings of a man of faith, but when he speaks, he speaks the words of the dragon. He is the mouthpiece of Satan himself. He will be a religious man, but the religion he is promoting is the worship of Satan! His true nature will be revealed by the words which he will speak.

By the way, it doesn't take too long to determine what a preacher or a church believes. Just listen to their words and they will reveal their hearts in short order. Take some of these TV preachers for instance. One of the most popular never mentions the name of Jesus, nor does he mention sin. He just tells a few stories and builds everyone up. Others are always talking about money and prosperity. It doesn't take long to separate the wheat from the chaff, if you know a little bit about the Word of God!

Verse 12 begins to show us the power of this beast! We immediately see the source of his power! *"He exerciseth all the power of the first beast"*. This individual will receive his power from the same source that the Antichrist will receive his power. It will come from the devil. The world will accept this man as a *"man of God".* He will be hailed worldwide as the greatest religious leader the world had ever seen. The world will be deceived and will not grasp the truth that he is the agent of Satan until it is too late.

Then we begin to see the scope of his power! The man will be the facilitator of a vast worldwide religion. He will be able to unite all world religions under one banner. He will convince the world that the Antichrist is a god and that he alone is to be worshiped. Men and women from every conceivable religion will bow down in worship of the Antichrist as the leadership of this False Prophet.

This man will solve the problems between the religions of the world. Take the situation in the Middle East. The problems there are not political, they are religious. The problems in that part of the world predate the forming of Islam. The Jews and the Arabs have been bitter enemies since the days of Moses and Joshua. Now, the Muslims hate the Jews, and they are bent on the destruction of the nation of Israel. No one can seem to solve their differences today, but this False Prophet will, during the Tribulation. He will find the common ground that will allow all the religions of the world to exist under one umbrella.

In our day, when there is news of a religious nature, the world often looks to the Pope to see what he has to say about the matter. In that world, the eyes and ears of the world will rest on the False Prophet.

Why will the world worship the Antichrist? As we learned in a preceding chapter, the Antichrist will be wounded and die and he will rise again from the dead, **v. 3-4**. The world will fall at his feet in stupefied wonder and worship.

At some point, the Antichrist will enter the Jewish Temple in Jerusalem. He will go in to the Holy of Holies and he will place his throne there. He will declare himself to be God and he will demand to be worshiped as God. We also see this in **2 Thes. 2:4**. The False Prophet will support the claims of the Antichrist and will lead the world to worship this Man of Sin. The phrase *"before him"* in **verse 12** means *"in his presence"*. The two men, the Antichrist, and the False Prophet, are the devil's duo. They will work hand in hand to accomplish the devil's will here on earth during the dark days of the Tribulation Period.

Remember, Satan is an imitator! We are told that the Holy Spirit will magnify Jesus, **John 16:13-14**. Satan's anti-spirit will spend his time magnifying the Antichrist and he will lead the world to worship the Beast!

Verses 13-15 tell us the miracles this beast will work! We are told that the False Prophet will be a man of miracles. He will duplicate the miracles of the Two Witnesses, **Rev. 11:5**. He will duplicate the miracle of Elijah in **1 Kings 18**. When Elijah called fire down from Heaven, men fell to their faces and worshiped Jehovah. When the False Prophet calls down fire from the sky, men will fall on their faces and worship the devil!

This False Prophet will lead the world to build an idol, an image of the Antichrist. He will cause this image to come to life. This image will speak to the people. They will be deceived by his power and his miracles, and they will fall down in worship of the beast and his image. The ministry of the False Prophet will be marked by exciting and powerful miracles. His miracles will deceive the world.

We are living in a world where most people worship nothing but themselves. It is hard to imagine people all around the world bowing down to worship an image. In our day of advanced technology, and sophisticated people it is hard to see the world falling down before a statue to worship the devil. But try to put yourself in that time period!

We need to understand the world around us! Millions have gone missing in the Rapture. The world is falling apart at the seams as war rumbles from country to country. Disease, war, starvation and other plagues have claimed nearly one-half the world's population. Men in that day will be looking for something to believe in. they will be looking for someone who has the answers.

Then, the Antichrist will appear. He will have the solution to the problems of the world! He will have the solution to war, to hunger, and to every problem know to humanity. He will die at the height of his power and the world will mourn his passing. Then, miracle of miracles, he will rise from the dead! The world will see it live and in living color on their television sets.

The False Prophet will speak, and he will set the world at ease. He will declare the Antichrist to be the world's savior and they will bow at his feet and worship him. It will be a time of mass deception on a world-wide scale!

Verses 14-15 tell us of his motive. The False Prophet does all for the sole purpose of getting the world to worship the Antichrist. The world will fall for this deception. Those who refuse, orthodox Jews and those who have been saved during the Tribulation, will be hunted down, and destroyed.

Today, you can worship any god you please to worship, or you can worship no god at all, if that is your choice. In that day, you will either worship the Antichrist or you will pay for your disobedience with your life.

The world will come together one day. It will not be the United Nations that will bring about that unity. It will be the work of Satan and he uses the Antichrist and the False Prophet to accomplish his goals in the world.

There are dark times ahead for our world! The time to escape the coming nightmare is now! If you have never trusted Jesus as your Savior, I challenge you to come to Him for your salvation.

THE MARK OF THE BEAST

Revelation 13:16-18 is a passage of Scripture that has caused more speculation that possibly any other. For centuries people have been trying to decipher the Mark of the Beast. People actually fear the number 666.

There is a lot of speculation concerning what the Mark of the Beast is all about. There is much misinformation concerning this subject. These verses give us some of the information we need in order to understand the Mark of the Beast. We won't learn everything we would like to know, but we will learn enough to know that anyone that has accepted Jesus Christ does not need to be afraid of the Mark of the Beast.

So, let's look at these three verses today to dispel some of the mystery surrounding the Mark of the Beast.

Let's read from God's Word!

16 And he causeth all, both small and great, rich and poor, free and bond, to receive a mark in their right hand, or in their foreheads:
17 And that no man might buy or sell, save he that had the mark, or the name of the beast, or the number of his name.
18 Here is wisdom. Let him that hath understanding count the number of the beast: for it is the number of a man; and his number is Six hundred threescore and six.

In **Verse 16,** we see the mark of the Beast is a mark of identification. There has been much speculation concerning what the Mark of the Beast might be. Some believe that it might be some sort of a barcode system that is tattooed into the skin. People would then have to scan their code to access their money to buy and sell.

Scientists have developed tiny microchips the size of grains of rice. These chips can carry all of your medical and financial information and they can be read with a simple scanner. These chips are already being used in pets, and there is talk of placing these microchips in babies to prevent kidnappings and mistakes at the hospitals. It is possible that technology of this nature could be used to fulfill this passage. It is also possible to place GPS transmitters in chips the size of jellybeans. With these transmitters, people can be tracked regardless of where they are in the world.

Of course, technology has advanced to the place where people can be identified instantly by scanning their fingerprints, facial recognition, and the retinas of their eyes. DNA technology is advancing at such a rate that simple genetic testing will soon be possible almost instantly. Who knows what the devil will use? There are certainly enough resources available to him in these days.

As you know, plastic currency is quickly replacing cash as the standard in business transactions. It has been suggested that the Mark of the Beast will actually be a credit card system. This is already used in many cases for food stamps and other government services. Whether we like it or not, we are headed toward a cashless society. It makes sense! Without cash, crooks and drug dealers have a more difficult time. Without cash, people are less likely to hide their income from the IRS. We are moving in that direction.

Again, whether we like it or not, we have already been reduced to a number. Everywhere you go, you need your Social Security number and your driver's license number. It's already this way in Sweden and Israel. Everyone has a number! Computers like numbers better than names, and you can be sure that computers will be involved with whatever system the Antichrist devises. The stage is set, and people's minds are prepared for some system of public identification.

We are on the verge of a seeing a national identification card for citizens of our country. Given all the problems we are having with illegal immigration, there is a rising cry for some sort of identification card or system that can identify who is and who isn't an American citizen.

While we cannot know for sure what the Mark of the Beast is, we can learn something about how it will be utilized in that day.

The scope of this mark *"causeth...all"*. The word *"causeth"*, means *"to force"*. We are told that all people of all classes will be required to wear this mark in the bodies. Everyone, from the most common of men to the most famous of celebrities, will bear this mark in their bodies. It will be a universal mark. For once in this world there will be no favoritism and no discrimination. Every person from the savage in the darkest jungles of Africa to the executive living in the New York penthouse will receive the Mark of the Beast.

We also see the mark's location *"in the right hands, or in their foreheads"*. This mark will apparently be place either in the hand or in the forehead. The word *"mark"* comes from a word that means *"a stamp, an imprint, something carved"*. Whatever this mark is, it will reside in the flesh and be permanent. People will not be able to alter it or counterfeit it. It will be placed where it can be easily seen.

Then we see the source of the mark. The *"he"* in **verse 17** refers to the False Prophet. If you remember, he is the one who causes the world to worship the Antichrist. He is the one who causes the image of the Antichrist to move and speak. He is the leader of the one world religion that will dominate the world during the Tribulation. He will devise this marking system and he will see that it is carried out.

It might help us understand what happened in the Roman world during John's Day. In the Roman world, there were millions of slaves. A slave would be marked by his master with either a brand or a symbol or number tattoo. It was Roman law in those days for people to worship the emperor. The Roman emperors had declared themselves deity and they demanded the worship of their subjects. This emperor worship involved the Roman citizen entering a temple set apart for emperor worship. The citizen would take a pinch of incense, place it on a flaming altar and say, *"Caesar is god!"* the worshiper would them receive a mark, signifying that he had fulfilled his duty to the emperor.

This is exactly what we see in this passage. The world will worship the Antichrist, as we see in **Rev. 13:4, 15**. When they do, they will receive his mark. It will be a statement of their allegiance to him and to his government. They will be identified as his servants.

In **Verse 17**, we see the mark will be a mark of isolation. People will be required to produce the Mark of the Beast in order to be able to buy or sell. This, in itself, will be a great enticement for people to receive the Mark of the Beast. In order to hold a job, to get credit, to access bank accounts, or to do something so mundane as buy a loaf of bread, will require a person to have the Mark of the Beast.

Think about this for a moment and let's look at examples of the requirement for this mark. A young mother goes to the store to buy formula for her baby. She lacks the mark of the Beast, and she is not allowed to purchase her products. A man stops for gas at the gas station. He does not have the mark and he is not allowed to buy. A family shivers in the dark and the cold because they cannot buy utilities without the Mark of the Beast. This mark will instantly divide the world into two camps. The Mark of the Beast will declare who worships the Antichrist and who does not. It will prove to be a mark of isolation.

The Antichrist will use the Mark of the Beast to control the world. Everything in the world during the Tribulation will be controlled. Food, housing, medicine, and medical care will all be dispensed only to those who have the Mark of the Beast. This mark will give the Antichrist instant power over every person everywhere in the world.

A man who had lived under Bulgaria's communist regime remarked: *"You cannot understand and you cannot know that the most terrible instrument of persecution ever devised is an innocent ration card. You cannot buy and you cannot sell except according to that little, innocent card. If they please, you can be starved to death, and if they please, you can be dispossessed of everything you have; for you cannot trade, and you cannot buy and you cannot sell, without permission."* [6](Cited in W. A. Criswell, Expository Sermons on Revelation [Grand Rapids: Zondervan, 1969], 4:120–21)

There will be persecution for this isolation. Many will refuse to accept the Mark of the Beast. The 144,000 Jewish evangelists will not take the mark. Their converts will refuse to take the mark. There will be literally millions of people around the world who will refuse to bow to the Beast or to his image. They will reject the ministry of the False Prophet. These people will suffer greatly for their decision.

---

[6] Criswell, Expository Sermons on Revelation

They will not be able to buy food, clothing, or medicine. They will be refused medical treatment. Many, no doubt, will starve to death in order that they might not dishonor the name of the Lord Jesus. These people will be hunted down and persecuted to the death because of their defiance. These people will pay a terrible price for their faith in Jesus, but they will be rewarded greatly when they leave this world, **Rev. 7:9-17!**

We are not being actively persecuted for our faith in Jesus today, but we are a marked people. In the United States alone, there are many that refer to Christians as a political organization, not as members of the family of God. The world is ramping up its hatred of the Lord Jesus and of those who follow Him. We can expect to see this kind of hatred intensify as we move closer to the end.

Believers in this day need to continue to take a stand for Jesus in spite of what they might face for doing so. **Verses 17-18** tell us this is a mark of information. We are told that the mark is tied to a number and that this number is tied to the name of the Beast. This has led to some wild speculation over the years. In ancient times, number values were attached to Greek and Hebrew letters. Using what is known as "***gematria***", which is an ancient form of numerology, a number is assigned to each letter in the alphabet. These numbers are then used to seek hidden meaning in words. The people who believe in such things believe that numerical equivalents in names and words in not coincidental, but providential. The Beast's name, when it is known, will yield the number "***666***".

People have used this system to propose many different possibilities as to who the Antichrist might be. They have taken the letters in people's name added up the numerical value and declared that this person or that person had to be the Antichrist. They have suggested Adolph Hitler, Napoleon Bonaparte, and several American Presidents. Back in the 1980's some people believed that Gorbachev was the Antichrist because that huge birthmark he had on his head.

The fact is, we do not know who the Antichrist is. We can do all sorts of numerical gymnastics, but we will still be in the dark concerning his identity. But, when he appears, the people living in that day will have all the information they will need to be able to identify the Antichrist.

The mark reveals the nature of the beast! We are told the Beast's number is *"**the number of a man**"*. His number is *"**666**"*. Six in the Bible is the number of mankind. Man was created on the sixth day. This number is just short of the number of completion or perfection, the number 7. The number six is seen several times in the Bible. When it is in view, it always comes up short.

When Nebuchadnezzar made his idol in **Daniel 3:1**, it was 60 cubits by 6 cubits. When Goliath came out to meet David in **1 Sam. 17**, he was six cubits and a span tall and carried a spear whose head weighed 600 shekels.

The Antichrist will be the pinnacle of human achievement. He will be the brightest, most powerful human the world has ever seen, outside of the Lord Jesus Christ. He will be a remarkable man, but he will still fall short of completion and perfection. His number declares his deficiency.

Man is represented by the number six. God is represented by the number seven. Seven speaks of completion and perfection. God is perfect and complete, whether you are speaking of the Father, the Son, or the Holy Spirit. He is a *"777"*. Satan and his unholy trinity can never compete with God. They will give it their best but still be just *"666"*. They will never be complete and perfect because they lack God!

Why would anyone choose this number? We have to assume that if the Antichrist is the world's ruler, he must be able to choose his own number. Why 666? He may do it to stand in defiance to God. After all, the Lord has declared that the devil's Superman will wear this number and be defeated. He may do it out of pure rebellion.

Of course, this number might just be for God's people to be able to recognize him when he comes. Either way, this number will declare his name and his nature. When he comes, the people of God will be able to identify him and thus refuse his mark.

One of the practical lessons we can take away from this passage is this truth. Satan always marks his people. He marks their bodies, their souls, and their minds. He marks his people. On the other hand, God seals. (**2 Cor. 1:22; Eph. 1:13; 4:30; Rev. 7:2-8**). Satan marks those who give themselves to him. God seals those who come to Him through Jesus. He seals them for Himself and He seals them for all eternity!

There are some terrible days coming on this earth! Satan is going to have freedom on planet earth for several years and billions will be brought under his grip for time and eternity. Every one of these people who take the Mark of the Beast are destined for a horrible eternity. **(Rev. 14:9-12)**. They cannot take the Mark of the Beast, worship Satan and then be saved. If they bow to him, they are lost forever! That is a terrible truth!

As one of my professors once said, To Satan, you are nothing but a number. If you come to God, He will call you by your name, **Rev. 2:17; 3:5**. You can have a name, or you can have a number. If you have a name you will have a place in Heaven when you leave this world. If you receive a number, you will go to Hell forever. Where will you spend eternity?

AFTER THE STORM

As we have moved through this amazing book, the last two chapters have been dark, depressing and discouraging. We have studied about the devil, the Antichrist, and the False Prophet. We have witnessed the depths of depravity as man abandons his Creator to worship the devil through his false Christ.

Revelation 14 is like a glorious rainbow after a fierce storm. In **verses 1-5** God takes the brush of His grace and repaints the landscape of the Revelation. He gives us a breath of heavenly air in these verses. Only God can do that! Only God can take that which is horrible beyond words and turn it into a thing of glory. That is just what He does in these verses.

In this passage we are allowed to get a little glimpse of heavenly glory. We are allowed to see the Lamb of God. He is the book's theme, and He is center stage in these verses. It would be a blessing to learn how to keep Jesus at the center of everything we do as individuals and in the church's life.

In these verses, we again meet the 144,000 Jewish evangelists selected and sealed in **chapter 7**. These men have preached the Gospel of the Kingdom during the darkest days of the Tribulation. They were persecuted by the Antichrist, but God preserved them. At some point during the Tribulation, when they have served their purpose, God will allow the 144,000 to be killed by the Antichrist. These men will then join their Redeemer, the Lamb of God, in His glory in Heaven.

That is the scene we are going to investigate today. These men have weathered a terrible storm here on the earth. Now, for them at least, the storm is over, and they are home with the Lamb. I want to show you the facts revealed in these verses concerning the 144,000. I want us to move ahead and look at what happens after the storm.

Let's read from the Word of God!

14 And I looked, and, lo, a Lamb stood on the mount Sion, and with him an hundred forty and four thousand, having his Father's

> *name written in their foreheads.*
> *² And I heard a voice from heaven, as the voice of many waters, and as the voice of a great thunder: and I heard the voice of harpers harping with their harps:*
> *³ And they sung as it were a new song before the throne, and before the four beasts, and the elders: and no man could learn that song but the hundred and forty and four thousand, which were redeemed from the earth.*
> *⁴ These are they which were not defiled with women; for they are virgins. These are they which follow the Lamb whithersoever he goeth. These were redeemed from among men, being the firstfruits unto God and to the Lamb.*
> *⁵ And in their mouth was found no guile: for they are without fault before the throne of God.*

We immediately see in **Verse 1**, they are a rescued army and are protected by God. When we first met this group of men, it was in **Rev. 7:3-4**. There the Bible says, *"Saying, Hurt not the earth, neither the sea, nor the trees, till we have sealed the servants of our God in their foreheads. And I heard the number of them which were sealed: and there were sealed an hundred and forty and four thousand of all the tribes of the children of Israel."*

These men have been sealed by God and protected by Him through the darkest days of the Tribulation. Hundreds of millions, perhaps even billions of people, have died, but these men have been protected through it all because they have been sealed by God. The earth will be stained red with the blood of holy martyrs, but these men will be protected through it all! Satan will hunt them and harass them, but he will be powerless to kill them because they have been sealed by God. They have His Name in their foreheads, and they are untouchable! Satan marked His people, and they are headed to Hell, God sealed His servants, and they are bound for glory!

I want you to see that God has preserved these individuals! When these men arrive on Mount Zion, there are just as many as when they were sealed back in chapter 7. God sealed 144,000, and now 144,000 stands with the Lamb in glory. There are not 143,999; there are 144,000. He brought in just as many as He called out!

The same is true for all of God's saints! According to His Word, we have been *"sealed unto the day of redemption"*, **Eph. 4:30**. We are also told that Jesus will not lose a single one of those given to Him by His Father, **John 6:37-40**. Those who are saved are as assured of Heaven as if they were already there, **Rom. 8:28-30; Eph. 2:6**. Jesus gives eternal life and security to everyone who trusts Him for their salvation.

Not a single person will be missing when the roll is called in glory. When the family gathers for the Marriage Supper of the Lamb, an open seat will be at the table! God will bring *ALL* His children home!

We are told these men meet the Lamb on *"Mt. Zion"*. This is an ancient name for Jerusalem, as in **2 Sam. 5:7; Psalm 48:2**. Jerusalem is referred to as Mount Zion at least 21 times in the Word of God. Some commentators believe that John is referring to the earthly city of Jerusalem. They think we see a vision of the coming Millennium when Jesus will rule on the earth for 1,000 years. I'm afraid I have to disagree with this thought process. We are looking at a heavenly scene! These men have served their time. They have fulfilled their mission and been brought in the presence of the Almighty. **Verse 3** talks about heavenly singing. **Verse 5** shows them standing before the throne of God in glory. These men have been rescued from a world gone mad, and they are at home in the presence of the Father and the Lamb of God.

I am going to refrain from preaching through the written word! But sometimes, I just can't help myself. I praise the Lord that there is a better place waiting on the people of God! If this world was Heaven as some groups claim, I would want it. No, there is a better place waiting on the children of God when we leave this world! Jesus told us a little bit about it in **John 14:1-3**. John told us a lot about it in **Rev. 21-22**. My mind has tried to think about that place. But, one day, I will see its glory with a new pair of eyes. These will be eyes eternal that will actually be able to stand in the glory of Heaven and view its magnificence! I will have new feet that will walk its endless streets. These ears will hear the sweet songs of Zion and they will hear the sweetest sound to ever fall upon them. They will hear the Savior say, *"Enter thou in to the joy of thy Lord!"* Praise God! One day, we are going home!

In **verses 2-3**, we see they are a rejoicing army! In Verse 2 we see these men have been rescued from the terrors of the Tribulation. They have witnessed death and destruction on an unprecedented level. They have watched the world turn its back on God and embrace the devil as their new god. They have seen this world fall at the feet of the Antichrist and worship him as a god. They have seen things more horrible than anything you and I could imagine. But this verse finds them home, in Heaven, in the presence of the Lord Jesus. They are home! And Heaven is filled with the sounds of their worship and their praises. Heaven is filled with joy because of the presence of the Lamb. What a contrast there is between this world and Heaven. This world is a world filled with pain, sorrow, and tears. None of those things will be allowed in heaven as we see in **Rev. 21:4**. This world is marred by disease and death. That will not be found in heaven. This world is in the grip of sin and Satan. Both will be banned in Heaven, **Rev. 21:28**. This world is perishing. The world to come will endure for all eternity! One day, we will take our last steps in this wicked, harsh world. We will leave and we will fly away to be with our Christ, the one who died for us on Calvary's cross.

In **Verse 3**, we see a new miracle. This is the <u>**New Song**</u>. The 144,000 are overcome with joy because they are in the presence of God and the Lamb. They are overwhelmed and they burst into song. They sing a song that is <u>**unique to them**</u>. It is a new song, and no one is qualified to sing it but them! The word *"learn"* as it is used here, means *"**to understand**"*. No one can understand their song because no one has had their experiences.

Here is a little theology lesson! <u>**A new song**</u> is mentioned some seven times in the Old Testament. It is always used as a means to praise the Lord for some great, amazing thing He has done, Ill. **Psa. 98:1**.

There was a day when the Lord saved my soul. When He did, He placed a *"new song"* within my heart! The only songs my soul knew were the songs of the world. All my soul knew were the laments and dirges of a life of sin and sorrow. But, when He saved me, He gave me an amazing new song as identified in **Psa. 40:1-3**.

Now in **Verses 4-5** we see they are a redeemed army. These 144,000 are a special group of people. They represent the choicest of God's servants down through the ages. Many men and women have made their mark for

Jesus, but these men stand a little taller than the rest. These next two verses describe these men. What the Bible says about them should be true of every saint of God. These men have not even been saved yet, but their dedication to the Lord Jesus is a model for every believer.

Verse 4 shows us they are spotless! We are told that these men have maintained their physical purity. They have not fallen prey to the sins of the flesh that will mark the last days. Beyond that, they have not succumbed to the spiritual fornication that will run rampant in the world during the Tribulation days. The world will go after the *"great whore"* as identified in **Rev. 14:8 and Rev. 17:1**. However, these men will state separated and holy during an apostate age.

Verse 4 also tells us how these 144,000 evangelists followed the Lord Jesus wherever He led them. They did not turn back through fear. They did not turn away from their task, even though it was dangerous and costly. They stayed the course. They followed the Lamb. The word *"follow"* means *"to be in the same way as"*. These men walked in the ways of the Lord. They made His way their way and they stayed the course for the glory of God.

This is just what God expects from each one of us. He saved us to walk in His will and to follow His ways. He wants us to be obedient, surrendered followers. He wants us to make His way our way! Of course, this means that we have to see things the way He sees them and do things the way He does them. The Lord wants us to follow Him wherever He leads us with no regrets, refusals, or reservations. He is looking for obedient servants!

Let me show you just one such example. William Borden was born into wealth as an heir to the Borden dairy fortune, but he soon recognized true wealth was to be found in a different inheritance by being a child of God and an heir with Christ. Borden lived a short but high-impact life. He graduated high school at age 16 and quickly decided to become a missionary after seeing the global need for Christ on a trip through Asia, the Middle East, and Europe. He memorialized this decision by writing *"no reserves"* in the back of his Bible.

After revolutionizing the campus of Yale University by starting a weekly prayer and Bible study group attended by three-fourths of the student body, Borden could have started his career with any corporation he desired.

Rather, he stood firm in his decision to become a missionary and enrolled at Princeton Seminary. Once again, he recorded his decision in the back of his Bible: "***no retreats***" was his entry.

After finishing Princeton Seminary, Borden studied Arabic in Egypt to reach Muslims in China. He died from spinal meningitis shortly thereafter. Though he never reached his intended mission field, Borden impacted many people during his life. The last entry in the back of his Bible was "***no regrets.***"

God wants all of His children to live lives of great impact, and He gave us the example of William Borden as inspiration.

- **No reserves**—Sacrifice yourself, **Rom. 12:1**. Offer your entire being (body, mind, and soul) to God as a living sacrifice. Allow Him to use you as He desires and discover His perfect will for your life.
- **No retreats**—Press on **Phil. 3:14**. After totally surrendering to God, you will face distraction and discouragement that will make you want to revoke your sacrifice and not follow God's will. Stay focused on God and rely on His resurrection power to reach forward for what lies ahead.
- **No regrets**—Finish the course **2 Tim. 4:7**. Offering yourself unreservedly and unrelentingly requires great faith. But God honors your faith, and He will help you fight the good fight so that you can live without regrets and hear Him say: "***Well done, thou good and faithful servant***", **Matt. 25:21**.

Verse 4 also shows us the symbolism of the 144,000. These 144,000 were chosen, saved, and sealed at the beginning of the Tribulation. They went out and preached the Gospel to the ends of the earth.

Just as the first sheaves of grain were taken into the Temple and waved before the Lord as a symbol of the harvest that was to follow, these men are symbolic of all those who will be saved through their ministry (**Lev. 23:10-11**). They were the first, and they were the guarantee of more to follow! (**Rev. 7:9-17**.)

I cannot imagine how hard the ministry of these men is going to be. It is hard in these days, but it will be far harder then. What a comfort it is to know that God is going to use them to reap a vast harvest of souls during the Tribulation. Only in Heaven will they know the impact of their ministry.

Verse 5 shows us the sanctification of these men. These men stand in the presence of God complete and perfect. The Bible says that there was no *"guile"* found in them. The word *"guile"* means *"deceit"*. The word was used to speak of something that was *"a decoy"*. Something that gave the appearance of being real but wasn't. These men claimed to be the servants of Almighty God and their walk matched their words. The word *"fault"* means *"blemish"*. These men had no flaws in their lives that could be pointed out by men. Now, even in the presence of God, they are declared faultless by Him!

Again, there is a word here for saints living in this day and age. Like the 144,000 our walk is to match our words. We should live lives that are without blemish so that we might stand in His presence with confidence one day. (**1 John 2:28**).

WHEN THE END COMES

Where will you be five seconds after death? It all depends on what you do with Jesus. (**John 3:18, 36; 1 John 5:12**) Jesus has already experienced the undiluted wrath of God on the cross. He suffered on that tree because you and I are sinners. He took our place on the cross and suffered the wrath of God so that we would not have to. (**Isa. 53:4-6**. Now, the only hope of salvation is Jesus Christ. Those who believe on Him by faith will be saved and they will spend eternity in Heaven. Those who reject Him will spend eternity in Hell. **Verse 11** will be their future.

Revelation chapter 14 is an interesting chapter. In its verses, God takes care of some Tribulation housekeeping. In **verses 1-5** the Lord shows us the fate of the 144,000. If you will remember, the 144,000 are saved Jewish preachers who travel the world preaching the Gospel of grace. These men are divinely sealed and protected as they carry out their ministry. When their time is completed, the Antichrist is allowed to take their lives and **verses 1-5** picture them home, in Heaven, in the presence of the Lord Jesus Christ.

Verses 14-20 speak about the horrific battle of Armageddon that will occur at the end of the Tribulation. We will consider that text in our next study. For now we are going to focus our attention on **verses 6-13**. This passage speaks about the future that awaits two distinct classes of people. **Verses 6-11** deal with the future of the lost sinner, while **verses 12-13** speak to the future of the faithful saint.

While these verses speak about future events, they are still relevant to us today. Every person reading this book will reach the end of your earthly journey someday. There will an end of the road for each of us! We do not like to think about it, but we need to know what is coming so that we can be properly prepared for that hour. When the end comes, you and I need to be ready! When the end comes, there will be no more time to prepare. When the end comes, how we leave this world will be how we enter eternity. In **Eccl. 11:3**, Solomon said, *"...if the tree fall toward the south, or toward* *the north, in the place where the tree falleth, there it shall be."* The same is true about your life and mine. However, the end finds us, whether saved or lost, is how eternity will preserve us. We must be ready!

Today, let's consider these verses of Revelation 14:6-20 which clearly declare what the end holds for both the Tribulation sinner and the Tribulation saint.

Let's read from God's Word!

⁶ And I saw another angel fly in the midst of heaven, having the everlasting gospel to preach unto them that dwell on the earth, and to every nation, and kindred, and tongue, and people,
⁷ Saying with a loud voice, Fear God, and give glory to him; for the hour of his judgment is come: and worship him that made heaven, and earth, and the sea, and the fountains of waters.
⁸ And there followed another angel, saying, Babylon is fallen, is fallen, that great city, because she made all nations drink of the wine of the wrath of her fornication.
⁹ And the third angel followed them, saying with a loud voice, If any man worship the beast and his image, and receive his mark in his forehead, or in his hand,
¹⁰ The same shall drink of the wine of the wrath of God, which is poured out without mixture into the cup of his indignation; and he shall be tormented with fire and brimstone in the presence of the holy angels, and in the presence of the Lamb:
¹¹ And the smoke of their torment ascendeth up for ever and ever: and they have no rest day nor night, who worship the beast and his image, and whosoever receiveth the mark of his name.
¹² Here is the patience of the saints: here are they that keep the commandments of God, and the faith of Jesus.
¹³ And I heard a voice from heaven saying unto me, Write, Blessed are the dead which die in the Lord from henceforth: Yea, saith the Spirit, that they may rest from their labours; and their works do follow them.

Verses 6-7 show a final proclamation! These verses depict an angelic messenger flying above the earth, proclaiming *"**the everlasting Gospel**"*. This angel declares the same message preached by Paul, Peter, John and the rest of the Apostles. It is the same message preached by the true church for the last 2,000 years. The message this angel delivers is the message of salvation through the finished work of the Lord Jesus Christ.

Here is the gospel:

- It is the *"**power of God unto salvation to everyone that believeth**"*, **Rom. 1:16**.
- It is a simple message, **Rom. 10:9**.
- It is an available message, **Rom. 10:13**.
- It is a message of love, **John 3:16**;
- Of hope, **John 6:37**;
- Of eternal salvation, **John 6:47; John 10:28**;
- And of peace with God, **Rom. 5:10**.
- It is the same message that was proclaimed in Eden, **Gen. 3:21**;
- pictured in the Law; and purchased on Calvary, **John 19:30**.
- It is a message as fresh as the need of today; yet it is older than creation, **1 Pet. 1:18-20; Rev. 13:8**.
- It is the only message that will save the human soul from the wrath of God and an eternity in Hell, **John 14:1-6; Acts 4:12**.

Yet, it is a message that has been, is, and will be rejected by sinners until the end of time! This message has been preached for 2,000 years. It has been ignored by most of those that have heard it. It is still being ignored in this day. It will be ignored during the dark days of the Tribulation. Many people will be saved, thank God for that, but many, many more will be lost.

The people in the Tribulation will refuse to hear the 144,000 evangelists. They will refuse the preaching of the two witnesses in **Rev. 11**. The world will even rejoice when they are dead and gone. The world will refuse the steadfast, faithful testimony of the Tribulation saints. The world will be unmoved by their love for Jesus, their testimony and even by their blood when they are martyred for their failure to worship the Beast.

The world will turn a deaf ear to all human efforts to bring them to Jesus. In a final effort to reach them, God will entrust the Gospel to an angel. He will preach the message to a universal audience. He will call all people, everywhere, to flee the wrath to come. He will invite all people to come to Jesus for salvation. He will call them to refuse the Antichrist and to embrace the true Christ. It will be a powerful proclamation by a powerful preacher. But the world will remain defiant in their rejection of the Gospel! The salvation offered through the blood of Jesus is humanity's only hope.

If Jesus is rejected, *"there remaineth no more sacrifice for sin"*. **(Heb. 10:26)**. When the end comes, it will be too late to believe the Gospel. Today is the day of salvation, **2 Cor. 6:2**.

We have seen the final proclamation. **Verse 8** tells us of a fatal pronouncement. A second angel appears and pronounces God's final judgment on Babylon. You may notice that the angel says *"is fallen"* twice. This indicates that Babylon's judgment is **absolutely certain**! We will consider Babylon in greater detail when we come to **Rev. 17-18**. In this chapter, we will try to understand why this city, above all others, is singled out for a special pronouncement of judgment.

One thing we need to understand is that Babylon is more than a city, Babylon is a philosophy! Babylon represents everything the world is. Babylon represents everything that stands opposed to God and His perfect will. Babylon represents a system of unbelief.

In **Genesis 10:8-10**, we are introduced to the descendants of a man named Cush. One of his sons was named Nimrod. Nimrod founded the city of Babel, **v. 10**. It was here that mankind rebelled against the Lord and attempted to build the Tower of Babel, **Gen. 11**. This tower was a place dedicated to the worship of the zodiac and the heavenly bodies. Babel was one of the first centers of false, idolatrous worship in this world and Nimrod was the ringleader. He is called *"a mighty hunter"* in **Gen. 10:9**. The phrase *"mighty hunter"* has been interpreted by some as *"a mighty hunter of souls"*. In other words, many scholars believe that Nimrod was the father of a religious system that was designed to seduce men and turn them away from the one true God.

So, when they build their tower dedicated to the worship of idols and heavenly bodies, God intervened and confused their languages. But that did not destroy the seeds of false religion that had been planted in the hearts of men. People left Babel and carried their false doctrines with them around the world. Babel later became Babylon. It was a city that was the capital of false religion and idolatry. It represents everything in this world that stands opposed to God. In the Tribulation, it speaks of the economic and religious kingdom of the Antichrist.

In this verse, Babylon is pictured as a harlot. She is seen seducing the foolish sinners of this world. She has led them away from God with her lies and she is about to pay a terrible price. The judgment of God is coming upon her and her heresies and **NONE** can stay the hand of His judgment. The philosophy behind all of mankind's religious heresies and rebellion against God will be destroyed. Their foundation will be shattered by the wrath of God.

Verses 9-11 give us a fearful as a third angel appears. He preaches a message of judgment to all those who receive the mark of the Beast and who worship the Beast. This angel reveals what will happen to all those who refuse to receive the Gospel of salvation through Jesus Christ. This angel preaches a fearful message, but it is one that we need to take note of today.

We are told in **verse 10** that *"The same shall drink of the wine of the wrath of God, which is poured out without mixture into the cup of his indignation; and he shall be tormented with fire and brimstone in the presence of the holy angels, and in the presence of the Lamb:"* What a horrible picture! Let's dissect that verse a phrase at a time.

1. *"The wine of the wrath of God"* – The word *"wrath"* translates the word *"thumos"*. It is a word that pictures *"an explosion of wrath; a sudden outburst; a passionate display of anger."* When God's wrath is poured out on this world, it will be a time of sudden judgment from which there will be no escape.
2. *"Poured without mixture"* – When the wrath of God comes on this world, it will be pure and undiluted. Sinners and Satan have never experienced the undiluted fury of an offended God, but they will one day. **(Heb. 10:31; 12:29)**.
3. *"The cup of His indignation"* – The word *"indignation"* translates the other New Testament word that is often translated *"wrath"*. It is

the word "*orge*". The word speaks of a "*slow rising anger*". It was used to refer to the sap rising in a tree. It is the picture of water rising behind a dam, until the pressure of the water becomes too great and the dam bursts. It is the image of a person holding back their anger, becoming red-faced, until they finally explode in wrath. It is similar to the OLD PASTOR MIKE, that when faced with evil and deceit, used to start counting to 10, and only got to 3 before righteous anger exploded. And when it did, you did not want to be anywhere around me when the M Bomb exploded. Wrong has always been a hard pill for me to swallow. It still is.

Ok, some of you are starting to make that big round knowing "O" with your mouth as to why and how a *preacher* can lose his temper. Shame! Shame! You have heard me say this before and you will hear me say it again. If you are putting your pastor on a pedestal and worshipping him, you are worshipping the wrong person! That pastor or minister is born under the same sin of Adam as you, and, like me, God is still working on him and will continue to do so until the day he dies. By the way being too pious is also a sin!

However, God's wrath is just and justified. One day the dam of God's wrath will burst and all those who are outside of a relationship with Jesus are going to be doomed!

4. "*In the presence of the holy angels, and in the presence of the Lamb*" – The heavenly host and the Lamb of God will stand as a constant reminder to the lost sinner that they did not have to arrive at this horrible place. They would have been saved if they would have turned to Jesus Christ by faith.

Most horribly of all, we are given a glimpse of the horrors that await the lost sinner in the flames of Hell. **Verse 11** is very clear; Hell is a place of unending, unimaginable torment for the lost sinner. Remember our first lesson in this series, *The Final Countdown? **HELL IS REAL!*** When they die without Jesus, they will go to Hell. Once there, they will never know one second of rest or relief. They will go to a place where they will never die! They will suffer throughout eternity as they endure the wrath of God in Hell.

It did not have to end this way for these people. It does not have to end that way for you! When Jesus Christ died on the cross, He bore our sins in His body, **1 Pet. 2:24**. You see, our Savior took our sins to the cross. Can you imagine that terrible weight? Jesus took the sins of ALL mankind, from the beginning of time, with Adam and Eve, until the end when his judgment was complete, to the cross, and they died with him. The judgment was so complete that Jesus even cried out in His anguish. **Matt. 27:46.** That cry was also a proclamation and a direct quote from the opening verse from **Psalm 22.** The Old Testament is not simply some piece of history meant to be separated from the rest of the Bible with a big red bow, as if to say, "OK, we are done with that now!" No, we are not under the Old Law. I cannot even say all of the Old Testament is fulfilled. If you think it is, look at the book of Isaiah for a quick view. It is not, but it still points straight to the book of Revelation. Read the Old Testament. It points straight to the New Testament and to our Lord and Savior Jesus Christ!

Now that we have explored what will happen to the SINNER let's look at what the end holds for the SAINT!

As we studied **verses 6-11**, we listened as angels announced the fact that God had pronounced a sentence of damnation on this world system and all those who refuse to believe the Gospel message. Those verses tell us about a horrible place called Hell where the lost will suffer in the flames of God's wrath for all eternity. That is a sad, horrible picture of the future that awaits every person who lives and dies outside of a relationship with the Lord Jesus Christ.

What a contrast there is when we come to **verse 12**! We leave the wrath and judgment of **verses 6-11** and we are exposed to the sweet fragrance of God's grace. Having declared His judgment against the wicked, God now demonstrates His grace toward the righteous. Having shown us the wicked, God now casts the spotlight on His faithful remnant. He says, ***"You have seen the wicked ones, now take a look at my children!"***

These verses show us what will happen to the saints of God when they leave this world. We have seen the hellish side of death; now let's examine the heavenly side of death. What waits on the sinner is ghoulish; what waits on the saint is glorious.

In **verse 12,** there is a proclamation of their faithfulness. The word *"patience"* literally means *"steadfast endurance"*. It is the picture of a person who cannot be swayed from his simple faith in, and devotion to, the Lord Jesus Christ.

In spite of the horrors of the Tribulations Period and the threats of the Antichrist, these believers have remained faithful to their Lord. They refused to bow to this world. They refused to give their worship to the Devil. They have endured every attack and every affliction with the confident knowledge that their God was executing an eternal plan. They were faithful even unto the death, knowing that, in the end, their faith would be vindicated, and Satan and his kingdom would be judged.

These people knew that they were part of the victorious people, even while they suffered! That is a lesson that we would do well to learn in our day. This world and the devil are always trying to get us to compromise. There is a constant barrage designed to cause us to abandon God and the way of righteousness. The devil would love nothing better than for us to get our eyes off Jesus and His will for our lives and our church. He would love for us to lower our standards, as our politicians continue to press America to do today! They want us to relax our hold on our convictions and abandon the way of righteousness in these days.

After all, it would be easier! It would cause the church to be more accepted in the community. It would take some of the pressure off. The only problem is that it would offend God! It would cause Him to remove His power from our midst as in countless other churches. The world might not appreciate your efforts for the Lord; but God does! He sees every sacrifice for His name, and He will reward His people in due time. (**Matt. 10:41-42; 1 Cor. 3:10-15**).

In **Verse 12**, these people demonstrated their faithfulness to the Lord in two ways. They kept His commandments, and they kept the faith. By keeping the faith, these people had refused to deny Jesus. They had maintained their faith in Him even when doing so was costly. Many in the Tribulation will die rather than deny the Lord Jesus. How much easier would it be for them to deny Him with their lips, even as they embrace Him in their hearts? But they are not hypocrites! They will not deny Him even though it will cost them everything. By refusing to worship Antichrist, they will suffer greatly. They will not be able to buy or sell. They will be hunted and hounded and executed for their allegiance to Jesus. Still, they will remain faithful!

These suffering saints set a shining example for those of us living in these days! As we know, the trend in churches and among church people in our day is to become more like the world. That is the easy path to follow. It gains you favor with the world and helps you grow in numbers. God blessed me with a good education. A PhD and an MBA teach you may things. Not the least of these if the power of the written word and the power of numbers. You can use numbers to demonstrate almost anything you want. And in our society, numbers are used to praise, and to punish.

When you compromise the Word of God and water down the Gospel message, you forfeit the presence and power of God. You might have a full house, huge crowds and mountains of cash, but if there is no power and touch of God, those things amount to less than nothing!

Verse 13 shows us the profit of their faithfulness! From a worldly perspective these people gave up a lot for their faith in Jesus Christ. They suffered, they starved, and they endured hardships that we cannot even begin to imagine. Men watched their wives and children starve to death. Mothers watched their children suffer. What did it profit them? What payoff was there in such suffering and pain? This verse tells us about their future. If you are saved it tells how you are paid. God is a great banker. If you are saved, he has already given you part of your payoff, which you did not deserve and could never earn. He gave it to you while you still walked this earth. The last part of that payoff comes when you stand before him in heaven!

First, we are told that these people who will die in and for Jesus are *"blessed"*. This word has the idea of being *"happy."* It means to be *"supremely blessed; fortunate; well off"*. The idea here is that those who die in the Lord leave a harsh, unfriendly world for a better place.

We have often heard it said, when a believer dies, *"**Well, they are better off.**"* It is so true! Paul knew this truth, **Phil. 1:23; 2 Tim. 4:6**. Death, for the child of God is not the horrible monster we have made it out to be! It is nothing more than a doorway that allows us to step out of time and into eternity! It is a portal that allows us to leave this land of death and step into that land of life. Death, for the child of God, is not a grinning devil; it is a smiling friend that comes to usher us home into the waiting arms of our Savior!

There is no comparison between what we have in this world and what will be ours when we get home to glory! This verse touches on two of the blessings that will hold special importance for those saints living through the horrors of the Tribulation.

1. **They Will Rest from Their Labors** – These people have labored for Jesus in a difficult day, now they are going home to rest. The word *"labour"* does not refer to the act of working, but to the weariness that comes from working. The word literally means *"a beating; grief; sorrow; trouble.* The idea here is of the soldier who has fought in the campaigns and battles and has grown weary. I can relate.

At the age of 22, I learned about the dark side of life, as I peered through the Leupold rifle scope on my highly modified XM24A1 sniper rifle, chambered in the .300 Winchester Magnum. That rifle was built for one thing and one thing only. And in the hands of the right man, it did its job remarkedly well. Like the gospel, it had the power to reach out and touch someone! These saints gave their all for Jesus here on the earth, and all they got in return was the weariness of the flesh, grief, and sorrow. Now, they can go into the presence of the Lord to rest. They have heaven to look forward to. (**Rev. 21:1-6; 21:10-22:5**.) The word *"rest"* means *"to cease from labor to in order to recover and collect strength"*. It speaks of being in a state of *"refreshment"*. There is weariness in the work of God! God's faithful servants get tired, but a day of rest and refreshment is coming!

2. **They Will Be Rewarded for Their Labors** – We are told that *"their works do follow them."* In other words, their labor for the Lord in that dark day was not in vain! God saw everything they did for His glory and rewarded them for it all. That is how it will be for the children of God one day! We will stand in His presence, and He will reward us for the things He allowed us to do for His glory, **1 Cor. 3:10-15**. He saved us by His grace. He gave us His Spirit. Anything we have ever done for

Him has been because He enabled us to do it. Yet, He is going to reward us! Isn't that amazing! But I know what we will do with those rewards. We will cast them at His feet and praise Him for His grace in salvation and service, **Rev. 4:9-11**. We sing *"What A Day That Will Be"*, and it will be glorious when we leave this world to go to our reward!

The contrast in the lost and saved destinations could not be more different! Those who reject Jesus Christ will spend eternity apart from His presence in Hell. Those who receive Him will enjoy an eternity spent in His presence in Heaven.

Five seconds after you die you will already be where you are going to spend eternity. Look at your heart right now. Where would you go if you died within the hour? Would you go to Heaven? Would you go to Hell? Are you content with the place you are headed right now?

The clock is ticking. Where will you spend eternity?

WHEN THE JUDGE CALLS HIS COURT TO ORDER

I have already said this. However, at the risk of being repetitive, I want to remind you that the Book of Revelation is not written in chronological order. The first three chapters tell of our Lord's letters to seven actual churches that existed in John's Day. Those chapters also paint a clear portrait of the church all the way from Pentecost to the Rapture. **Chapters 4-11** tell us about the chronology of the Tribulation Period. They take us all the way from the beginning to the end of that terrible seven-year period of time. In **chapters 12-14**, we are taken back to the beginning. These chapters give us the same time period from a different perspective. We are no longer talking about the chronology of the book; now, we are confronted with the book's characters. Through a series of seven visions, John takes us once again through the days of the Tribulation.

We have arrived at the seventh of these visions in our study of this book. These verses close out the pause in the action we have been in since **chapter 12 verse 1**. When this chapter ends, we will be thrown back into the heat and the horrors of the final days of the Tribulation. Before we deal with those things, John gives us a vision of our Lord when He comes again in power and glory.

When Jesus came the first time, He came as a Savior. He came to give His life on the cross so that sin might be paid for, and sinners might be set free. When He comes the second time, He is coming as a Judge. He is coming to destroy sin, Satan, and all those who stand in defiance of God. When Jesus returns, He will come in power, glory, and judgment and none will be able to withstand Him! There will be no cross for Jesus the next time He comes. There will be a crown! There will be no tree for Him to hang upon; but there will be a throne for Him to sit upon.

Let's move through these verses and catch John's vision of the Lord

Jesus Christ and the coming days of His terrible judgment. I want to focus on the court of the judge! As I do, I want to show you the *parts* of John's vision.

Let's explore **Revelation 14:14-20** as we read from the Word of God!

> *¹⁴ And I looked, and behold a white cloud, and upon the cloud one sat like unto the Son of man, having on his head a golden crown, and in his hand a sharp sickle.*
> *¹⁵ And another angel came out of the temple, crying with a loud voice to him that sat on the cloud, Thrust in thy sickle, and reap: for the time is come for thee to reap; for the harvest of the earth is ripe.*
> *¹⁶ And he that sat on the cloud thrust in his sickle on the earth; and the earth was reaped.*
> *¹⁷ And another angel came out of the temple which is in heaven, he also having a sharp sickle.*
> *¹⁸ And another angel came out from the altar, which had power over fire; and cried with a loud cry to him that had the sharp sickle, saying, Thrust in thy sharp sickle, and gather the clusters of the vine of the earth; for her grapes are fully ripe.*
> *¹⁹ And the angel thrust in his sickle into the earth, and gathered the vine of the earth, and cast it into the great winepress of the wrath of God.*
> *²⁰ And the winepress was trodden without the city, and blood came out of the winepress, even unto the horse bridles, by the space of a thousand and six hundred furlongs.*

In **Verse 14**, he first image we are given is of the Lord Himself, sitting upon a cloud, wearing a crown with a sickle in His hand. Let's examine this image in more detail.

If we look at the person of this individual, there is no doubt about whom John is writing. He is writing about ***"The Son of Man"***. As you may remember, this was one of the titles given to the Lord Jesus when He came to this earth the first time. Jesus used this title to refer to Himself some 84 times in the Gospels. It was the way He most often referred to Himself. This title identifies Jesus with mankind. It is His human title. It speaks to His sufferings, His service, and His sacrifice. When John sees the Son of Man in the clouds, he is seeing the One Who came to this earth and gave His life as a ransom for sin. John is seeing Jesus Christ.

Of course, we are promised that Jesus Christ will come in this fashion. **Rev. 1:7 and Luke 21:27** spell it out. John gives us a preview of that glorious day when Jesus Christ will return in glory and power.

When John sees Jesus, he sees Him wearing a "*golden crown*". The word "*crown*" translates to "*a victor's crown*". It refers to the laurel wreaths that were given out to victors in the ancient Olympic Games. The fact that this crown is "*golden*" identifies the wearer as a King.

When John sees Jesus Christ this time, he does not see a carpenter. He does not see a humble Jewish rabbi. He does not see Jesus of Nazareth. He does not see the son of Mary. When John sees Jesus here, He sees the King of Kings and the Lord of Lords. He sees the One Who invaded Satan's territory and carries off a great victory, he sees the one who walked valiantly into the jaws of death, shedding His blood on the cross to defeat sin and Satan and liberate sinners. He sees the one who conquered death and walked victoriously out of that tomb on the third day. John sees the King Who has dome to take possession of His domain.

When Jesus comes back, there will be no debate. The United Nations will not convene to see whether He can reign or not. When He comes, He will be wearing the golden crown of the victor. This just means that all the battles have already been fought and He is the winner! Jesus will not rule by the leave of men. He will rule by His right at Creator, Lord, Savior, and King!

When John sees the King, he sees his power! He has "a sharp sickle in his hand". A sickle is an instrument used to harvest wheat. When Jesus returns, He is coming to both gather His people into His barn as a farmer gathers his wheat; and He is coming to cut down the wicked like a farmer cuts down his wheat. We will see this truth unfold in the next few verses.

For now, it needs to be said that Jesus can either be your Savior or He can be your Judge. If you receive Him in these days of grace, He will save you and take you to Heaven. If you reject Him, He will judge your life one day. He will either be your Savior, or He will be your Judge. The choice is yours! Verses 15-19 unfold our Lord's plan to bring judgment to this earth. When He came the first time, He came as the Sower. He moved through this world, sowing the seeds of the Gospel of Grace. When He returns, He will come as the Reaper. He will separate the saint from the sinner. He will take the saints home to Heaven, and the sinner will be cast into hell.

There are two harvests described in these verses. Harvest time in the Bible is often used as a picture of souls coming to God for salvation, **John 4:34-35**. In these verses, the harvest is used as a picture of judgment. Let's see what these verses say about the harvests the Lord will reap someday.

Verses 15-16 describe the Lord Jesus thrusting in His sickle to reap the earth. The world is pictured as a field of wheat ready to be harvested. The Lord takes His sickle, and He reaps the field.

What we see in these verses is the fulfillment of a parable Jesus told in the Gospels. In **Matthew 13:24-30**, Jesus told the parable of *"**The Wheat and the Tares**"*. It is a story of a farmer who sowed a wheat field expecting to reap a bountiful harvest. But his enemy came and sowed tares among his wheat. The servants wanted to pull up the tares, but the farmer knew that doing so would destroy the wheat. His council was for both to grow together until the time of the harvest, then the tares could be gathered and burned, and the wheat could be gathered and placed in the farmer's barn.

In the same chapter, **Matthew 13:36-43**, Jesus told His disciples what this parable meant. The good seed represented genuine believers while the tares represented false believers. The good seed represents the saved and the tares represent the lost.

The problem with the wheat and the tares is that they cannot be told apart while growing. The tares, a plant called the Bearded Darnel, look just like wheat as it matures. The difference between the two plants becomes clear when they near harvest time. The head, or top, of the tare turns black and stands up straight. It is filled with tiny black seeds that can cause nausea, or even death. It is a natural emetic and when tares are harvested with the wheat, every kernel must be inspected. On the other hand, the wheat has a head filled with heavy wheat kernels. These kernels cause the head of the wheat plant to bend toward the earth. (***This is the obvious contrast between the saved and the lost.***)

One day Jesus will gather His wheat, the genuine believers, unto Himself. The wicked will be cut down and *"cast into a furnace of fire"*. The judgment of the Lord is coming and *"the Lord knoweth them that are his,"* **2 Tim. 2:19**.

The word *"ripe"* is an interesting word. It means *"to be dry or withered"*. It speaks of a crop that is *"overripe"*. What a picture of the grace and longsuffering of God! The harvest of sin has been ripe since the first sin was committed in Eden. Yet, God in His grace, love and mercy as withheld judgment, giving lost men and women ample time to repent. One day His patience will be exhausted, and His judgment will come on sinners. You must search your heart and *"give diligence to make your calling and election sure,"* **2 Peter 1:10**.

The scene changes in **Verses 17-19** and we move from the field to the vineyard. The lost are compared to a field of grapes *"ripe to the bursting"*. They are ready to be harvested.

When harvested, grapes are placed in a *"winepress"* and. In those days, grapes were processed by placing them in a winepress. A winepress usually consisted of two vats connected by a channel. The grapes were placed in the upper chamber, and people would climb into the winepress and use their feet to crush the grapes, extracting their juice. The juice would run out of the upper vat through the channel and into the lower vat, where it would be collected for wine making.

Again, we are given a picture of a world slated for judgment! This world has rejected Jesus the True Vine, **John 15:1-8**. They have attached themselves to the vine of this world, and they have drunk deeply of the wine of sin and have rejected the God of glory. This world has rejected God and His Son Jesus. But one day, He will come, and they will face Him in judgment. He will crush this world system, and all those who hold to it, under His feet like a man crushes a grape. This is the very image Isaiah paints of the coming King in **Isa. 63:1-6**. Jesus is coming in wrath and judgment and there will be no escape! The enemies of God will be thrown into *"the winepress of the wrath of God,"* and they will be judged!

Verse 20 concludes John's vision. It gives us some insight into where this great judgment will take place. There is coming a day of reckoning and this verse gives some much-needed insight into that horrible event.

This verse tells us that "the winepress was trodden without the city". This does not tell us where this event will take place. However, what we are seeing in these verses are a vision of a coming battle called *"Armageddon"*. According to **Rev. 16:16**, a terrible battle will take place here. I believe it is this battle that is being pictured in one of our next chapters.

Armageddon means *"the hill or city of Megiddo"*. Megiddo is located in the *"Plain of Esdraelon"*. This location is the site of some famous biblical battles. Here, Barak and Deborah defeated the Canaanites in **Jud. 4-5**. It was here that Gideon defeated the Midianites in **Jud. 6-8**. This same valley is the place that both King Saul and his son Jonathan were killed in battle in **1 Sam. 31**. King Josiah also met his death in the valley of Megiddo in **2 Chron. 35**.

It is in the same valley where the armies of the earth will come together to destroy the King of Kings. It is here in this place that Napoleon described as *"a natural battlefield"* that the earth's final battle will be fought.

We are told that the winepress will be *"trodden"* and this will be the pain of His reckoning! This word means *"to crush with the feet"*. This is a very vivid description of what Jesus will do to those who have despised and rejected Him. Like a man crushing grapes in a winepress, He will crush the enemies of God under His feet. This is the promise of the Word of God! (**1 Cor. 15:24-28; Heb. 10:12-13**).

A person can either be crushed under His feet or be held in His arms. The sinner can either be the focus of God's wrath or of God's grace. If I were you, I would be certain that I was saved so that I might miss out on this terrible time of judgment.

This is a permanent reckoning! What we are witnessing here is total destruction of the enemies of the Lord. This is not a probation period. This is not a judgment that will be lifted after a while. This is total annihilation as far the physical man is concerned.

The image here is one of violence and death. We are told that the blood will run as high as the horses' bridles. This is between four and five feet deep. It will flow in a river some 1,600 furlongs long. This is about 200 miles. Can you imagine such carnage? Our minds cannot conceive of this amount of blood. Josephus said that so much blood flowed through the streets of Jerusalem when Titus sacked the city that many of the fires that had been set to destroy Jerusalem were actually extinguished by the blood that poured from the bodies of the slain Jews.

The world's armies gather in a final attempt to defy God. Jesus will return and by His word, destroy the enemies of God and tread them down in the winepress of His wrath! Hundreds of millions of soldiers will die in this catastrophic battle. **(Rev. 19:11-21)**. The blood of the fallen will fill the valley of Megiddo from Dan in the north to Beersheba in the south. Men have rejected the precious, saving, life-changing blood of Jesus; now they will wallow in their own blood!

We read of these events as we cannot comprehend such total devastation. Yet, the Bible says it is coming! Some of the Old Testament prophets wrote about these very events in **Zech. 14:1-4 and Joel 3:11-14**. This battle will take place, and God will be victorious.

I don't know whether anyone reading this chapter may be where Joel spoke of in **Joel 3:14**. You may be in the *"valley of decision"*. You need to decide whether you will claim the blood of Jesus and the salvation it supplies, or whether you will face Him someday to shed the blood of destruction. His blood saves! Your blood condemns you to judgment and Hell!

Thousands of years ago in Egypt, God saved His people by the lamb's blood. They killed that lamb, placed its blood on the doorposts of their houses and went in. when they did, they were saved, safe and secure. They were under the blood. When the death angel passed through that night, they were spared because they were under the blood.

What about you? Are you under the blood today? Has the blood of Jesus been applied to the doorposts and lentils of your heart? Have you trusted Jesus as your Savior? I hope so, for if you haven't, you will face Him as your Judge one day.

If you are in the valley of decision, come to Jesus right now! One day Jesus will call His court to order; you need to be sure that you are saved before that day comes! Where will you spend eternity?

THE BOWL JUDGMENTS

The book of Revelation is a book of contrasts. As we move through the book, we are taken back and forth between Heaven and the earth. We are allowed to witness scenes of joy in the heavens, and we are confronted with scenes of judgment on the earth. In the heavens, you see scenes of worship. On the earth, you see scenes of wrath.

In this chapter we are once again taken into Heaven. In these eight verses of **Revelation 15:1-8**, which comprise the shortest chapter in Revelation, we are allowed to see a vision of Heaven as God prepares for His final judgment of earth's tribulation. There has already been great suffering as the judgment of God has been unleashed on the earth. When these judgments are poured out on the earth, they serve to increase the agony of the wicked.

We want to examine John's vision today. We are given a glimpse of Heaven as it prepares for final judgment. Up to this point, God has mingled mercy and judgment. Until now, God has been leaving the door to repentance ajar. Now, humanity has made its final choice. The world has chosen Satan over God, and judgment is coming. There will be no mercy. There will be no more opportunities. There will be no longsuffering or grace. There will only be judgment and the wrath of God for all those who have rejected Jesus Christ. Let's join John as he looks in on this scene of heavenly preparations. I want us to study *The Preparation For The Bowl Judgments*.

Let's read from the Word of God:

> *15 And I saw another sign in heaven, great and marvellous, seven angels having the seven last plagues; for in them is filled up the wrath of God.*
> *² And I saw as it were a sea of glass mingled with fire: and them that had gotten the victory over the beast, and over his image, and over his mark, and over the number of his name, stand on the sea of glass, having the harps of God.*

> *³ And they sing the song of Moses the servant of God, and the song of the Lamb, saying, Great and marvellous are thy works, Lord God Almighty; just and true are thy ways, thou King of saints.*
> *⁴ Who shall not fear thee, O Lord, and glorify thy name? for thou only art holy: for all nations shall come and worship before thee; for thy judgments are made manifest.*
> *⁵ And after that I looked, and, behold, the temple of the tabernacle of the testimony in heaven was opened:*
> *⁶ And the seven angels came out of the temple, having the seven plagues, clothed in pure and white linen, and having their breasts girded with golden girdles.*
> *⁷ And one of the four beasts gave unto the seven angels seven golden vials full of the wrath of God, who liveth for ever and ever.*
> *⁸ And the temple was filled with smoke from the glory of God, and from his power; and no man was able to enter into the temple, till the seven plagues of the seven angels were fulfilled.*

In **Verses 1 and 7**, we see a vision of judgment. Here, John tells us that he saw *"another sign"*. The word *"sign"* as it is used here is the same word translated as *"wonder"* in **Rev. 12:1 and 3**. In Greek, the word is "απορώ." Not only does it translate to "wonder." It also translates to *"marvel."*

In **Rev. 12:1**, John saw a *"woman"* representing the nation of Israel. In **Rev. 12:3**, John saw a *"great red dragon"* representing Satan. In these verses, John sees *"seven angels"* who will be God's instruments of final judgment upon the earth.

John tells us that this vision is both *"great and marvelous"*. The word *"great"* in Greek is the word "σπουδαίος". It means **"important, serious, significant, grand."**

John speaks of something that is *"important and astonishing."* The word "marvelous" has the idea of *"something to be wondered at"*. John is calling our attention to this vision because what is happening here is something important and amazing.

You see, in the last chapter, we saw the horrifying judgments of God as they were visited on earth. Here, we can see the judgment from Heaven's perspective as it prepares for judgment.

In **Verse 1,** we see that it is a scene of final judgment. John sees seven angels, and these angels have "the seven last plagues." In Greek, the word *"plague"* is *"πληγή"*. It is an accusative, plural feminine noun. It means *"a blow, stripe, a wound, a public calamity, heavy affliction"*. We see God striking the earth and wounding it in judgment. The lashes of God's whip of judgment have begun to fall on this world system, and there is nothing that can stop the damage that is about to be inflicted on those who have rejected the Gospel of grace.

When these seven judgments are poured out on the earth, they will complete the judgments of the Tribulation Period. **Verse 1** says that through these judgments, the wrath of God is *"filled up"*. This phrase translates the Greek verb *"telos"*. This is the same word used by Jesus when He was dying on the cross. Just before He died, He cried, *"It is finished"*, **John 19:30**.

This word is very expressive, and it was used in many ways in that society. Servants used it when they had completed an assignment. Priests used it when they had located a worthy animal to be used as a sacrifice. Farmers used this word when a perfect specimen had been born into their flock. Artists used it when they had put the finishing touches on a work or art. Merchants used it when a deal had been struck. Often your receipt would contain this word. It meant that the debt had been paid in full. Soldiers used it when they placed their foot on the neck of a vanquished foe. Homeowners used it when they had paid the last payment on their mortgage. They would often inscribe the word of a plaque and nail it to the front of the house, revealing to all that the final payment had been paid.

Jesus used this word on Calvary to let everyone know that He had finished the Father's work and that redemption's price has been fully and finally paid. Praise God, salvation is finished!

It is used here to signify completion as well. When these seven last plagues are poured out, God's judgment on this world will be finished. What we see depicted is a full judgment. The seven angels are given seven *"vials"* or *"bowls"*. These bowls are said to be *"full of the wrath of God"*. The word *"full"* means *"to be swelled"*. It was used in that day of a ship that was filled with cargo. Here, it refers to the wrath of God that reached the busting point. Up until now the wrath of God has been like water flowing over a dam. The damage has been severe, but the dam has held back the worst part. In these verses, the dam of God's wrath is about to break, and the waters of judgment are going to drown both sin and sinner. As **Rev. 14:10** says, *"The same shall drink of the wine of the wrath of God, which is poured out without mixture into the cup of his indignation..."* Judgment is coming and there will be no escape.

In **Verses 2-4** we see a vision of jubilation. Even as Heaven prepares to unleash judgment upon the earth, there is rejoicing in Heaven. I praise the Lord that there is a land free from the cares, sins and sufferings of this world. We see the same thing every time we are privileged to look into Heaven. We see the saints of God rejoicing in the presence of their Redeemer. This vision is no different.

Verse 2 gives us the setting of this jubilation. These saints are standing on a *"sea of glass mingled with fire"*. This glassy sea speaks of God's judgment as being firm and fixed. On this earth, there is nothing more constantly changing than the ocean. The sea is never still, and it is never the same. This sea is solid and unmoving! Judgment is fixed and it cannot be altered! It is *"mingled with fire"* to remind us that God is a God of wrath who is in the process of judging this world.

If you will remember, there was a *"sea of brass"* called *"the laver"* outside the tent of the Tabernacle. Before the priests entered the tent, they were required to wash in the laver. It symbolized cleansing and forgiveness of sin. How many times have I stopped at the laver of **1 John 1:9** and washed my sins and my stains away? I thank God that there is a place of forgiveness and restoration today.

In Heaven, that sea of brass has become a sea of glass. There will be no more need for the saints to come to God for cleansing. We will never fail Him again! That will be a blessing. But, for the lost sinner, this sea reminds us that it has become too late for repentance. Judgment is set and fixed. Man has reached his limit and God is about to pour out His wrath on a lost and sinful world. What a horror awaits the *"earth dwellers"*!

Verse 2 also gives the source of this jubilation. These Heaven dwellers are rejoicing, and with good reason! These are the Tribulation saints that we met way back in **Rev. 7:9-17**. These people heard the Gospel when it was preached during the Tribulation. They heard the call of God, repented of their sins, and they were saved. Many of them were called upon to give their lives for Jesus. This they did, dying horrible deaths at the hands of the Antichrist.

They are home in Heaven, safe, secure, and saved. And they rejoice in the victory they have been given. While those who dwell on the earth writhe under the lashes of God's whip of wrath, these saints of God stand perfect and saved in God's presence and praise Him for His grace in salvation!

Verses 3-4 give us the song of this jubilation. These Tribulation saints lift their voices in song to praise the God who redeemed their souls. We are told that they sing two songs. They sing the *"song of Moses," and they sing the "song of the Lamb."* The Song of Moses is found in **Exodus. 15**. It is the first song in the Bible. The Song of the Lamb is the last song recorded in the Bible. The Song of Moses was sung by the children of Israel when they had been delivered from Egypt and Pharaoh. The Song of the Lamb is sung by the saints of God when they are delivered from Antichrist. The Song of Moses was sung by the Red Sea. The Song of the Lamb is sung on the glassy sea. The Song of Moses was to praise God for bringing His people out. The Song of the Lamb is sung to praise God for bring His people in. These songs are songs of redemption and praise for the God who delivers His people from sin.

The song spans Verses 3 and 4. Let's take a moment to examine this song.

- Verse 3 **They Sing of His Works** – They sing of the God Who works in power and moves in glory.
- Verse 3 **They Sing of His Ways** – They sing of the God whose ways are always right and just.
- Verse 4 **The Sing of His Wonder** – They exalt His greatness and magnify the God Who alone is worthy to be praised!
- Verse 4 **They Sing of His Worship** – They sing of the God Who is worthy to receive and will receive the worship of all mankind.

- Verse 4 **They Sing of His Wrath** – They sing of the God Who alone is worthy to judge sin and sinners because He alone is holy and just.

These saints have been through a horrific time, but they found God to be faithful. He saved them. He kept them. He carried them home to glory. And they stand in His presence and lift their voices in song to the God of their salvation. Just as surely as Heaven will be a place of praise, it will be a place filled with singing.

Finally, in **Verses 5-8** we see justice! The scene changes and our attention is focused on the Tabernacle in Heaven. What John sees here is the original Tabernacle. The one Moses built in the wilderness was patterned after this heavenly place of worship. From this Tabernacle, God's judgment issues forth onto the earth.

In **Verse 5**, we see justice is decreed! This place John sees is called *"the temple of the tabernacle of the testimony."* The word *"testimony"* refers to the Law that was handed down to Moses on Mount Sinai. The ancient Law set God's standard for living. Through the Law God manifested His glory and His holiness. The Law also showcased the sinfulness of man. The Law was given so that men might understand the holiness of God and what He expected from people. The tables of the Law were placed in the Ark of the Covenant as a permanent witness to Israel of the holy demands of a righteous God.

Here in Heaven, John sees that the Law is still in force! The Law of God has always served as God's standard of righteousness. And it always will! Man has tried to alter the standards of God, but they are carved in stone, and they are unchanging. Men have broken the Law of God, and the Law demands that men be judged. God will defend His righteousness and judge all those who violate His Law. That is what is about to take place in the next chapter.

By the way, Jesus came to fulfill the Law for all who will put their faith in Him. He has not abolished the Law, but He has fulfilled it for those who are saved, **Col. 2:13-14**. When a person's faith rests in the finished work of the Lord Jesus Christ, they are not required to keep the Law to please the Lord. They are, however, expected to live holy lives for the glory of God!

The Law no longer stands in judgment over the redeemed saints of God, for in Jesus, we are seen as righteous!

Then in **Verses 6-7**, we see justice is delivered! Angels appear out of the Temple in Heaven. They are clothed in *"**pure and white linen**"*. This signifies their holiness, and it reflects the holiness of the One they serve. They wear *"**golden girdles**"* around their chests. This speaks of the majesty and glory of the God they serve. These angels have the seven last plagues that will be poured out on the earth. These are the four beasts we met in **Rev. 4:4-8**. They exist to glorify the God of all creation. These beasts give the angels seven bowls filled with God's wrath. This signifies the fact that the plagues of the Tribulation will be carried out because of God's wrath and anger against sin and sinners.

God's wrath had been building against sin ever since Adam and Eve sinned in Eden. One day, the wrath of God will boil over, and absolute judgment will be the end result. The only refuge a sinner has, whether it is now or in that future day, is the blood of Jesus Christ.

Then in **Verse 8**, we see that judgment is dispensed. The Temple that was standing open has been closed. No one is allowed to enter because it is filled with the glory and presence of Almighty God. This image indicates that the **day of mercy has passed**. The door will be opened again during the Millennium, but it has been closed for the duration of the Tribulation and will not be opened! Man's access into grace and salvation has been forever cut off. The door has been closed, God is going to judge sinners, and there is nothing they can do to stop Him. It is too late to pray. It is too late to repent. It is too late to change. It is too late! There is no more hope, no more grace and no more opportunity. The door is shut, and it will not be opened again!

Matt. 25:1-10, Jesus tells a parable about 10 virgins. Five are wise and five are foolish. The five wise virgins were ready when the bridegroom came, and they entered in with Him and His bride. The five foolish virgins were not ready. They had no oil in their lamps and the door was closed while they were gone to get their oil. and they were shut out of the wedding chamber.

That parable will be a reality in many people's lives one day. Do not let it be true in your life! You need to be sure that you know Him! You need to be sure that you are saved. Today, God is offering salvation to whosoever will come to Jesus. In that day, He will offer salvation to no one. All He will give then is judgment, wrath, and damnation. Where will you spend eternity?

THE FINAL JUDGEMENT

Revelation 16 ushers in the final judgment. There is no denying that the book of Revelation is a book of judgment. It is also a book of love. If you noticed in our preceding lessons, even while God is angry, he is still in the business of saving souls. But now, that time is past. He is no longer an angry father who punishes his children so they will return to the ways he has given them. He is now a very angry and very JUST God. God has a plan for the judgment of all those who have rejected Him.

Let's read from God's Word:

16 And I heard a great voice out of the temple saying to the seven angels, Go your ways, and pour out the vials of the wrath of God upon the earth.
² And the first went, and poured out his vial upon the earth; and there fell a noisome and grievous sore upon the men which had the mark of the beast, and upon them which worshipped his image.
³ And the second angel poured out his vial upon the sea; and it became as the blood of a dead man: and every living soul died in the sea.
⁴ And the third angel poured out his vial upon the rivers and fountains of waters; and they became blood.
⁵ And I heard the angel of the waters say, Thou art righteous, O Lord, which art, and wast, and shalt be, because thou hast judged thus.
⁶ For they have shed the blood of saints and prophets, and thou hast given them blood to drink; for they are worthy.
⁷ And I heard another out of the altar say, Even so, Lord God Almighty, true and righteous are thy judgments.
⁸ And the fourth angel poured out his vial upon the sun; and power was given unto him to scorch men with fire.

⁹ And men were scorched with great heat, and blasphemed the name of God, which hath power over these plagues: and they repented not to give him glory.

¹⁰ And the fifth angel poured out his vial upon the seat of the beast; and his kingdom was full of darkness; and they gnawed their tongues for pain,

¹¹ And blasphemed the God of heaven because of their pains and their sores, and repented not of their deeds.

¹² And the sixth angel poured out his vial upon the great river Euphrates; and the water thereof was dried up, that the way of the kings of the east might be prepared.

¹³ And I saw three unclean spirits like frogs come out of the mouth of the dragon, and out of the mouth of the beast, and out of the mouth of the false prophet.

¹⁴ For they are the spirits of devils, working miracles, which go forth unto the kings of the earth and of the whole world, to gather them to the battle of that great day of God Almighty.

¹⁵ Behold, I come as a thief. Blessed is he that watcheth, and keepeth his garments, lest he walk naked, and they see his shame.

¹⁶ And he gathered them together into a place called in the Hebrew tongue Armageddon.

¹⁷ And the seventh angel poured out his vial into the air; and there came a great voice out of the temple of heaven, from the throne, saying, It is done.

¹⁸ And there were voices, and thunders, and lightnings; and there was a great earthquake, such as was not since men were upon the earth, so mighty an earthquake, and so great.

¹⁹ And the great city was divided into three parts, and the cities of the nations fell: and great Babylon came in remembrance before God, to give unto her the cup of the wine of the fierceness of his wrath.

²⁰ And every island fled away, and the mountains were not found.

²¹ And there fell upon men a great hail out of heaven, every stone about the weight of a talent: and men blasphemed God because of the plague of the hail; for the plague thereof was exceeding great.

While some passages allow for rejoicing in the chapters of this book, Revelation is still a chronicle of God's final judgment of sin, sinners and Satan. In Revelation, there is a series of three judgments executed in seven stages each. There are the seven seal judgments, the seven trumpet judgments, and finally, the seven bowl judgments. As the judgments progress, the intensity and severity of the judgments increase. Remember the number seven? Seven is the number of God's fulfillment. Seven is the number of God's completion.

As we have already seen, the number seven is widely used throughout Revelation, including about the seven churches, seven bowls, seven seals, seven trumpets, seven thunders, seven Spirits of God, seven stars, seven lampstands, seven eyes, seen horns of the Lamb of God, seven heads of the dragon. . . . I think you get the idea.

We have arrived at the final set of judgments. In **Rev. 15:7** shows one of the four beasts giving to seven angels seven bowls *"full"* of the wrath of God. As a reminder, *"full"* means *"to swell"*. It is the image of a dam, under pressure, nearing its bursting point. This is a good description of the wrath of God.

Ever since Adam sinned in Eden, the wrath of God against sin and sinners has been building. The grace and mercy of God have served as a powerful dam, which has held that wrath in check. In the judgments of the Revelation, the dam of God's wrath bursts and a Christ rejecting world is swept away in the wave of judgment that issues forth.

Up to this point, God has always tempered His wrath. God has been faithful to honor the request of the prophet Habakkuk. In **Hab. 3:2**, the prophet prayed, *"in wrath remember mercy."* But now the time for judgment has come. There will be no mercy any longer. The wrath of God is about to be poured out. God is preparing to commence His final judgment of the earth.

In **Rev. 14:10**, John writes, *"**The same shall drink of the wine of the wrath of God, which is poured out without mixture into the cup of his indignation.**"* In these verses, the world is about to experience the undiluted wrath of an offended God.

In **Verse 2**, we see the plagues poured out on planet Earth! When the first bowl is poured out, all those who have worshiped the beast and received his mark are afflicted with sores in the bodies. The word *"sore"* literally means *"an ulcer"*. It has the idea of an open, running, ulcerated place on the skin. It probably refers to an oozing boil.

These sores are described using the Greek adjective *"βλαβερός"* which translates to *"noisome"*. This word means *"of a bad nature, troublesome, injurious"*. They are also described as *"grievous"*. This word refers to something *"annoying, painful, or bad"*. These two words reveal that these sores will be extremely painful, festering, and incurable.

No doubt the greatest medical minds of the age will do their best to find a cure, but they will fail. There will be no cream, poultice, or drug that will relieve the people suffering from these boils.

A sore on the outside is a sign of rottenness on the inside. God is clearly revealing the condition of these lost sinners. He is displaying the corruption of their hearts through the corruption in their bodies. These people have rejected God and His Christ. And they must face Him in judgment!

These festering ulcers bring to mind the ancient plagues in Egypt. The sixth of those plagues is found in **Ex. 9:8-12**. In that plague, the people of Egypt suffered from incurable, painful boils all over their bodies. This seems to be the same kind of physical problem Job experienced as well, in **Job 2:7**. Just as it was in ancient Egypt, these boils only afflict the enemies of God. Those who trust the Lord are spared this judgment.

Verse 3 shows us the plagues in the sea. When the second bowl is poured out, the waters of the earth's oceans are corrupted and become like a corpse's putrid, fetid blood. In **Rev. 8:8-9**, when the second trumpet judgment was administered, one-third of the ocean was affected. Here, the cataclysm is worldwide.

Every creature in the sea will die when this plague is poured out. The seas will become vast cemeteries. Beaches will no longer attract the sun worshipers and the pleasure seekers. The beaches will wreak with the stench of death. Instead of being thronged with crowds of sunbathers, the word's beaches will be choked with the rotting carcasses of billions of dead sea creatures.

This kind of plague has already been seen on a very small scale in our world. Occasionally, something called a *"red tide"* will occur. *John Phillips* vividly describes this phenomenon in his commentary on the Revelation. "From time to time, off the coast of California and elsewhere, a phenomenon known as "the red tide" occurs. These red tides kill millions of fish and poison those who eat contaminated shellfish. In 1949, one of these red tides hit the coast of Florida. First, the water turn it was thick with countless billions of dinoflagellates, tiny one-celled organisms. Sixty-mile rows of stinking fish fouled the beaches. Much marine life was wiped out, even bait used by fishermen died upon the hooks. Eventually the red tide subsided, only to appear again the following year. Eating fish contaminated by the tide produced severe symptoms caused by a potent nerve poison, a few grams of which, distributed aright, could easily kill everyone in the world. An unchecked population explosion of toxic dinoflagellates would kill all the fish in the sea. (*Exploring Revelation*, rev. ed. [Chicago: Moody, 1987; reprint, Neptune, N.J.: Loizeaux, 1991], 190–91)[7]

This time, when it occurs, the entire world will be affected. When you consider the fact that 70% of the surface of this planet is covered in ocean, you can see how great of a plague this will be. Imagine the impact this will have on the environment. Most of the rainwater the earth receives comes from moisture that evaporates from the world's oceans. No more evaporation means greatly diminished rainfall on the earth. This will cause a drought of worldwide proportions.

Consider the fact that this world is largely dependent on the oceans for its food supply. Billions of people receive the abundance of their daily food supply the ocean. Without this source of food, millions will face starvation. Not only will food supplies be drastically affected, but so will commerce and shipping. The socio-economic impact of this plague will devastate the earth.

One by one, God is tearing down all the things' men take for granted. First, their health is destroyed. Then, the oceans are destroyed. The coastal regions of every nation in the world will become abandoned wastelands as the oceans are transformed into vast seas of death.

---

[7] *Exploring Revelation*

Verses 4-7 tell us when the third bowl is poured out, the freshwater sources of this world are stricken. Again, we saw this in miniature in **Rev. 8:10-11**, when one-third of the world's fresh water supplies were poisoned when a comet, a meteor, or some other heavenly body fell into them.

Here, they are turned to blood. This is an appropriate judgment because, by the time this plague is poured out on the earth, the world has become absolutely bloodthirsty. Millions of martyrs have been slain by the Antichrist and his forces. Millions of saints have had their blood shed by the enemies of God. He honors their desire for blood by giving them blood to drink. When Jesus was here, His first miracle was to turn water into wine. That miracle was designed to draw men to Him. Here, He turns the water into blood to remind men of Him. One by one, the Lord removes every prop, every comfort, everything mankind leans on for support and takes for granted.

This plague reminds us of the first of the ten plagues in Egypt. In **Ex. 7:20-24**, the fresh water in the land of Egypt was turned to blood and men searched in vain for water to quench their thirst. In this judgment, every source of fresh water is turned to blood. Whether it is a spring, a well or a municipal water system, the world's fresh water supply will be removed.

Our bodies can survive several weeks without food but only about three days without water. Imagine a world with no water! Imagine turning on your faucet, and instead of cool, clean, thirst-quenching water, it outpours putrid, foul, deadly blood. No doubt death from disease and thirst will skyrocket during these horrible, evil days.

When this plague comes, the angels praise God for His wisdom in sending this judgment. The world is merely reaping what it has sown. We see this in **Gal. 6:7-9**. The world has been guilty of murdering God's people and God's evangelists, and they are given blood to drink in return.

Another angel declares the righteous nature of God's judgments. Our human minds cannot comprehend the judgments of these verses. We shrink back from them and think that they are horrible. We recoil when we think about people having to suffer like people will suffer during the Tribulation. We might even fell that there must be a better way.

One day, when we are home in glory, and our minds have been transformed and glorified, we will see things from God's perspective. Then we will understand just how hateful and horrible sin truly is. We will feel as God feels. We will think as He thinks, and we will understand. In fact, I am 100% sure that we will voice our own "***Amens***" as He judges the world that has denied Him and defiled His creation.

We will understand that the time for judgment has come. We will know that the only thing that has held judgment off for this long has been the **pure grace of God**.

When judgment comes, we can rest assured that God will judge the right individuals in the right amount in the right way. He can do nothing but the right thing. As **Genesis 18:25** says, *"That be far from thee to do after this manner, to slay the righteous with the wicked: and that the righteous should be as the wicked, that be far from thee: Shall not the Judge of all the earth do right?"*

Verses 8-9 show us the fourth plague touches the sun. Its heat is allowed to burn the bodies of men. *"Scorch"* means *"to be burned with heat; to be tortured with intense heat."* By some means, God will allow the heat of the sun to be intensified, and the bodies of men will be burned.

This universe is an amazing place. God created everything and placed it exactly where it needed to be. The sun is some 93 million miles away from the earth. It sits at exactly the precise distance to allow life to exist. If the sun were any closer, we would be burned up. If the sun were any farther away, we would freeze to death. God placed it exactly where it needs to be.

The sun is a giant nuclear reactor. It is so large that 1.3 million, of our earth could fit inside of it. It is hot too. The surface of the sun is nearly 10,000 degrees. If that heat were to hit the Earth in full force, the planet would burn up instantly. Surrounding the earth is a band of radiation called the magnetosphere. This radiation band filters out the sun's rays, allowing exactly the right amount of heat and light to enter our atmosphere.

During this plague, God may either turn up the sun's heat or allow more of its heat to enter the earth's atmosphere. As a result, men will experience intense burns in their bodies.

The pain of sunburn is an intense, nagging pain. Imagine having that pain intensified many times over. Imagine the agony that will result from this plague.

Another of mankind's crutches is kicked out from under him. Since the dawn of time the sun has risen every morning and sat every evening. It has yielded life-giving, dependable heat and light for thousands of years. One day, mankind will awaken to a sun blazing in flaming heat. It will scorch their bodies. But it will be nothing compared to the pain they will feel when they are cast into Hell's fire. This is just a warning of something far more terrible and final!

Now we see the final judgment conclude. In **Revelation chapter 5** the Lamb of God took a seven sealed book from the hand of His Father. This book represented the title deed to planet Earth. Jesus owns this world because He created it out of nothing. He owns this world because He redeemed it when He died on the cross. When Jesus took that seven-sealed-book, He began to open the seals. When He did, the Tribulation Period began on the earth.

By the time we reach these verses, the world has been smiting under the wrath of a holy God for seven years. Now, the Tribulation is about to come to an end. As the final three seals are opened, God prepares to conclude His judgment of this world and its inhabitants.

When the events of these final three judgments are concluded, Jesus Christ, the King of Kings will return to the earth in glory and power. He will take possession of the throne of this world, and He will rule in righteousness. These three last plagues set the stage and prepared the way for the coming of the Lord.

When Jesus returns, He will finally receive the glory and honor He deserves. Today, the Lord Jesus is rejected, maligned, and hated by the world. That hatred will only intensify as the days go by and grow more and more evil.

In the following verses, we see the conclusion of the Final Judgment.

In **Verses 10-11, we see the Beast is finally** plagued! Up until now, the Beast has been somewhat sheltered from direct attack. When this fifth bowl is poured out, it is directed at the very seat of his power. Like Pharaoh in ancient Egypt, the Antichrist, with all his power is helpless against the judgment of God Almighty. This plague begins at the very throne room of the Antichrist and then spreads to cover his entire kingdom. He may be a powerful ruler, energized and supported by Satan, but he is helpless to defend himself against the God of Heaven.

In **Verse 10**, we see the world is darkened. When the fifth bowl judgment is unleashed upon the world, the world is suddenly engulfed in darkness. This darkness is not the darkness we normally think of. Instead, it is absolute, inky blackness. The darkness will be so complete that nothing can penetrate it. Surely, this darkness represents some change in how light reaches the planet. It also suggests that the power grids we use to light the earth will be eliminated. Whatever causes this darkness, it will be severe, and it will be complete.

This supernaturally imposed darkness is a tangible representation of the darkness already engulfed the world. The world has already rejected the Light of the World, the Lord Jesus because they loved darkness rather than light, **John 3:19**. This world chose moral, spiritual, intellectual, and emotional darkness over the light that was available in the person of Jesus Christ and in the Word of God. They favored darkness over light, and God gave them more darkness than they ever bargained for!

We are also told that when this darkness descends, men will literally chew their tongues because their pain is so great. The combined misery of the sores in their bodies, starvation from the ruined oceans, the lack of drinkable water, and the terrible burns they have suffered from the intense heat of the sun all combine to cause the inhabitants of the earth to writhe in pain.

What we see here is a tiny glimpse of Hell. God is letting the Antichrist, and his followers know what is waiting on them because they have rejected Jesus. Once, when speaking of Hell, Jesus in **Matt. 25:30**, *"**And cast ye the unprofitable servant into outer darkness: there shall be weeping and gnashing of teeth.**"* What we see here is a small glimpse of what those who reject Jesus will face when they go to Hell.

In **Verse 11**, we see the lesson has been declared! When the plagues and pains come, you would think people would have enough sense to repent of their sins and turn to God. Not these people! They shake their puny fists in the face of God, and they curse Him and blaspheme Him! What a tragedy! But what a window into the human heart!

There are those who tell us that mankind is bad, but there is a divine spark within him. They believe that man fell when Adam sinned but that his fall was not complete. The fact is man is totally depraved! This does not mean that He is as bad as he can be at all times. It does mean that there is no spiritual good in mankind at all, **Rom. 3:10-23**. Man, left to himself, will only grow more and more corrupt, **Eph. 4:22**.

If this judgment proves anything, it proves the absolute sinfulness of humanity! It proves that man is an incorrigible sinner, and that salvation is totally the work of grace! It proves that even when man is confronted with the power and judgment of God he will not repent of his sins. It proves that *"salvation is of the Lord," as in Jonah 2:9, and that people don't just "get religion" or "turn to Jesus."* It proves that salvation requires direct, divine intervention. If God did not come to us on a personal basis, convict us of our sins, quicken our dead spirit, and save us by His grace, **Eph. 2:1-10**, we would all go to Hell. You see, the same rebellion and hatred of God would be revealed in you and me were it not for the grace of God!

When people do die and go to Hell, we have the image of them trying to get saved, as they confess their sins and cry out to Jesus. I do not believe it will be that way! Look at the Rich Man in **Luke 16:19-31**. There is no hint of remorse over the life he lived. There is only sorrow over the sentence He received! When people go to Hell, they will lift their voices in blasphemy against God. They will curse Him and even His judgment will not bring them to a place of repentance! May God help this sin-cursed, fallen world!

Then in **Verse 12-16**, we see a great battle is planned! The sixth bowl is poured out on the earth, and it sets the stage for the battle of Armageddon. When this angel pours out his bowl, we are told that the Euphrates River will dry up. The Euphrates begins in Turkey at Mount Ararat and flows south, through Iraq, and into the Persian Gulf. For centuries, this river, which is over 1,700 miles long and 3,600 feet wide at places, has been the dividing line between the east and the west. As we know, no river really poses a problem for a modern mechanized army, but God will remove every obstacle and prepare the way for a massive invasion of the Middle East.

How will the river be dried up? Consider the fact that the oceans and all fresh waters have been turned to blood, and the amount of rainfall the earth has received has been dramatically reduced. Some have speculated that water levels would be far lower than normal anyway. In addition to many dams being built along the river, it would be very easy for human engineers to cut off the water. However, the fourth bowl intensified the heat of the sun. This would cause the snow and the ice cap on Mount Ararat to melt, causing the Euphrates to overflow its banks. Either way, it will be the result of divine intervention. God will speak and the waters of the Euphrates will cease to flow so that a massive army can pass through.

In **Verse 12**, we are told that a vast eastern army will use the highway created by the drying up of the Euphrates River to move toward Israel. The intention of this army is the total destruction of Israel. The phrase **"*kings of the east*"** literally means **"*the kings of the rising sun*"**. The Greek word ἀνατολή is a genitive, singular, feminine noun. Translated it means **"*rising sun and stars*"**. This is a genitive, singular, feminine noun. This reference has caused many to speculate that China and her allies will be the source of this army. In our study in **Rev. 9:16**, the Bible speaks of an army that numbers some 200 million. Only one nation on earth could raise an army of that size. That is the nation of China.

However, I would like to propose a different interpretation. The way things are shaping up in our world, we are headed toward a showdown between Islam and the Jews. Ever since the United Nations took Palestinian lands and gave it to the Jews, there has been conflict in that region. The Arab nations that surround Israel have repeatedly tried to oust the Jews from Palestine, and they have failed in every attempt. Though outnumbered some seven to one, the Israelis have defeated their Arab enemies every time they met on the field of battle. This has created great hostility in the hearts of the Arab nations. We see this in our present hostilities between Israel and Hamas and the horrible atrocities committed by Hamas against the Jews!

Imagine returning home to land in your family for centuries only to find someone else living there and you and your family evicted with no place to go. The Arabs hate the Jews and they long for the total destruction of the nation of Israel. I think that is what we are seeing in these verses.

While Islam paints itself in colors of peace and love, the religion also calls for the deaths of all Jews and Christians. Anyone who is not a Muslim is an infidel in their eyes, and infidels must either repent or die! Dr. Ken Trivette, in a sermon on these verses, shares the following quotations from the Qur'an:

- **Qur'an 59:14** *"The Jews are devoid of sense. There is a grievous punishment awaiting them. Satan tells them not to believe so they will end up in Hell."*
- **Qur'an 4:55** *"Sufficient for the Jew is the Flaming Fire!"*
- **Qur'an 88:1** *"Has the narration reached you of the overwhelming (calamity)? Some faces (all disbelievers, Jews and Christians) that Day, will be humiliated, downcast, scorched by the burning fire, while they are made to drink from a boiling hot spring."*

It would be for radical Islam to field a massive army bent on the annihilation of the Jews and their state. It may be Islam that leads a final, fatal Jihad against the nation of Israel.

In **Verses 13-14** we see a clear picture of the antagonists. When this judgment is poured out, three frogs emerge from the mouths of the Dragon, the Beast, and the False Prophet. Frogs are unclean creatures used here to refer to evil spirits, or demons. The mouth is the source of influence. So, it seems that Satan will inspire the words of these hellish world leaders, and they will whip their followers into a frenzy for a final assault against Israel. They can form a coalition between the world's armies. This final war will be satanically inspired and energized.

In **Verse 15, a heavenly announcement is made on the heels of this judgment**. Ever since Jesus ascended back into Heaven, it has been prophesied that He would return. (**Acts 1:9-11**). Seven years before these events, Christ did return, and He received His bride into Heaven. That was the Rapture. This verse is referring to the Second Coming. Jesus is telling His precious people to hang on for a little longer. His coming that has been imminent has become immediate! He is at the door! The saints of God are encouraged to keep the faith for a few more days, the Lord is coming! He is coming like a thief. The world will not see the signs, but He will come instantly and bring judgment with Him. Jesus lets His people know, however, that their waiting is over.

In **Verse 16** we see the great battle of **Armageddon**. This army has been assembled by Satan to destroy the people of God. The devil still thinks that he is in control! A quick glance at the Scripture paints a different picture altogether. **Verse 14** tells us this army is being gathered *"to the battle of that great day of God Almighty"*. Then, **verse 16** says, *"He gathered them together..."* Satan may think that he controls these events, but the real leader is God Himself. He gathers the world's nations in the valley of Megiddo so that He might engage and destroy them in one precious moment. For a creature that is supposed to be so very wise and intelligent, it is beyond me how Satan can believe he can still take on God and win. Perhaps he doesn't. Perhaps he realizes he has gone so far beyond the point of no return and can take no different path. Or perhaps he is truly that narcissistic. There are sociopaths who actually talk themselves into believing what comes out of their mouths. I don't know which one fits Satan best. But one thing for certain is this evil character has a date with destiny!

We have already considered the Valley of Megiddo in a previous chapter. But a little refresher never hurt anyone. Armageddon means *"the hill or city of Megiddo"*. Megiddo is located in the *"Plain of Esdraelon"*. This location is the site of some famous biblical battles. Here, Barak and Deborah defeated the Canaanites, **Jud. 4-5**. Here, Gideon defeated the Midianites, **Jud. 6-8**. This same valley is the place that both King Saul and his son Jonathan were killed in battle, **1 Sam. 31**. King Josiah also met his death in the valley of Megiddo, **2 Chron. 35**.

In this valley, the armies of the earth will come together to destroy the King of Kings. It is here in this place that Napoleon Bonaparte described as *"a natural battlefield"* that the earth's final battle will be fought. We will consider this battle in detail when we come to **chapter 19**.

In **Verses 17-21** we see Babylon is plundered! The seventh bowl is poured out. When it is, the awful wrath of God and His judgments against the earth are ended. Also, in this final judgment, this world system is destroyed. Since the dawn of time man has moved in rebellion to God. He has rebelled in his personal life, his public life, his political life and his productive life. In these verses, that entire world system is brought crashing down and man is left with nothing! Let's look in as Babylon is plundered.

Verse 17 shows us a sentence is rendered! As this bowl is poured out, a voice from the throne says, *"It is done!"* **This statement signals the fact that judgment has reached an end**. The Lord Jesus is on His way. He is prepared to take back everything Adam lost in the fall. He is preparing to claim everything He purchased at the cross. Jesus is about to receive the glory He is due. Jesus cried when he was on the cross, *"It is finished!"* There He announced His victory. Here, He cries, *"It is done!"* Here, He announces His verdict. There He cried out in joy; here He cries out in judgment. He is letting us know that we have reached the end of judgment; glory is just around the corner.

In **Verses 18-21** we see a ruined system! God has been in the process of judging the earth all the way through the Tribulation. Wave after wave of divine wrath has washed over this world and its inhabitants, and still, this world system stands in continued defiance of the will of God in Heaven. Here, in one final stroke, God destroys the last vestiges of human power. In one final judgment, God removes the last of man's props. God destroys everything that man has built and glories in. In a moment of time, the world is brought to its knees. Let's take a minute to unpack these verses.

In **Verse 16** a great earthquake shatters the world causing devastation! Earthquakes have always been a part of living in this world. Earthquakes happen around the world daily. Most, thankfully, go unnoticed by the inhabitants of the world. Some, however, have brought profound loss of life and severe damage. We all remember the earthquake in December 2004 that triggered a tsunami that devastated the South Pacific. Some statistics and data on earthquakes are shown in the table on the next page.

Description	Richter Magnitudes	Earthquake Effects	Frequency of Occurrence
Micro	Less than 2.0	Micro earthquakes, not felt.	About 8,000 per day
Very minor	2.0-2.9	Generally, not felt, but recorded.	About 1,000 per day
Minor	3.0-3.9	Often felt, but rarely causes damage.	49,000 per year (est.)
Light	4.0-4.9	Noticeable shaking of indoor items, rattling noises. Significant damage unlikely.	6,200 per year (est.)
Moderate	5.0-5.9	Can cause major damage to poorly constructed buildings over small regions. At most slight damage to well-designed buildings.	800 per year
Strong	6.0-6.9	Can be destructive in areas up to about 100 miles across in populated areas.	120 per year (1994 Northridge quake, San Francisco, CA, 6.5; 5.6 megatons)
Major	7.0-7.9	Can cause serious damage over larger areas.	18 per year
Great	8.0-8.9	Can cause serious damage in areas several hundred miles across.	1 per year (1906 San Francisco, 8.0; 1 gigaton)
Rarely, great	9.0 or greater	Devastating in areas several thousand miles across.	1 per 20 years (1964 Alaska 9.0; 5.6 gigatons) (2004 Indian Ocean Earthquake, 9.3; 32 gigatons)

To get an idea of how powerful this earthquake was, consider the fact that all the atomic and nuclear tests throughout history only equal 510.4

megatons. The South Pacific quake was 64 times larger than all nuclear explosions combined!)

Dr. Ken Trivette wrote, *"The earthquake and tsunami that hit Seward, Alaska in 1964 was so massive it deposited a cargo ship on the top of a mountain several thousand feet inland. Fourth Avenue, the main street in Anchorage at the time, dropped 15 feet, swallowing whole cars into a crevasse. The entire Anchorage neighborhood of Turnagain slid into the Cook Arm of Prince William Sound."* And that was only a 9.0 quake!

This quake will transcend the power of any quake ever measured. The devastation will be immense!

Verse 19 tells us that the cities of the earth are affected. *"**The Great City**"* probably refers to Jerusalem. That ancient city suffers terrible damage. The Old Testament speaks of great geological changes in and around Jerusalem.

The rest of the cities of the earth are devastated. Washington, New York, Los Angeles, Tokyo, London, Moscow, Paris, Rome- all the cities of the earth are likely to be destroyed in a moment. All the centers of pleasure, economics, and power are taken away momentarily.

Verse 19 tells us that Babylon is judged. We will see this fleshed out in greater detail in **chapters 17-18**, but for now we need to understand that the seat of the Antichrist's power, and the seat of the False Prophet's power, will be destroyed. This city and the system behind it will suffer more than the rest of the world.

Verse 20 tells us the islands and mountains are destroyed. The entire topography of the world will change. The continents will shift. Islands will be swallowed up in massive tsunamis. The mountains will crumble and disappear. The Lord is preparing the world for His millennial reign!

In **Verse 21, we see gigantic hailstones falling** on men. In Verse 21 we see the size of these large balls of ice. A talent was the weight a full-grown man could reasonably lift. A talent weighs somewhere between 100 and 125 pounds. Can you imagine 125-pound balls of ice raining down from the sky? Everything that is left behind from the devastating earthquake will be pulverized and the earth will be covered with shards of ice. Any crops that are in the fields will be destroyed. Cars, houses, and everything of value will be totally wiped out by this terrifying plague.

Then, in Verse 21, we see that all sinners will be revealed. Even after all they have been through, the world's inhabitants refuse to repent. They continue to blaspheme God. It is hard to imagine that the human heart can be so hard. Yet, the condition of sinners under judgment proves that lost people are totally depraved and will not repent.

We read the Bible, and we understand that these plagues are God's judgment on sinners who refuse to come to Him for salvation. These plagues are designed to judge those who have defied a holy God at every turn. We read it, and we understand the source and the solution. What strikes me as amazing is that these people also understand what is happening. They understand that God is behind these plagues. Instead of repenting in the face of His wrath, they stand in continued defiance of Him and His will. The Bible tells us in **verse 9** that they *"blaspheme"* the name of God. That word means *"to revile; to speak evil of"*. They shake their puny fists toward God and revile His holy name!

They have the audacity to blame Him for their troubles and suffering. Of course, that has been the human way since the dawn of time. Even in Eden, Adam and Eve sought to blame their problems on others (**Gen. 3:11-13**). That trend continues today.

Grown men and women are running around blaming their parents for the problems they have in life. If they are angry, if they are substance abusers, if they have other problems in their adult lives, they lay the blame at their parent's feet. Still, others blame God for their perversion. They claim God made them the way they are. That is foolish! Husbands blame wives and wives blame husbands. Everybody blames somebody else for their problems. Even under judgment, men will blame God for what they are suffering.

But the problem is not with God. The problem is clearly stated in **verse 9**, **"*and they repented not to give him glory.*"** They refuse to repent of their sins for God's glory and pay a heavy price for their choice. They have no one to blame but themselves!

If you put off salvation, die, and go to Hell, you will have no one to blame but yourself. You could stop anywhere and call on the name of God and trust Him for salvation if you would. If you do not, you will have nothing but judgment to look forward to!

The time for repentance is now. If you are not saved, you need to come to Jesus today. You need to be saved today! If you are saved and want to praise Him for delivering your soul from death, Hell, and judgment, the time is now. I call your attention back to **verse 15**. Jesus is coming! His counsel is for people to be ready. We do not know when He will come. He may come today in the Rapture. He may come for you today in death. If He were to come for you would you be ready? Or would you be caught unprepared?

If you have not experienced our God's free, unbridled love today and accepted his son, Jesus Christ, as your Lord and Savior, I urge you to please do that today. If you have strayed away from the Lord, remember where you were headed before He saved you by His grace. Amid all you have just read, I'd like to ask you this question again. It is the time of *The Final Countdown. Where will you spend eternity?*

THE JUDGMENT OF THE BABYLONIAN HARLOT

In **chapter 16**, we witnessed God's final judgment against this world. We saw God destroy this world through a series of powerful plagues. We also witnessed the defiance of fallen man. Even in the face of judgment, man refused to repent.

Of course, this shouldn't surprise us. Man refused to repent in the face of Law, and man has refused to repent in this age of grace. Man is a horrible sinner, and apart, from the grace of God, mankind is hopelessly lost.

As we continue our study into the Final Countdown, let's read from the Word of God, in Revelation 17:1-18.

> *17 And there came one of the seven angels which had the seven vials, and talked with me, saying unto me, Come hither; I will shew unto thee the judgment of the great whore that sitteth upon many waters:*
> *² With whom the kings of the earth have committed fornication, and the inhabitants of the earth have been made drunk with the wine of her fornication.*
> *³ So he carried me away in the spirit into the wilderness: and I saw a woman sit upon a scarlet coloured beast, full of names of blasphemy, having seven heads and ten horns.*
> *⁴ And the woman was arrayed in purple and scarlet colour, and decked with gold and precious stones and pearls, having a golden cup in her hand full of abominations and filthiness of her fornication:*

⁵ And upon her forehead was a name written, MYSTERY, BABYLON THE GREAT, THE MOTHER OF HARLOTS AND ABOMINATIONS OF THE EARTH.

⁶ And I saw the woman drunken with the blood of the saints, and with the blood of the martyrs of Jesus: and when I saw her, I wondered with great admiration.

⁷ And the angel said unto me, Wherefore didst thou marvel? I will tell thee the mystery of the woman, and of the beast that carrieth her, which hath the seven heads and ten horns.

⁸ The beast that thou sawest was, and is not; and shall ascend out of the bottomless pit, and go into perdition: and they that dwell on the earth shall wonder, whose names were not written in the book of life from the foundation of the world, when they behold the beast that was, and is not, and yet is.

⁹ And here is the mind which hath wisdom. The seven heads are seven mountains, on which the woman sitteth.

¹⁰ And there are seven kings: five are fallen, and one is, and the other is not yet come; and when he cometh, he must continue a short space.

¹¹ And the beast that was, and is not, even he is the eighth, and is of the seven, and goeth into perdition.

¹² And the ten horns which thou sawest are ten kings, which have received no kingdom as yet; but receive power as kings one hour with the beast.

¹³ These have one mind, and shall give their power and strength unto the beast.

¹⁴ These shall make war with the Lamb, and the Lamb shall overcome them: for he is Lord of lords, and King of kings: and they that are with him are called, and chosen, and faithful.

¹⁵ And he saith unto me, The waters which thou sawest, where the whore sitteth, are peoples, and multitudes, and nations, and tongues.

¹⁶ And the ten horns which thou sawest upon the beast, these shall hate the whore, and shall make her desolate and naked, and shall eat her flesh, and burn her with fire.

^{17} For God hath put in their hearts to fulfil his will, and to agree, and give their kingdom unto the beast, until the words of God shall be fulfilled.
^{18} And the woman which thou sawest is that great city, which reigneth over the kings of the earth.

This chapter and the one to follow explain everything discussed in **chapter 16.** This is where we see the fulfillment of those prophecies. In this chapter, we will witness the fall of the great worldwide church that will flourish after the rapture of the church. This system is already at work even today. All around the world, a great move is underway to bring all religious groups under one central umbrella. We are witnessing the great falling away which the Bible says will come about in the last days. (**2 Thes. 2:3; 1 Tim. 4:1-3; 2 Tim. 3:1-3; 2 Tim. 4:3-4**). It has already reached the place where Bible believing Christians, people who take the Bible literally and who try to live a holy life for the Lord, are under increasing attack. In the eyes of the world, the only way to succeed is to conform and be tolerant of other's beliefs and opinions. I believe that all Christians can worship together. But sometimes, people begin to practice eisegesis. We talked about this early in this book. Eis·e·ge·ses [ahy-si-jee-seez] is an interpretation, especially of scripture that expresses the interpreters' own ideas, bias, or the like, rather than the meaning of the text. And that is dangerous theology.

Let's look at this awesome chapter and identify the fall of this religious Babylon.

The last plague in **Rev. 16:17-21** brought about a great earthquake that destroyed the world's cities. This final, great quake devastated all the places that man had created. This earthquake destroyed everything that represented the greatest accomplishments of humanity. All of mankind's centers of pleasure and profit are wiped out.

Since the dawn of time, man has been in the business of trying to get by without God. Mankind rests on his power, his accomplishments, his ability to produce and his ability to enjoy pleasure. In that last great judgment, everything man trusts is taken away.

We are also told that **"great Babylon came in remembrance before God, to give unto her the cup of the wine of the fierceness of his** *wrath,"* **Rev. 16:19**. Babylon is a city, but it is also a system. Babylon represents everything mankind has accomplished apart from God. This system is judged in the seventh bowl judgment.

What we have in **chapters 17 and 18** is another parenthetical passage. These two chapters give us the details of the destruction of the Babylonian system. In **chapter 17,** we will see the destruction of religious Babylon. In **chapter 18** we will see the destruction of economic Babylon.

Let's walk through these verses today and seek insight into them. I want to preach from this chapter on *The Judgment of The Babylonian Harlot*. Notice the *facts* this passage reveals.

Note that **Verses 1-6** describe the Babylonian Harlot. The first verse tells us that we are going to witness *"the judgment of the great whore."* The word "πόρνη" or *"whore"* is a word that we do not use in decent company. But it is a word the Bible uses, so we must deal with it. It translates the Greek word *"pornay"*, which refers to *"a woman who sells her body for sexual uses; a harlot; a prostitute."* It is also used to refer to a woman who is an *"idolatress"*. In this passage the word refers to the whole system of false religion embraced by this world. These verses teach us about this system of false religion and how it will be judged someday.

Verses 1-6 tell us about this Babylonian mother. Verse 1 describes her popularity and her worldwide influence. This religious system will have the ear of the world! (i.e. power and wealth.

Verse 2 shows us her perversion. This is illustrated by the word whore. She will use her charms to deceive the world into thinking she is the right way.

In **Verse 3** we see this church is upheld by the beast's power. It will be headquartered in Rome. (**Verse 9**). She will be defended by the ten-nation confederacy of the revived Roman Empire. The church will once again wed the state. Look at what happened to Constantine in 325 AD. Christianity began to change. We had Christmas, Lent, Baptism, Relic Worship, Saint Worship, Popery, etc. Some say this is the Catholic Church. It absolutely is not. Catholicism will surely be involved, but so will Methodism, Lutheranism, Presbyterianism, the Islamic faith, Buddhism, Church of Christ and even the Baptists. That said, the connection between the history and practice of Roman Catholicism and the description of this religious system cannot be lightly passed by.

In **Verse 4,** we see her prosperity and garments, wealth, and ritual! In short, we see the trappings and wealth of religion.

Verse 5 shows us how she is identified. We see the origin of the Babylonian Mother in Gen. 10:8-11; 11:1-4.

Verse 6 tells us of her persecutions. This system is responsible for the deaths of the saints of the Lord. From Cain and Abel to the Tribulation saints, this religious system has been responsible for the martyrdom of tens of millions of Christians. Note it has never been the denomination that determines a person's salvation. It is the Blood of Jesus that makes the difference!

Now that we have looked at this mother let's look at the scope of this system. **Verse 1** tells us this harlot *"sitteth upon many waters"*. **Verse 15** gives us the commentary on this verse. What we see here is a one-world religious system. Today there are thousands of religions on this planet, and there is little agreement between them. The primary religions recognized by most people are Christianity, Judaism, Islam, Buddhism and Hinduism. Most of the world's population observes one of these religions.

There will come a day when all the world religions will be brought together under one banner. The Antichrist, or the False Prophet, will have a plan to iron out all the differences between these belief systems. One day there will be a one world religion.

There is already a great push in that direction now. An ecumenical movement working in our day is seeking to bring all the world's religions together.

Christianity is different from all other religions because it is not really a religion. It is a faith. When the Rapture occurs, all true Christians will be removed from this world. What will be left will be those who *"have a form of godliness but deny the power thereof"*. Those people will be easy prey for the devil and demonic religion.

According to **verse 2,** the entire world will come under the spell of this great end-time religion. Kings and world leaders will be a part of the movement. The whole world will be intoxicated by the teaching of this false system of belief. Like a slick seductress, this great harlot will seduce the world with her promises and her power.

Verse 3 tell us this harlot is supported by the Antichrist. The Antichrist is the *"beast"* and he carries this religious system to great power in the world.

The phrase *"full of names of blaspheme"* reminds us that Antichrist will set himself up as God. He will enter the Jewish Temple and he will demand that the world worship him. **(2 Thes. 2:3-4)**. He will demand worship and a deluded world will give him what he desires. **(2 Thes. 2:11)**. He will give this religion its power.

According to **verse 9**, this system sits on *"seven hills"*. This could be a reference to ancient Rome built on seven hills. Some people think that this reference ties this system in with Roman Catholicism. However, the seven hills could also reference the seven continents, which would indicate that this system is worldwide in nature.

In our society, there is a tendency to try and determine which religion this passage refers to. I believe that it will contain Roman Catholics, Mormons, Jehovah's Witnesses, Muslims, Presbyterians, Methodists, Church of God, Church of Christ and yes, Baptists. What we do best is to blame someone else for our woes, which hasn't changed since the days of Adam and Eve. Mankind has always looked o blame another religion for their problems. I believe the final construction of this end-time religion is best left in the hands of the Lord!

Verse 4 shows us the success of this system. Just as a prostitute usually dresses provocatively to draw attention to herself, so does this false religious system. This religion wears the colors *"purple and scarlet"*. These are the colors of royalty and nobility. She is *"decked with gold and precious stones and pearls"*. This speaks to her wealth and prosperity. This system will be wealthy beyond words. This is true of many of the *"great religious systems"* of our day. There is big money in religion! Some people grow very wealthy at the expense of others!

The Bible tells us that this system is well-connected and prosperous, but it is all a pretense. This harlot holds *"a golden cup full of abominations and filthiness of her fornications."* While this religion appears healthy, good and prosperous on the outside, it is really filled with corruption. It is an abomination to God! As any church or denomination grows, there is a danger that it will thrive on its prosperity and forget its allegiance to the Lord. A subtle seduction in money and power can easily lead a system off the course of holiness and godliness. Many movements that begin well have gone away from God, having been seduced by power, popularity and prosperity! There is a tendency to change so that the trends may continue!

Verse 5 tell us of the spirit of this system. In ancient times, it was common for prostitutes to wear identification so that prospective customers could recognize them. This system is identified by God as *"**the mother of harlots and abominations of the earth.***

When we speak of Babylon, many people immediately think of a city. And it is a city located in the country of Iraq. Babylon, the city, was once the grandest capital of the most powerful nation in the world. Today, it is abandoned by everyone by archaeologists and historians. But Babylon is also a system. Babylon is described as the system from which every false religious system originated. That is what the title *"mother"* implies.

This Babylonian system first appears in **Genesis 11:1-9**. The city was called Babel then and was founded by a very wicked man named Nimrod. The people of Babel decided to build themselves a tower to leave their mark on the world. **Gen. 11: 4** says, *"And they said, Go to, let us build us a city and a tower, whose top may reach unto heaven; and let us make us a name, lest we be scattered abroad upon the face of the whole earth."*

The flood was fresh in their minds, and they wanted to leave their mark on the world. This tower was not designed to reach into Heaven as some think. It was designed as a temple of Heaven. The constellations were placed on the top of this tower and men climbed it to worship the heavenly bodies. (**Gen. 11:4**). This tower, and the religion in represented, is the first of many false religions started by man. They were the first false religionists, but they would not be the last. However, the same seeds of humanism and pride found in their attempt to form their own religion can be found in every religion founded by man!

God judged these people for their rebellion and for their foolish worship. Just as He judged them, He will one day judge all the false religions of the world. That is what we see here in **Revelation 17**. This chapter clearly reveals what will happen to the false religions of this world at the end of the Tribulation Period.

Verse 6 shows us this system of belief is responsible for the deaths of every saint of God who has ever died at the hands of false religion. From the death of Abel to the prophets, to the early Christian martyrs, to the martyrs of the inquisition, through the millions of martyrs of the Tribulation, every single death can be laid at the feet of the Babylonian harlot. She is responsible for the deaths of God's children, and she will be judged for her bloodthirsty ways!

Verses 7-15 show the Babylonian Harlot demystified. These are confusing verses. **Verse 8** refers to the miracle of the Antichrist's death and resurrection. **(Rev. 13:3)** Whether his death and resurrection are real or fake, it doesn't matter. The result will be the same. Most of the world's lost people will believe the miracle and follow the Antichrist.

Verse 10 refers to the seven great world kingdoms. Five were established in John's Day (Egypt, Babylon, Medo-Persia, and Greece). One was ruling Rome. The one to come is the kingdom of the Antichrist.

Verse 11 refers to the reign of the Antichrist. He will be a world leader, but after the miracle of his death and resurrection, he will become the ruler of the world. But his judgment is set in stone. Despite all his power and popularity, the Antichrist is headed to perdition! The word *"perdition"* means *"utter destruction"*.

Verses 12-13 demystify the benefactors of Babylon. These two verses refer to ten kings who will give their allegiance and power to the Antichrist. In return, he gives them great power and authority. These kings are wholly committed to the reign of the Antichrist. They are given a kingdom, but their reign is short-lived, i.e., "one hour."

In Verse 14, we see the battle itself demystified. As we mentioned in our last study, the nations of the world under the direction of the Antichrist and his kings will gather to do battle with Jesus Christ at Armageddon. They are fighting a losing battle because they are foolish enough to attack the Lamb. The Lamb they attack is the *"king of Kings and the Lord of Lords."* He will destroy them with the word of His mouth. **(Rev. 19:11-21)**. We will get to that in a subsequent chapter.

This verse also refers to those with the Lamb when He battles with the world. These people who are *"**called, and chosen and faithful**"* refer to the Bride of Christ. This, my friends, is us! When He comes, we are coming with Him! We will watch the Lamb do battle and shout for Him as He claims victory over all His enemies!

We have witnessed the fall of the religious Babylon. Let's examine the destruction of economic Babylon. The Bible paints a horrific picture of the end of all false religion. One day, every belief system in the world that bypasses the Lord Jesus Christ will be utterly destroyed and will cease to exist. That will be a devastating day for the devil and his followers, but it will be a glorious day for the God of Heaven and His Son Jesus.

While **chapter 17** reveals the demise of ecumenical Babylon, this chapter reveals the doom of economic Babylon. In **verses 1-2**, a mighty angel, shining with the glory of Heaven, appears on the scene. This angel comes to announce the condition and the condemnation of this world's economic system. Mankind will not only be deprived of the religion he created; he will also suffer the loss of the wealth he craves.

Nothing seems to devastate people more than destitution. Take away a man's money, and often, you have taken away his reason for living. This was the case in 1929 when the stock market crashed. October 29, 1929, became known as *"**Black Tuesday**"*. When the stock market crashed, the world was plunged into *"**The Great Depression**"*. Over the next few years, the economic structure of the U.S. economy was nearly destroyed. Over 9,000 banks closed their doors between 1930 and 1933. Production in U.S. manufacturing plants ground to a halt, leaving millions unemployed. Many thousands lost their homes to foreclosure; many others lost their health to malnutrition.

All across this nation, people waited in soup lines for their meals. All across this nation, *"**hobo jungles**"* and *"**Hoovervilles**"* sprang up. The *"**hobo jungles**"* were places near train yards where the hobos who travelled the country on freight cars set up camp. *"**Hoovervilles**"* were shanty towns filled with shacks made from crates and other cheap materials. They were named after President Hoover, who received much blame for the economic conditions of the times. People who lived through those dark and difficult days were changed forever by the hardships they suffered.

These verses tell us of an economic collapse that will make the stock market crash of 1929 seem like nothing! This economic disaster will be worldwide in its scope, and it will take away mankind's favorite god: money! Our money has the words *"In God We Trust"* printed or stamped on every piece. For far too many, the *"god"* they trust is that piece of money they hold.

We have already considered the destruction of the one-world religious system that will dominate the end times. In this study, we will consider the demise of the one-world economic system that dominated the world in those days. Whether we realize it or not, the world's economy is already headed toward being one vast system. Just a few months ago, a sharp decline in China's stock market impacted stock markets all around the world. It even caused a 400-point drop in our own stock market. People lost billions of dollars in an instant. These verses talk about a time when the entire economic structure of the world would come crashing down in a moment.

Let's consider the facts in this chapter that are revealed as God judges this world's economic system. I want to teach these verses on *The Destruction of Economic Babylon*.

In **Verses 2-8**, we see the spirit of a corrupted system. The angel tells us about the spirit behind the system. It will be a system energized and controlled by demons and evil spirits. It will be utterly vile and corrupt. We look at our world today and think it can't get much worse. What this verse describes is a world that has literally gone to the devil. Things can get worse, and they will!

Verse 3 tells us this Babylonian system will seduce the entire world. Kings and merchants will all tie their futures to what happens in this economic boom. Billions of dollars will be made as the wealthy people of the earth give everything, they have to get their hands on all they can get.

We live in a world obsessed with money. How many have sat around and imagined what we would do with millions of dollars? How many are spending money they don't have buying lottery tickets to try and get rich quick? How many always have some scheme cooking that will make them rich? The love of money is the greatest corrupter of mankind ever conceived.

(**1 Tim. 6:10**). Money in and of itself is not evil. But, when a person loves money to the point that it controls their life and lifestyle, it becomes evil.

Verses 4-8 tell us how the sentence this system receives. The angel is preparing to pronounce God's judgment upon this corrupt system. Before he does, he calls for God's people to avoid being caught up in the wickedness of that hour. The angel calls for the people of God to reject this system and the sins of this system. God expects His people to come out of this world's system and to be different. (**2 Cor. 6:17**). He expects us to be motivated by different values.

We will never win the world by being like them! We will impact the world the most when we separate from their ways and allow them to see Jesus living through our lives.

Let's look at what happens as the Lord's sentence is passed on the Babylonian economic system.

Verse 5 tells us of her deeds. The sins of this system have "*reached unto heaven*". The word "*reached*" means "*to glue, cement, fasten together*". The ancient tower of Babel failed to reach the heavens, but the sins of this system have succeeded in reaching the throne of God. God, in His patience, has held back His judgment. Now, the sins of Babylon come up in the remembrance of God, and the day of His judgment has arrived.

I praise the Lord that those in Jesus do not have to worry about their sins being remembered. Consider the wonderful promise of **Isaiah 43:25**, "*I, even I, am he that blotteth out thy transgressions for mine own sake, and will not remember thy sins.*"

Verse 6 tells us of her doom and her reward! The word "*reward*" here means "*to pay a debt; to give back that which is due*". Babylon has sinned much, and she is about to be punished much! Her sins have been doubled, and her punishment will be doubled, too!

You never get away with sin! **Gal. 6:7** tells us that we always reap what we sow. We always reap more than we sow, whether good or bad.

In **Verse 7,** we see her judgment. This system glorifies itself. It thinks it is so powerful and so glorious that it is above sorrow and judgment. The Babylonian system is about to learn a harsh lesson. Lots of people have this same attitude about their lives. They think that they are safe and that they will never be judged. God has a word for people with that attitude, **1**

Thes. 5:3, *"For when they shall say, Peace and safety; then sudden destruction cometh upon them, as travail upon a woman with child; and they shall not escape."*

In **Verse 8,** we see her destruction. Her power, glory, and pride will not stave off the judgment of the Lord. Her destruction will be swift and sure. In one day all that man has built over thousands of years will be brought to nothing! Judgment will come, and there will be no escape. It is settled!

In the second part of **Verse 8,** we see her destroyer! God makes promises and not threats. This system has defied His Word and defiled His ways. He will come in judgment, and none can stay His hand or stop His purposes. He can judge the world, and none can stop Him!

The entire world is plunged into grief when the Babylonian economic system is judged. The world cries, "Alas, Alas" as they realize their wealth and power are gone. Notice how the different groups react to the fall of Babylon.)

In **Verses 9-10**, all the leaders of the nations of the earth who have risen to power and prosperity on the back of this system now mourn over her destruction. Every economy of every nation on the earth will crash to the ground in a moment of time. The crash of this system will be accompanied by the wailing and weeping of the world's rulers.

In **Verses 11-17,** we see the merchants as the businessmen and CEOs of the world's great businesses. In an instant, their financial empires are brought to desolation. They weep and mourn because no one has any money to buy their goods. (**Verse 12**). Suddenly, all their goods, worth so much (**Verse 13-14**), are worth nothing! **Verse 12** tells us that the luxuries of life are out of reach. Houses, cars, jewelry, and other fine things of life will be unobtainable. **Verse 13** tells us that the basic necessities of life will be impossible to obtain. Spices, bread, meat, and other foods will be out of the reach of every man. **Verse 14** tells us that the exotic things men long for will also be taken away. Notice this list. The first item is *"gold"*. (**Verse 12**). The last item is *"the souls of men"*. (**Verse 13**). This reveals where this world system places its priorities. It elevates profits over people. This system has built its power and gained its prosperity through the oppression and enslavement of the common man. Those days are over.

Verse 15-17a shows the formerly wealthy merchants weeping over the city's destruction. They have witnessed the devastation of the word's economic system, and they are shattered by what they have seen.

We live in an hour when anything we want is readily available, and most people in our society can afford about anything they want. People talk about the economic downturn in our area, but you can't prove it by the parking lot at Wal-Mart! People still have plenty of money. That will change one day! The money of the world will be worth nothing. Goods will cease to be available. The destruction of economic Babylon will bring the world to its knees.

Verse 17-19 says that the mariners of the earth will mourn her. All the people who made a fortune carrying the goods produced by this system mourn when they see its destruction. Their source of wealth is taken away and they are left destitute. All hope of profit and prosperity are taken away in an instant.

In **Verse 20**, we take note as the multitudes of heaven consider her. While earth weeps over the fall of Babylon, Heaven worships! This system has been responsible for the death and destruction of many of God's people. Now, this system is judged, and Heaven is filled with joy. Observing Heaven's perspective concerning the events of the Earth is interesting. What brings sadness to earthly men's hearts brings shouting to heavenly men's hearts.

In **Verses 21-24,** we see a system that has been condemned. In Verse 21, her condemnation is categorized. A mighty angel casts a millstone into the sea. A millstone was a huge, round stone used to grind grain. A typical millstone was around four to five feet in diameter and about a foot thick. A stone of that nature would sink to the bottom of the sea and not float back to the surface.

This stone is used to illustrate the judgment that is coming upon Babylon. Babylon will be destroyed, and it will not rise to power ever again. This is what Jeremiah prophesied many years ago. **Jeremiah 51:64, "*And thou shalt say, Thus shall Babylon sink, and shall not rise from the evil that I will bring upon her: and they shall be weary. Thus far are the words of Jeremiah."*** The judgment of Babylon will be sudden, swift, and sure. It is also a judgment that is forever settled!

In **Verses 22-23,** we see her condemnation completed! When Babylon is judged and ceases to exist, her passing will also signal the passing of life as the world knows it. There will be no more music. **(Verse 22)**. Music has always been associated with happiness and joy. There will be no more reason for rejoicing. Music will cease. There will be no more manufacturing. **(Verse 22).** People have always been industrious. Man has always found a way to work with his hands and provide for his family. Man works because he has hope for the future. When Babylon falls, all hope for the future vanishes with her.

There will be no more merriment. **(Verse 23)**. The *"light of a candle"* speaks of habitation and home. A light in the window of a home suggests happiness, hope, family, and home. All these are taken away when Babylon falls. The homes of the world will be plunged into darkness and despair! There will be no more marriages. **(Verse 23).** No longer will love bring the hopeful couple to an altar to exchange their vow. There will be no more beautiful brides in their white dresses. There will be no more nervous grooms in their tuxedos. There will be no flower girls, ring bearers and wedding bells. Weddings are times filled with hope and happiness. A couple meets at the altar with their hearts full of love and hope for the future. They begin their relationship with great expectations. When Babylon falls, there will be no more love, no more marriages and no more hope for the future!

In **Verses 23-24** we see how this system is judged because she stood for everything God was against. This system was ***domineering***. A few got rich while the rest suffered. This system was ***deceptive***. People were led to believe that salvation was in achieving riches and success. That is the lie of the devil! It is better to have none of this world's goods, than for this world's goods to have you. Listen to the Word of God: ***Pro. 11:4***, *"Riches profit not in the day of wrath: but righteousness delivereth from death." **Pro. 11:28**, "He that trusteth in his riches shall fall: but the righteous shall flourish as a branch."* This system was ***deadly***, v. 24. The Babylonian system has been responsible for the deaths of many of God's precious people down through the ages. In fact, most of the faithful martyrs who have been killed have been sacrificed on the altar of power and profit.

In **Verses 16-17** we see the reality and reason for her destruction. After the Antichrist and his minions use the harlot to achieve power, they will turn on her. When they have reached the pinnacle of success, they have no more need of a religious system. They turn on the Harlot and they totally destroy her. The Antichrist and his followers do not know it, but they are merely doing the will of the Lord. He is the one who puts it into their hearts to destroy the Babylonian religious system. God uses these wicked men to carry out His will against false religion.

God hates false religion! In the end of the world, He will use the ungodly to destroy the ungodly. Organized religion is a disgrace to God! When ritual, tradition and the doctrines of men take prominence over the Lord God, it is false worship. It does not matter what name they have over the door. It does not matter what they claim to be. When anything or anyone but Jesus Christ is the center of attention, it is a false religion, and it will be destroyed by God one day!

When the Tribulation Period ends, all false religion will have been destroyed. This will pave the way for the Millennial reign of Jesus. He will usher in a one-thousand-year period of time when people will worship no one but Him, at least openly!

This world economic system that has caused so much pain is going to be destroyed one day. I advise you to be sure that your treasure is in the right place. **Matt. 6:19-21**, *"Lay not up for yourselves treasures upon earth, where moth and rust doth corrupt, and where thieves break through and steal: But lay up for yourselves treasures in heaven, where neither moth nor rust doth corrupt, and where thieves do not break through nor steal: For where your treasure is, there will your heart be also."*

Did you know that man is a religious creature? That's right, all people worship something. Everyone believes something. Even the person who claims to be an atheist believes in his unbelief. When it is all said and done, this comes down to two simple choices: Jesus Christ or false religion!

Every belief system in the world that does not center on the Lord Jesus is a false system of belief. How can I say that? Listen to what Jesus said, **John 14:6**, *"I am the way, the truth, and the life: no man cometh unto the Father, but by me."* Listen again, **Acts 4:12**, *"Neither is there salvation in any other: for there is none other name under heaven given among men, whereby we must be saved."* Listen to one more, **John 8:24**, *"I said *therefore unto you, that ye shall die in your sins: for if ye believe not that I am he, ye shall die in your sins."*

These are not the words of Mike Letterman. This is the Word of God! So, what is it with you? Is it Jesus, or is it religion? Do not be satisfied to join a church or be baptized. Do not be satisfied to get your name on the role of some religious organization. Do not be satisfied with anything less than believing on Jesus Christ, and Him alone, for your salvation! Anything else is just religion. Anything less than Jesus is a prescription for Hell!

Ask yourself, if I died right now, where would I spend eternity? My brothers and sisters, we are in the time of The Final Countdown. And some of you would say, "Well, preacher, you don't know!" You are right. I don't know. I do not know the hour or day when our Lord will return to take home what is his. But I know this. In these chapters, as we have studied the Book of Revelation, how can you not say we live in the last days? History is being fulfilled right now, today, across the globe. The stage is set for the return of our Savior. There is only one thing missing. **God has not yet said it is time.**

Right now, God is still in the business of saving souls. There will come a time when invitations like this will no longer be given. The Bible says there will be weeping, wailing, and gnashing of teeth. And that is only the beginning for those who are not saved.

So, allow me to ask you again. Where will you spend eternity?

THE KING

The opening chapter of Revelation sets the tone for everything else in the book. **Rev. 1:1** tells us this book is *"The revelation of Jesus Christ."* **Rev. 1:7-8** says, *"Behold, he cometh with clouds; and every eye shall see him, and they also which pierced him: and all kindreds of the earth shall wail because of him. Even so, Amen. I am Alpha and Omega, the beginning and the ending, saith the Lord, which is, and which was, and which is to come, the Almighty."* This book is about Jesus and about His return to this earth to rule and reign.

Revelation **chapter 5** takes us into Heaven. God is shown holding a book sealed with seven seals, **5:1**. A search is made in heaven and on earth to find someone worthy to open the book, but no one is found **5:2-3**. John weeps at this news because he desperately wants to know what is written in the book, **5:4**. John is told not to weep because the Lamb of God is worthy to take the book, **Rev. 5:5-7**. When the Lord takes the book from the hand of God, Heaven erupts into praise and worship because the Lord Jesus has been found worthy to take the book and open the seals, **Rev. 5:8**.

When we studied that chapter, we discovered that the seven-sealed books was the title deed of the planet Earth. You see, Satan is called *"the god of this world"*, **2 Cor. 4:4**. He may be the *"little g"* god of this world today, but he is not worthy to retain his grip on the world. This world belongs to Jesus, and to Jesus alone! The day will come when He takes possession of this world away from Satan.

This world belongs to Jesus because of three great truths.

1. *It is His by right of Creation – He made it!*
2. *It is His by right of Calvary – He redeemed it!*
3. *It is His by right of Conquest – He will retake it!*

The entire book of Revelation has been leading us to this great moment we will consider together in this chapter. The whole purpose of the

Tribulation Period, **chapters 6-18**, is to prepare the world for the coming of the King. The passage we are about to study today speaks of that great moment in the future when Jesus will return to this earth and have the power and glory to claim what is rightfully His. The first time Jesus came to this world, He came as a ***Redeemer***. The next time He comes, He is coming as a ***Ruler***! The first time He faced a ***Cross***. The next time, He will wear a ***Crown***. The first time He came there was a ***Tomb***; the next time He comes there will be a ***Throne**/*

Let's study these verses together and notice the *truths* contained in these verses. I don't mind telling you that these verses excite me greatly! I am tired of hearing the name of Jesus treated like a byword. I am tired of seeing His Gospel treated like a lie. I am tired of watching Satan and lost sinners live as though the Lord Jesus doesn't exist. I look forward to that day when Jesus Christ will return to this world in power and glory. On that day, He will destroy His enemies and rule this earth in righteousness. Let's study that great day together because *The King Is Here*!

Let us read from God's Word in **Revelation 19:11-21.**

> *¹¹ And I saw heaven opened, and behold a white horse; and he that sat upon him was called Faithful and True, and in righteousness he doth judge and make war.*
> *¹² His eyes were as a flame of fire, and on his head were many crowns; and he had a name written, that no man knew, but he himself.*
> *¹³ And he was clothed with a vesture dipped in blood: and his name is called The Word of God.*
> *¹⁴ And the armies which were in heaven followed him upon white horses, clothed in fine linen, white and clean.*
> *¹⁵ And out of his mouth goeth a sharp sword, that with it he should smite the nations: and he shall rule them with a rod of iron: and he treadeth the winepress of the fierceness and wrath of Almighty God.*
> *¹⁶ And he hath on his vesture and on his thigh a name written, KING OF KINGS, AND LORD OF LORDS.*

ⁱ⁷ And I saw an angel standing in the sun; and he cried with a loud voice, saying to all the fowls that fly in the midst of heaven, Come and gather yourselves together unto the supper of the great God;
¹⁸ That ye may eat the flesh of kings, and the flesh of captains, and the flesh of mighty men, and the flesh of horses, and of them that sit on them, and the flesh of all men, both free and bond, both small and great.
¹⁹ And I saw the beast, and the kings of the earth, and their armies, gathered together to make war against him that sat on the horse, and against his army.
²⁰ And the beast was taken, and with him the false prophet that wrought miracles before him, with which he deceived them that had received the mark of the beast, and them that worshipped his image. These both were cast alive into a lake of fire burning with brimstone.
²¹ And the remnant were slain with the sword of him that sat upon the horse, which sword proceeded out of his mouth: and all the fowls were filled with their flesh.

Verses 11-14 tell of the coming of the King. This is the second time a door has been opened in Heaven in Revelation. The first time the door in Heaven was opened, it was opened so that the church, the Bride of Christ, could join the Lord in Heaven. (**Rev. 4:1**). When this door is opened it allows the Lord to ride out of Heaven to return to this earth. That first door speaks of the Rapture of the Church. This second open door in Heaven speaks of the Return of the Christ.

Verses 11-13 tell us how the King will appear when He returns to the earth. When he returns, he will return in glory! When Jesus came to this earth the first time, He concealed His heavenly glory beneath the flesh of His body. (**Phil. 2:5-8**). Those who saw Him saw a common, ordinary Jew. (**Isa. 53:2**). Even though He was the Creator of the universe in human flesh, He didn't even have a place to lay His head. (**Matt. 8:20**).

The next time He comes, things will be different. He will come on a *"white horse"*. Ancient Roman generals often rode white horses in their triumphal processions. John sees Jesus returning as a Conqueror. The last time the world saw Jesus, they saw Him dead on a cross. The world looked at Jesus as a *victim*. This time, they will see Him as a *Victor*! He is not coming the second time to die. He is coming to reign!

Verse 12 describes Jesus as having eyes "like a flame of fire." This speaks of His power, glory, and right to judge sinners. Jesus is coming as one who sees, knows, and controls all. He is returning not as a Savior but as a Judge!

This verse shows he is faithful and true. Modern politicians rarely speak the truth. They usually tell us what they think we want to hear. They lie to keep their jobs and to fulfill their agendas. Jesus is not like those men! He always tells the truth and will do everything He says He will do. I am glad that we can depend on the promises of the Lord! Men will fail us, but my Lord and Savior never will! (**2 Cor. 1:20**).

We see that He fights with righteousness. Most of this world's wars have been fought over false pretenses and foolish objectives! But our Lord's cause is just and holy! He fights for the honor of His Father's Name and glory! He fights against unrighteousness and evil. He wages war for the glory of God alone! The Lord is a man of war. (**Ex. 15:3**)

In these verses, we see his name. It is a name of mystery. What is this mysterious name? No one knows but Him. You can study all the names of Jesus given in the Bible. However, He will still be more than our mortal, finite minds can comprehend! He may let us comprehend Him fully someday.

But here is the point. Mankind has refused to know Jesus. They would not use His name except as a by-word, slang, or curse word. Now, the day of grace has forever passed! Now, they cannot know Him even if they desire to.

Verse 13 tells us it is a name of ministry. He is called "***The Word of God***". The first time Jesus came, He came as God in human flesh. (**John 1:1**). He is the Word of God. He came to fulfill the promises and prophecies of the Word. He came to go to the cross and paid the price for sin and sinners.

The next time He comes, He is coming to fulfill the rest of the Word of God. Jesus is the "*author and finisher*" of our faith. (**Heb. 12:2**).

In **Verse 16**, we see he has a name of majesty. His Name is written on his thigh, symbolizing strength, stability, and power. When Jacob wrestled with the angel, the angel touched Jacob's thigh, and his power to resist was broken ((**Gen. 32**).

When Jesus comes the next time, He is not coming as the lowly Nazarene. He will not be the butt of cruel joking and mockery! He will not be mocked, stripped, beaten, spit upon, and crucified. He will come the next time as "*the King of Kings and Lord of Lords!*"

His name is also written on His vesture, which symbolizes His position. When Jacob gave Joseph that coat of many colors, he told everyone who his favorite son was. Joseph's brothers saw that coat and knew that Joseph was the apple of his daddy's eye! Jesus is the ultimate ruler, and His garments prove He is worthy of faith and worship!

In **Verse 13**, we see the apparel of this king! His garments are stained with the blood of His enemies. (**Isa. 63:1-6**). What a day it will be when the eastern sky rips asunder, and King Jesus rides forth in astounding and absolute victory in all His glory and power.

In **Verse 14**, we see the King's army. This verse tells us that Jesus will be accompanied by the redeemed saints of God when He returns in glory. How do we know these are the saints? Look at their apparel. They are "*clothed in fine linen, white and clean*". This is the same wording used to describe the appearance of the Bride of Christ in **verse 8**. On that day, I will saddle up and ride back with my Redeemer when He comes in glory!

In **Verse 15**, we see the King's Armament. When He comes, Jesus will need no carnal weapons. He will open His mouth and unleash the power of His Word. There is power in His Word! He created this universe, and everything contained within it with the Word of His mouth! His word can bring light out of darkness and life out of death! He speaks, and it happens! His Word is a living thing. (**Heb. 4:12**). It is an extension of Himself. It has the power to heal and give life, and it has the power to destroy and kill. Jesus spoke, and the waves lay at His feet like gentle ripples. He spoke, and a fig tree withered. He spoke, and a dead man named Lazarus walked out of his tomb. He spoke, and the scales fell from my eyes. In the depths of my sin and death, I heard His voice when He called me to come to Him. His Word came and brought light and life. There is power in His Word!

In **Verses 17-18** we see his commanding presence! In **Verse 17** God is about to prepare a feast for the fowls of the air. They will feast on the flesh of His enemies! There has been a sharp decline in the populations of the various scavenger birds worldwide. Scavenger bird populations are at dangerously low levels in Africa, Asia, and the Middle East. That fact shouldn't bother us! When this day comes, the Lord will call these birds to gather from around the world. They will come at His command. Just as they came when Noah built the ark, they will come for the great feast the Lord is about to place before them! In **Verse 18,** He commands the flesh to be consumed. In life these men had been separated by rank, title, and power. In death they are all made equal!

Death is the great leveler! You may be somebody in this life, but when death comes calling, you will find that you are nobody without Jesus!

Notice the word "*flesh*" is used five times in this verse. Some people want to blame all evil on the devil. The devil and the world are terrible enemies, but a third enemy is the flesh. Satan may tempt us to do evil, but it is our stinking flesh that follows Satan into sin. The world is filled with allurements and attractions that the flesh longs to indulge in. If it weren't for the flesh, Satan and the world would have no power over man at all.

Chances are you have been fighting some battles with your flesh. You have also been battling with the world and the devil. Well, I have some good news for you! The book of Revelation talks about the judgment and destruction of all three enemies. The world is destroyed in **Rev. 18**. The devil is destroyed in **Rev. 20**. And the flesh is taken care of here in **Rev. 19**. I praise the Lord that there is a day when my flesh will be changed and will cease to be a problem in my life. I praise the Lord that there is a day when the Lord of Glory will destroy the power of the flesh forever! In **Verses 19-21,** we see the day of his conquest.

In **Verse 19**, he draws the armies to Armageddon. In our study of this book, we have examined Armageddon's battle several times. That great and terrible day has finally arrived. All the armies of the world, many of whom are enemies today, will join forces to try and defeat the Lion of the tribe of Judah. Their mission will be to put an end to God, the saints of God, and even the mention of the Name of God. Their plans will all fail!

Man thinks that he is in control of his destiny. He thinks his decisions, plans, and desires make some difference. God is sovereign and not man! God determines destiny and not man! God rules and not man! The very fact that the armies of the world gather themselves together in the Valley of Megiddo at this very moment in time proves that God, and not man, is in control! These puny humans think they are going to defeat the Lord and His people. They think they are doing what they please. In reality, they are carrying out the perfect will of a sovereign God. He is pulling all the strings, calling all the shots, and directing every step to ensure His plan for the ages is perfectly and completely fulfilled! (**Psa. 115:3, Psa. 135:6, Isa. 46:10, Eph. 1:11**).

In **Verses 20-21**, our Lord and Savior Jesus Christ destroys Armageddon's enemy armies. Not only does the Lord have the power to draw the armies of the world to Armageddon. He also has the power to defeat them once they are there!

In **Verse 20**, we see the Devil's men are utterly destroyed! The Antichrist and the False Prophet are thrown alive into the Lake of Fire! The two demonically inspired individuals will be taken by the power of a sovereign God and cast alive into the Lake of Fire. These two minions of Satan will not experience physical death. They will be taken alive and sent immediately to their eternal doom! Hell is waiting with an open mouth to receive these two pretenders!

Imagine the shock of this world when, right before their very eyes, their leaders are taken and cast into Hell! The world will immediately see that their allegiance and faith have been misplaced. They will know that they were fools. It may even dawn on them that they are lost, doomed, and destined for Hell!

In **Verse 21**, the assembled armies of the world are defeated in a single moment by the power of the Word of the Lord Jesus Christ. They will die at His Word, and their blood will flow to the horse's bridle. (**Rev. 14:20**). Their souls drop off into Hell to await judgment at the Great White Throne, and their flesh is consumed by the fowls of the air!

That is a terrible scene, but it will be played out someday. The world has rejected the Lord Jesus as its Savior, and now it must face Him as its Judge! There is a truth here that we must attend today. The very Word of God that tells you about a Savior who loves you and will save you is the same Word that tells you about a judge who will judge you if you reject Him. The same Bible that preaches a saving Gospel to the repenting sinner today will be the means of slaughter on that awful day.

Here is what God says about that terrible day, **Psa. 2:1-5**. What would you rather hear? The voice of God as He says, *"**Well done thou good and faithful servant, enter into the joy of thy Lord?**"* or *"**Depart from me, I never knew you!**"* Would you rather hear Him speak peace or judgment to your soul? You can have either one you want!

Jesus is coming! Many do not believe it, but it is true, nonetheless. The Second Coming of Jesus is one of the major themes of the Word of God. There are 1,845 references to it in the Old Testament, and seventeen Old Testament books give it prominence. Of the 260 chapters in the entire New Testament, there are 318 references to the Second Coming, or 1 out of every 30 verses. 23 of the 27 New Testament books refer to this great event. For every prophecy on the First Coming of Christ, there are eight on Christ's Second Coming.

Jesus is coming! I was told a story in seminary about a man who made a covenant with Death. The contract stated that Death would not come to him unannounced and without warning. The years went by, and Death finally appeared before the man. The old man said, *"**Death, you have not fulfilled your promise. You have not kept your covenant. You promised you would not come unannounced. You never gave me any warning.**"* Death replied, *"**Not so! Every gray hair in your head is a warning. Every one of your lost teeth is a warning. Your eyes growing dim and your natural power and vigor abated is a warning. Oh yes, I have warned you and warned you continually.**"* With those words, Death swept the man into eternity.

Jesus is coming! You have been warned! Are you ready to meet Him? Are you saved by His grace? Is everything as it should be between your soul and the Lord?

Once again, I am asking you to consider your final state. We are in the times of *The Final Countdown*. Where will you spend eternity?

THE 1000 YEAR REIGN

Revelation 20 is surrounded by controversy. The controversy swirls around using the words *"thousand years"* in verses 2, 3, 4, 5, 6, and 7. The controversy concerns the 1,000-year period we call the Millennium. This study takes more than a little time. I would encourage you to grab a pen and paper to take notes.

Let's read from God's Word as we continue our study in *The Final Countdown* and look at the Millennium period.

> *20 And I saw an angel come down from heaven, having the key of the bottomless pit and a great chain in his hand.*
> *² And he laid hold on the dragon, that old serpent, which is the Devil, and Satan, and bound him a thousand years,*
> *³ And cast him into the bottomless pit, and shut him up, and set a seal upon him, that he should deceive the nations no more, till the thousand years should be fulfilled: and after that he must be loosed a little season.*
> *⁴ And I saw thrones, and they sat upon them, and judgment was given unto them: and I saw the souls of them that were beheaded for the witness of Jesus, and for the word of God, and which had not worshipped the beast, neither his image, neither had received his mark upon their foreheads, or in their hands; and they lived and reigned with Christ a thousand years.*
> *⁵ But the rest of the dead lived not again until the thousand years were finished. This is the first resurrection.*
> *⁶ Blessed and holy is he that hath part in the first resurrection: on such the second death hath no power, but they shall be priests of God and of Christ, and shall reign with him a thousand years.*
> *⁷ And when the thousand years are expired, Satan shall be loosed out of his prison,*
> *⁸ And shall go out to deceive the nations which are in the four*

quarters of the earth, Gog, and Magog, to gather them together to battle: the number of whom is as the sand of the sea.
⁹ And they went up on the breadth of the earth, and compassed the camp of the saints about, and the beloved city: and fire came down from God out of heaven, and devoured them.
¹⁰ And the devil that deceived them was cast into the lake of fire and brimstone, where the beast and the false prophet are, and shall be tormented day and night for ever and ever.
¹¹ And I saw a great white throne, and him that sat on it, from whose face the earth and the heaven fled away; and there was found no place for them.
¹² And I saw the dead, small and great, stand before God; and the books were opened: and another book was opened, which is the book of life: and the dead were judged out of those things which were written in the books, according to their works.
¹³ And the sea gave up the dead which were in it; and death and hell delivered up the dead which were in them: and they were judged every man according to their works.
¹⁴ And death and hell were cast into the lake of fire. This is the second death.
¹⁵ And whosoever was not found written in the book of life was cast into the lake of fire.

There are three dominant views concerning the nature of the Millennium. These are as follows:

1. **Postmillennialism** - This view says that the world will get better and better and when the world has reached the proper stage of perfection, Jesus will return and establish His kingdom on earth. This was a very popular view before World War II. Nearly anyone can look at this world and all the wickedness and evil and see that the world is getting worse. This is a false view of the Millennium.

2. **Amillennialism** – There are several variations of this view. The primary version says that there is no literal millennial kingdom. The

kingdom of God is spiritual in nature, and we are in the kingdom age right now. Many who hold this view believe that Satan is bound right now. The Amillennial view spiritualizes these verses. This is also a false view of the Millennium. (Ill. A branch of Amillennialism known as Preterism believes the Tribulation has already occurred and Jesus has already returned. The Preterist believes that Jesus returned in 70 AD and established His kingdom then. Their belief system is far more complex than that, but that is the condensed version of it.

3. **Premillennialism** - This view holds that humanity will continue to degenerate; the world will go through a literal Tribulation; Jesus will return and defeat the Antichrist and establish a literal kingdom on the earth and reign here for 1,000 years. This is the only view that takes these verses literally. From my studies, this is the only true view of the millennium.

These verses fulfill many great Old and New Testament promises and prophecies. They tell us about a literal 1,000 kingdom that will exist on this earth and describe the final kingdom in time.

Why is there even a need for the millennium? Why not just wind it all up, judge sin and sinners, and let the redeemed enter eternity? The millennium will allow the Lord to accomplish some much-needed goals. Among other things, the millennium will allow the Lord to:

1. To fulfill His Old Testament promises of a kingdom to Israel.
2. To put Jesus, in all His glory, on public display.
3. To answer the prayer, "*Thy Kingdom come.*"
4. To fulfill the promise that the saints will reign.
5. To bring about the complete redemption of nature.
6. To give man one final test under the sovereign rule of the Lord Jesus Christ.

While there are many great truths associated with the millennial kingdom, too many to share in one chapter, let me share a few of the things that will be a reality then. We will share a few of these. We will not print each verse. You may study the remaining verses at your leisure!

- **Peace** – All wars will cease. (**Isa.2:4; Isa.9:4-7; Isa.32:17-18; Isa.33:5-6; Isa.55:12; Isa.60:18; Eze.28:26; Eze.34:25, 28; Hos.2:18; Micah 4:2-3; Zech.9:10**)

    Isa. 2:4 He will judge between the nations and will settle disputes for many peoples. They will beat their swords into plowshares and their spears into pruning hooks. Nation will not take up sword against nation, nor will they train for war anymore.

    Isa. 32:17-18 The fruit of that righteousness will be peace; its effect will be quietness and confidence forever. [18] My people will live in peaceful dwelling places, in secure homes, in undisturbed places of rest.

    Micah 4:2-3 [2] Many nations will come and say, "Come, let us go up to the mountain of the LORD. to the temple of the God of Jacob. He will teach us his ways, so that we may walk in his paths." The law will go out from Zion, the word of the LORD from Jerusalem. [3] He will judge between many people and will settle disputes for strong nations far and wide. They will beat their swords into plowshares and their spears into pruning hooks. Nation will not take up sword against nation, nor will they train for war anymore.

    This will be a time of peace!

- **Joy** – The King's subjects will be happy. (**Isa.12:3-6; 14:7-8; 25:8-9; 61:7,10; 65:18-19; 66:10-14; Jer.31:18-19; Zeph.3:14-17; Zech.10:6-7**)

    Isaiah 12:3-6 [3] With joy you will draw water from the wells of salvation. [4] In that day you will say: "Give praise to the LORD, proclaim his name; make known among the nations what he has done, and proclaim that his name is exalted. ⁵ Sing to the LORD, for he has done glorious things; let this be known to all the world. ⁶ Shout aloud and sing for joy, people of Zion, for great is the Holy One of Israel among you."

Zech.10:6-7 "I will strengthen Judah and save the tribes of Joseph. I will restore them because I have compassion on them. They will be as though I had not rejected them, for I am the LORD their God and I will answer them. ⁷ The Ephraimites will become like warriors, and their hearts will be glad as with wine. Their children will see it and be joyful; their hearts will rejoice in the LORD.

This will be a time of JOY!

- **Holiness** - This kingdom will be a holy kingdom. **(Isa. 31:6-7; 35:8-9; 60:21; 61:10; Eze.36:24-31; 37:23-24; Zech.8:3; 14:20-21)**

Eze.36:24-31 ²⁴ "'For I will take you out of the nations; I will gather you from all the countries and bring you back into your own land. ²⁵ I will sprinkle clean water on you, and you will be clean; I will cleanse you from all your impurities and from all your idols. ²⁶ I will give you a new heart and put a new spirit in you; I will remove from you your heart of stone and give you a heart of flesh. ²⁷ And I will put my Spirit in you and move you to follow my decrees and be careful to keep my laws. ²⁸ Then you will live in the land I gave your ancestors; you will be my people, and I will be your God. ²⁹ I will save you from all your uncleanness. I will call for the grain and make it plentiful and will not bring famine upon you. ³⁰ I will increase the fruit of the trees and the crops of the field, so that you will no longer suffer disgrace among the nations because of famine. ³¹ Then you will remember your evil ways and wicked deeds, and you will loathe yourselves for your sins and detestable practices.

This kingdom will be a HOLY kingdom!

- **Glory** - This kingdom will be a glorious kingdom, with the glory of God in full display. All the citizens of the world will be able to travel to Jerusalem and see the glorified Savior face to face! (**Isa. 4:2; 35:2; 40:5; 60:1-9**)

Isaiah 40:5 ⁵ And the glory of the LORD will be revealed, and all people will see it together. For the mouth of the LORD has spoken."

This kingdom will be a glorious kingdom!

- **Comfort** - Jesus will fully minister to every need, so that there will be no want anywhere on the earth. (**Isa 12:1-2; 30:26; 40:1-2; 49:13; 51:3; 66:21-23; Jer.31:23-25; Zeph.3:18-20**)

Isaiah 40:1-2 40 Comfort, comfort my people, says your God. ² Speak tenderly to Jerusalem, and proclaim to her that her hard service has been completed, that her sin has been paid for, that she has received from the LORD's hand double for all her sins.

There will be comfort in this kingdom!

- **Justice** - Perfect justice will be administered to every individual. (**Isa. 9:7; 32:16; 42:1-4; 65:21-23; Jer.23:5**.)

Isaiah 65:21-23 ¹ They will build houses and dwell in them; they will plant vineyards and eat their fruit; ²² No longer will they build houses and others live in them, or plant and others eat. For as the days of a tree, so will be the days of my people; my chosen ones will long enjoy the work of their hands. ²³ They will not labor in vain, nor will they bear children doomed to misfortune; for they will be a people blessed by the LORD, they and their descendants with them.

There will be justice in this kingdom!

- **Fullness of Knowledge** - An increase in the teaching ministry of the

Holy Ghost (**Isa. 11:1-2, 9; Isa. 41:19-20; Isa. 54:13; Hab.2:14**)

Isaiah 54:13 All your children will be taught by the LORD, and great will be their peace.

God will impart His Knowledge.

- **Instruction** – King Jesus will instruct His people in the ways of God. (**Isa. 2:2-3; 29:1724; 32:3-4; Jer.3:14-15; Micah 4:2**)

Micah 4:2 ² Many nations will come and say, "Come, let us go up to the mountain of the LORD, to the temple of the God of Jacob. He will teach us his ways, so that we may walk in his paths."

The law will go out from Zion, the word of the LORD from Jerusalem.

- **The Removal of the Curse**

⁶ The wolf also shall dwell with the lamb, and the leopard shall lie down with the kid; and the calf and the young lion and the fatling together; and a little child shall lead them.
⁷ And the cow and the bear shall feed; their young ones shall lie down together: and the lion shall eat straw like the ox.
⁸ And the sucking child shall play on the hole of the asp, and the weaned child shall put his hand on the cockatrice' den.
⁹ They shall not hurt nor destroy in all my holy mountain: for the earth shall be full of the knowledge of the LORD, as the waters cover the sea.

In **Gen. 3:17-19**, God placed a curse upon the earth. This curse will be removed; resulting in an increase in the productivity of the earth, and in wild animals will losing their ferocity and ability to injure or kill. (**Isa 11:6-9; 65:25**).

The curse from Genesis will be gone!

- **The wolf and the lamb will feed together.** (Isaiah 65:25)

  The wolf and the lamb will feed together, and the lion will eat straw like the ox, and dust will be the serpent's food. They will neither harm nor destroy on all my holy mountain," says the LORD.

  Wild animals will no longer harm.

- **Sickness Removed (Isa 33:24; Jer.30:17; 33:6)**

  Jer.30:17 But I will restore you to health and heal your wounds, declares the LORD, because you are called an outcast, Zion for whom no one cares.'

  The King will be a healer.

- **There will be healing** - All will be healed. (**Isa.29:17-19; Isaiah 35:3-6**)

  Isaiah 35:3-6 Strengthen the feeble hands, steady the knees that give way; [4] say to those with fearful hearts, "Be strong, do not fear; your God will come, he will come with vengeance; with divine retribution he will come to save you." [5] Then will the eyes of the blind be opened and the ears of the deaf unstopped. [6] Then will the lame leap like a deer, and the mute tongue shout for joy. Water will gush forth in the wilderness and streams in the desert.

  Sickness will be overcome.

- **There will be unified worship** - The entire world will worship God through the Lord Jesus Christ. (**Isa.45:23; 66:17-23; Zeph.3:9; Zech.14:16; 8:23; Mal.1:11**)

  Isaiah 66:17-23 [17] "Those who consecrate and purify themselves to go into the gardens, following one who is among those who eat the flesh of pigs, rats and other unclean things—they will meet their end together with the one they follow," declares the LORD.¹⁸ "And I, because of what they have planned and done, am about to come[a] and gather the people of all nations and languages, and they will come and see my glory. ¹⁹ "I will set a sign among them, and I will send some of those who survive to the nations—to Tarshish, to the Libyans[b] and Lydians (famous as archers), to Tubal and Greece, and to the distant islands that have not heard of my fame or seen my glory. They will proclaim my glory among the nations. ²⁰ And they will bring all your people, from all the nations, to my holy mountain in Jerusalem as an offering to the LORD—on horses, in chariots and wagons, and on mules and camels," says the LORD. "They will bring them, as the Israelites bring their grain offerings, to the temple of the LORD in ceremonially clean vessels. ²¹ And I will select some of them also to be priests and Levites," says the LORD. ²² "As the new heavens and the new earth that I make will endure before me," declares the LORD, "so will your name and descendants endure. ²³ From one New Moon to another and from one Sabbath to another, all mankind will come and bow down before me," says the LORD.

All will worship the Lord.

- **The fullness of the Spirit (Isa.44:3; Eze.36:26-27; 37:14; Joel 2:28-29).**

Eze.36:26-27 I will give you a new heart and put a new spirit in you; I will remove from you your heart of stone and give you a heart of flesh. ²⁷ And I will put my Spirit in you and move you to follow my decrees and be careful to keep my laws.

All who are subject to the King will experience divine enablement and presence.

All the promises God has made to the earth's inhabitants will come to pass as his covenants are fully revealed and his promises made manifest before all mankind!

In **Verses 1-3**, we see the fulfillment of a prophecy concerning Satan. In Verses 1-2, we see a heavenly intervention as a strong angel descends from Heaven and *"laid hold on"* the devil. That phrase means *"to have power over; to be one's master"*. This angel is empowered by heaven to be the devil's master. He grabs Satan and binds him with a strong chain that will remain on him for 1,000 years. There is no disputing who the Bible is speaking about in these verses. He is called *"the dragon"*; *"that old serpent"*; *"the devil"* and *"Satan"*. Those names reveal all we need to know about his character. As a dragon, Satan is looking for those he might *devour*. As a serpent, he is always seeking those whom he might *deceive*. As the devil is the false accuser, always looking for someone to *defame*. As Satan, the adversary, he is always seeking someone to *defeat*. One day, he will get what is coming to him!

God will have the last word in the fate with the Devil! Satan is powerful, but he isn't all-powerful! Only God can lay claim to that title!

In **Verse 3**, we see a heavenly incarceration takes place. This angel removes the devil from the earth for 1,000 years. Imagine a world with no devil! It will be almost like Heaven! There will no one to tempt people to evil. No one will whisper lies into the ears of our minds. No one will remind us of how wicked we were and are. No will to set traps for us to fall into. A world without the devil will be a wonderful place! Without a devil, peace, prosperity, joy, holiness, and blessing will be the order of the day!

While the earth will rejoice in his absence, the devil will get a small taste of what awaits him in eternity. We are told that he will go to the *"bottomless pit"*. This term translates the word *"abyss"*. This seems to be an ancient prison where certain demon spirits are incarcerated by the Lord, **Jude 6**. We saw this abyss opened in **Rev. 9:1-12**. When the pit was opened, terrible demons issued forth to torment people on the earth. Satan will be confined to this prison for 1,000 years!

What will Satan do for 1,000 years? He will bide his time because he knows he will be released for *"a short season"*. We will talk about all that in a few minutes. For now, we should rejoice in the truth that Satan will be bound one of these days! Hallelujah!

In **Verses 4-6,** we see a prophecy concerning the saints. Verse 4 tells us a day is coming when the saints of God will rule with their Redeemer. Here's a reminder of the events leading up to this moment for the saints of God.

Jesus will return in the clouds above this earth in the Rapture. He will take His Bride home to Heaven. We will face Him at The Judgment Seat of Christ and join Him for the Marriage Supper of the Lamb. Jesus will return to this earth in power and glory, bring His people back with Him. He will defeat all His enemies, establish His kingdom on earth and allow us to reign with Him for 1,000 years. (**2 Tim. 2:12; Rev. 5:10**).

Verse 4 introduces another group of Saints. It speaks of those who endured the horrors of the Tribulation Period without tarnishing their testimonies or denying their faith. Some of these saints died during the Tribulation but have been resurrected. Others made it alive to the end of the Tribulation Period. They are allowed to enter the Millennium. These Tribulation saints join with the Bride of Christ, and we reign with Jesus for 1,000 years. **Dan. 7:27** also promises that the Old Testament saints will also reign during this period.

Imagine a world where there is no devil. Imagine a world filled with the redeemed saints of God from Pentecost to the Rapture. Imagine a world where the brave saints of the Tribulation will be living. Imagine a world where you might walk down the street and bump into Adam, Abraham, David, Moses or Elijah! That world will exist one day!

Verses 5-6 reveal that there are two resurrections. Some people believe in a general resurrection. They believe that all the dead will be raised at one time, and the sheep, which represent the saved, will be sent to Heaven while the goats, which represent the lost, will be sent to Hell. The Bible teaches very clearly that there will be two resurrections. (**Luke 14:14; John 5:29**)

The first resurrection occurs at the Second Coming of the Lord Jesus and includes the saints raised at the Rapture and all those resurrected at the end of the Tribulation. The Bible says that those who have a part in this resurrection are *"blessed"*. Why? They will not have to endure *"the second death"*. However, all those who have rejected Jesus as their Savior, from the time of Adam all the way to the end of the Millennium, will be raised in the second resurrection. The poor, unfortunate souls will all face Jesus at the Great White Throne and they will spend eternity in the Lake of Fire. If I were you, I would do everything in my power to show that I was part of the first resurrection.

In **Verses 7-10**, we see a prophecy regarding the sinners. Verse 7 shows us a peculiar circumstance surrounding Satan. After being bound in the bottomless pit for 1,000 years, Satan is turned loose. Why?

I asked one of my professors this very question. Why? He had a great answer! He said, *"If you can tell me why he was released the first time I will tell you why he was released the second time."*

There must be a reason because Verse 3 says, "he must be loosed." I am certain that we will never fully understand all the reasons why, but I will offer one or two for you to consider.

First, this event proves that the devil is incorrigible and unrepentant. Even after God has proven to the devil countless times that He is stronger, yet Satan still continues in his stubborn rebellion against God. God has thwarted every plan launched by the devil. And still, Satan stands in defiance and open rebellion to the Lord.

Second, this event will prove the total inability of man to save himself, even in a perfect world. It also proves, beyond a shadow of a doubt, that lost man is totally depraved. There is no good in him and left to himself; he will always go away from God. (**Eph. 2:1-3; Rom. 3:10-23**).

Verses 8-9 tell us of Satan and his forces! Where will the devil find this vast army? After all, the world is perfect! There is no poverty, no disease, and no war. It is a perfect world! Why would anyone fall for the devil's lies and rebel against God?

Remember, millions of people entered the Millennium in flesh and blood bodies. Some were Jews. Others were Tribulation saints. These people would likely marry and have children. In fact, because of perfect health and living conditions, the earth's population will likely explode. The children born during the Millennium will be raised in a perfect environment, and still, they will rebel against God.

Every one of those little children was born into this world with a sin nature. Every one of them would still need to be saved from their sins by faith in the finished work of Christ at Calvary. In a world where they will travel to Jerusalem and see King Jesus in Person, they will still refuse to bow to Him in faith and repentance. In a world inhabited by the characters from the Bible, the glorified saints of God, and those who endured the Tribulation Period, many millions will not be saved. They will keep the rules because they will be forced to. But, in their hearts, they are still rebels needing a Redeemer. They are still sinners in need of a Savior!

Then in **Verses 9-10,** we see Satan raises his vast army and leads them in one final assault against King Jesus in Jerusalem. They do not stand a chance! God Himself ends the battle by raining fire down from Heaven. The rebels are destroyed in an instant, and they all drop off into Hell to await judgment.

Satan himself is cast into the Lake of Fire, where he will spend eternity being tormented along with the Antichrist and the False Prophet. When the smoke clears and dust settles, the Lord God Almighty has last say in this matter! God wins, end of story!

So, whose side are you on? Are you on the side of the Lord Jesus Christ or are you on the side of Satan? There isn't any room here for a conscientious objector. You are either one or the other. We are nearing the end of this book and the Book of Revelation. I honestly believe we are in the Final Countdown. Otherwise, I don't believe God would have been so vehement I preach on this topic for so many months or invest His time in this book. So, I ask you, as I have asked in previous lessons. *Where will you spend eternity?*

THE GREAT WHITE THRONE JUDGMENT

Some time ago, a young foreign exchange student flunked out at the University of Tennessee. In shame, he decided to disappear. For the next year, he hid in the unused attic of an old Knoxville church. Taking great pains to conceal himself, he quietly prowled around only at night, living off food and water from the kitchen. He never left the building or spoke to a soul. No one ever suspected he was there. Then, one day, a slight mistake gave him away. Accidentally, the young recluse made some noise, the police were called, and he was finally discovered.

How foolish this young man was to try to hide from his failure. Still, he is not as foolish as someone who thinks they can hide from God! The world is filled with people who live as though they have no sin. They live as though God did not exist. They live as though they will never face God in judgment.

What they hope for will never come to pass. These verses tell us about judgment day. They speak about that terrible day when every lost sinner will face the Lord in judgment. There will be nowhere to hide on that day. No one will hide behind excuses, ignorance, false professions, etc. Everyone will face Jesus Christ as Lord and Judge and receive a just sentence for their sins.

Revelation 20:11-15 rolls in *The Great White Throne Judgment*. Before I begin, I want you to know that there will not be one single born-again individual that will stand in judgment here. This is a judgment seat for the lost. Let's notice this judgment's facts as I preach on *The Great White Throne Judgment*.

Let's read from God's Word!

¹¹ And I saw a great white throne, and him that sat on it, from whose face the earth and the heaven fled away; and there was found no place for them.
¹² And I saw the dead, small and great, stand before God; and the books were opened: and another book was opened, which is the book of life: and the dead were judged out of those things which were written in the books, according to their works.
¹³ And the sea gave up the dead which were in it; and death and hell delivered up the dead which were in them: and they were judged every man according to their works.
¹⁴ And death and hell were cast into the lake of fire. This is the second death.
¹⁵ And whosoever was not found written in the book of life was cast into the lake of fire.

Verse 11 shows us the Judge and the great white throne upon which he sits. There are two adjectives used to describe this throne. **It is called Great.** This word refers to *"its power"*. This is the highest court in the universe! This is no small claims court! When judgment is rendered from this throne, there is no appeal to a higher court, for there is no higher court! This is the place of highest authority and final judgment. We can best understand this court by comparing it to our Supreme Court. There is no higher court in the land. All judgments rendered here will be final!

It is called White - This speaks of *"the purity"* of this court. All human courts are tainted by sin, prejudice, and fallibility. Conversely, this court is perfect, and the judgment rendered here will be fair and righteous. The Judge who occupies this bench is infallible. He cannot be tainted by sin or prejudice but renders judgment in perfect righteousness and fairness.

Not everyone judged here will cry *"unfair"* when their sentence is handed down. Every sinner judged and sentenced will **know** they have received perfect and fair judgment.

The Bible tells us of the Person that occupies this throne! However, His identity is not revealed here. It does not have to be. The Bible tells us in other places who sits upon this throne! The man on this throne is none other than the Lord Jesus Christ, and on this day, the *Savior* becomes the *Sentencer!*

Look at **John 5:22**. *"²²Moreover, the Father judges no one, but has entrusted all judgment to the Son."*

Look at **Acts 10:40-42**. *"⁴⁰ but God raised him from the dead on the third day and caused him to be seen. ⁴¹ He was not seen by all the people, but by witnesses whom God had already chosen—by us who ate and drank with him after he rose from the dead. ⁴² He commanded us to preach to the people and to testify that he is the one whom God appointed as judge of the living and the dead."*

As we look upon His nature, we see this is no lowly Nazarene who occupies this throne. This is not a poor, humble carpenter. This is a resurrected conqueror. This is the King of Kings and the Lord of Lords. His appearance is described for us by the prophet Daniel, **Dan. 7:9-10**.

Look at Daniel 7:9-10. *"⁹ As I looked, "thrones were set in place, and the Ancient of Days took his seat. His clothing was as white as snow; the hair of his head was white like wool. His throne was flaming with fire, and its wheels were all ablaze.¹⁰ A river of fire was flowing, coming out from before him. Thousands upon thousands attended him; ten thousand times ten thousand stood before him. The court was seated, and the books were opened."*

His presence is so terrible and powerful that even the heavens and the earth flee from before Him. Nature has the good sense to bow before this judge! Why is it that sinners have such a difficult time doing the same?

2 Pet. 3:10-13 tells us of the earth that is purified by fire.*"¹⁰ But the day of the Lord will come like a thief. The heavens will disappear with a roar; the elements will be destroyed by fire, and the earth and everything done in it will be laid bare. ¹¹ Since everything will be destroyed in this way, what kind of people ought you to be? You ought to live holy and godly lives ¹² as you look forward to the day of God and speed its coming.[b] That day will bring about the destruction of the heavens by fire, and the elements will melt in the heat. ¹³ But in keeping with his promise we are looking forward to a new heaven and a new earth, where righteousness dwells."*

Revelation continues to tell us, *"Then I saw a new heaven and a new earth, for the first heaven and the first earth had passed away, and* *there was no longer any sea."*

God destroys this ruined creation and remakes the universe as it was before sin invaded and devastated it.

The Bible tells us here that there was found no place for the heavens and the earth to hide from the gaze of the One on the throne. It needs to be remembered that this righteous Judge sees all, and He knows all. There is no sin hidden from Him and no thought has ever been concealed. There will be no pretending and no pretence on that great judgment day, but only a sure recounting of every sinful deed and every sinful thought, **Luke 8:17; Eccl. 12:14**. Nothing will be hidden!

You will not hide from this righteous Judge! He knows all about you before you appear in His presence. He knows you intimately!)

Verses 12-13 tell us about those that appear before the Great White Throne! In these verses we are told those appearing before the throne are the *"dead"*. <u>**This proves that there will not be a single born-again believer in the group**</u>. Why? In **John 5:24**, the Bible tells us that we who have trusted Jesus as our Saviour have **"passed from death unto life." We have been given eternal, abundant life through the blood of the Lamb and can never lose that or be dead again for**ever.

This can only mean one thing. This mass of humanity will be made up completely of those who are spiritually dead. (**Eph. 2:1**). Note also that this group includes all the physically dead! God raises their dead bodies from their tombs. He knows where every particle of human dust is located, and He can bring it together and raise it to life. He calls their bodies from the ground and their souls from Hell. He reunites them in a pitiful procession of anguish and hopelessness.

None are left out! The king, the President, the rich, the poor, the general, the foot soldier, the master, the slave, the borrower, and the lender will all stand before God. None will escape and hide, but all will face the Righteous Judge in judgment that day! Preachers, deacons, church members, popes, priests, nuns, choir members, drunks, drug addicts, pimps, pushers, grandmothers, grandfathers, teenagers, moms, and dads, will all stand together with every other person who chose wickedness over righteousness, before the throne to face their judgment! There will be no escape and there will be no exceptions.

Every person who has ever died without Jesus Christ will face Him in this Judgment on that day! In **Verse 13**, it reminds us that all who died, regardless of where they died will appear before Jesus in judgment. Even those who are in Hell will be brought out for this judgment. Every lost sinner from the beginning of time to the last sinner slain in the Millennium will stand before the Lord Jesus Christ! The question is, *Will you be numbered among them?*

This horrible assembly stands trembling before the Lamb of God. They are forced to look on the face of the One they spit upon. They can see the nail prints in His hands. They can see where the thorns pierced His brow. They can see the awful things He suffered to atone for sin. They see Him as He is, and they are filled with fear!

There are documents used at the throne! The Bible tells us the "*books*" will be opened. Only one of these books is named and it is called the "*book of life*." I don't know all the books that will be used that day, but I am sure of a few that will be opened. Allow me to share them with you for a moment. One of these will be **The Bible**. Jesus reminded us that we would be judged out of His Word. (**John 12:48**). This Bible that sinners mock and refuse to heed will be used to render judgment upon their lives that day. Better to believe it now and go to Heaven than reject it and then face it in judgment and go to Hell!

The next is the **Book of Deeds**. In Heaven, a record is being maintained of the deeds of all men. One day, every lost person will stand before the Lord and hear the record of his life read from the throne. Every deed, both good and evil will be mentioned. Every sin will be read aloud. Sins of commission, sins of omission, flagrant sins, secret sins, sins of the heart and sins of the mind. All will be brought out into the open on that day. **Verse 12** makes it clear that the lost will be judged according to their works.

A man can either choose to stand on his own record and face God in his sins, or he can come to Jesus and have his record expunged. Faith in Christ wipes our record clean. Faith in Christ gives us the innate ability to stand before God, covered in the blood of the Lord Jesus Christ. When we do so, God can no longer see our sin. All he sees is the pure untainted blood of our Lord.

The next book is **The Lamb's Book of Life**. This book contains the names of those who are redeemed by the blood of Jesus. When a sinner repents, their name is written in this book. This is the reason Jesus told His disciples to rejoice. **(Luke 10:20).** This book records who has and who has not accepted Jesus as their Saviour. When the Great White Throne Judgment comes about, both this book and the book of life will match perfectly!

Imagine the horror of standing there that day and hearing your sins recounted. Imagine being forced to admit your sins and the fact that you are a sinner. Then imagine Jesus opening the book of life and showing you where your name was removed. Then imagine Him opening the Lamb's book of life and showing you that every slot in that book is filled and that your name does not appear!

Is this fantasy? I don't think so! It is a time of such horror that nothing in life can compare with it! You need to be sure that your name is written in the Lamb's book of Life. If you have a doubt, get it settled right now!)

The last phrase in **Verse 13** tells it all. When these books are opened, judgment is rendered based on the evidence found in the books. You can be sure that the evidence is accurate, and that the record is complete.

Verses 14-15 tell us this is a fearful judgment. The sentence rendered from this bench is "**Death**". Not just physical death, but the second death which is eternal separation from God in the fires of the Lake of Fire. **(2 Thes. 1:9-10).** This death involves no dying! There will be no end to the torment, to the hell, to the awful nature of what the sinner will face. It will be an eternal state of dying apart from the presence of God or anything good! It will be Hell! It is the "*death*" Paul refers to in **Rom. 6:23** as the "*wages of sin*".

Imagine the horror of hearing Jesus say the words that will condemn you to eternal torment! Imagine hearing Him say, "**DEPART FROM ME, YE CURSED, INTO EVERLASTING FIRE, PREPARED FOR THE DEVIL AND HIS ANGELS**". **(Matt. 25:41).** Imagine living your life the way you wanted, without regard for God or His will and then having to hear the Lord Who loved you enough to die in your place speak those awful words. There could be nothing so terrible!

This is a final judgment. There will be no appeals; all judgments rendered from this bench will be final and binding. This will be the last day any of these sinners ever see. This will end the road for them, for they are forever consigned to the Lake of Fire to suffer torment for eternity! Do you remember the first sermon in *The Final Count Countdown?* Do you remember the difference between Hell and the Lake of Fire vs. Hades and Gehenna?

This is one of the most horrible scenes mentioned in the Bible. I think the concept of people perishing forever is terrible beyond description. However, as horrible as it is, as sad as it is, it is true nonetheless!

If you have never been saved, you need to come to Jesus. You need to be saved today! If you receive Jesus by faith, He will save you and spare you from this terrible time of judgment that is coming upon all the lost.

To those who are saved, this passage reminds us of the terrible need of the world around us. If nothing else, it should move us to come before the Lord and cry out for the souls of our friends and loved ones who need Jesus. It should stir our hearts so that we will not rest until we have tried to tell every lost person that salvation is available if they come to Jesus! It is my prayer we've not become so hardened that the thought of Hell no longer moves us.

An old preacher from northeast Tennessee worked in the coal mines and pastored a small country church. His work took him to many places in the mine all day. One day an inspector who needed to consult with him about safety conditions in the mines came to find him. And of course, he was impatient and frustrated when he found my friend. Here's the conversation that occurred.

The inspector said, *"I've been looking all over hell for you."*

"That's one place you will never find me," was my friend's calm reply. *"I'll never be in hell because I've been saved from hell by the blood of the Lord Jesus."*

No more was said, and the two men settled their business. But at the end of the workday, the inspector again came looking for Elmer just before the whistle blew.

"I've been thinking all day about what you said today," he said. *"I wish that I could know that I am saved from hell."*

"You can know," Elmer assured him. With verses from his ragged,

coal dust-stained pocket New Testament he explained God's plan of salvation, and standing there outside the mine, the inspector prayed to receive Christ.

That can be your testimony today! Wouldn't like to be able to say about Hell, *"That's one place you'll never find me!"* You can come to Jesus right now!

Thousands of years ago in Egypt, God saved His people by the lamb's blood. They killed that lamb, placed its blood on the doorposts of their houses, and went in. When they did, they were saved, safe, and secure. They were under the blood. When the death angel passed through that night, they were spared because they were under the blood.

What about you? Are you under the blood today? Has the blood of Jesus been applied to the doorposts and lentils of your heart? Have you trusted Jesus as your Savior? I hope so, for if you haven't, you will face Him as your Judge one day.

We are getting closer to the end of this book. Where will you spend eternity?

THIS EARTH IS NOT OUR HOME

In **Revelation 21:1-8** we learn a very important lesson! This earth is NOT our home!

Let's read from God's Word:

21 Then I saw "a new heaven and a new earth,"[a] for the first heaven and the first earth had passed away, and there was no longer any sea. ² I saw the Holy City, the new Jerusalem, coming down out of heaven from God, prepared as a bride beautifully dressed for her husband. ³ And I heard a loud voice from the throne saying, "Look! God's dwelling place is now among the people, and he will dwell with them. They will be his people, and God himself will be with them and be their God. ⁴ 'He will wipe every tear from their eyes. There will be no more death'[b] or mourning or crying or pain, for the old order of things has passed away."

⁵ He who was seated on the throne said, "I am making everything new!" Then he said, "Write this down, for these words are trustworthy and true."

⁶ He said to me: "It is done. I am the Alpha and the Omega, the Beginning and the End. To the thirsty I will give water without cost from the spring of the water of life. ⁷ Those who are victorious will inherit all this, and I will be their God and they will be my children. ⁸ But the cowardly, the unbelieving, the vile, the murderers, the sexually immoral, those who practice magic arts, the idolaters and all liars—they will be consigned to the fiery lake of burning sulfur. This is the second death."

Aleah just wanted to go home. Aleah was a young female Belgian Malinois who decided to chase a deer through the woods that surrounded our country home. Again, she was young and still in training. At that time in her life, her "*fas*" (attack) was fast and her "*ous*" (out) was slow. She was very headstrong. I watched her chase that deer through the woods while I chased behind her, screaming at the top of my lungs. Aleah was gone.

Did Aleah know where she was going? No. The high energy drive and adrenalin pumping through her at the time knew no bounds. She was focused. She was focused on one thing! The thrill of the chase!

I walked through the woods around our home every day. I drove the backroads looking for our missing family member. I screamed from the back yard. I fired a pistol into the ground as Aleah was being trained to protect her pack and come home at the sound of a gunshot. There was no sign of her. I talked to neighbors, and nobody had seen her. After several days, I almost gave up hope. A week passed. In desperation, I made yet another call to Sumner County Animal Control. I still remember the conversation like it was yesterday.

"Did anyone bring in a female fawn color Belgian Mal?" I asked.

"Does she have white socks on her feet?" the animal control officer asked.

My heart skipped a beat.

"Yes!" I replied.

"Black on her face with a white star?" she asked.

"Yes, and a pink collar?"

The officer was as happy as I was.

"Yes, she sure does!" the officer said triumphantly. "They just brought her in. She was hungry and looking for a home. She jumped an eight-foot privacy fence and landed in this woman's backyard. The woman was sitting outside preparing to eat her dinner. Needless to say, your dog got the food. She was starving!"

I immediately went to animal control and retrieved my Mal. She came to me, dragging the Animal Control officer behind her, dropping huge amounts of fur. Mals can shed heavily under times of stress. Aleah jumped up on my shoulder and started licking my face. She was finished with this terrible ordeal. She wanted to go home! And so, do we.

There's no telling what Aleah went through as she tried to find her way home. I am sure that danger after danger marked her steps. But when she finally arrived home, she found love, peace, safety, and food. You see, the things that had troubled Aleah along the way home could not follow her there!

According to God's Word, every person saved is a *"pilgrim and a stranger"* in this world, **1 Pet. 2:11**. As we go through this world, we are headed home, **John 14:1-3**. But, along the way, there are many elements of this life that trouble us and hinder our progress. Evil bullies like death, disease, discouragement, depression, and the devil make our journey home treacherous and difficult. But, when I read a passage like **Revelation 21:1-8**, I am reminded that everything that troubles us here will not be allowed to follow us home.

Like Aleah, there will come a day when the journey will be over, and we will be safely at home in the Father's house. We will be in a place of peace, safety, and perfection. While I travel, I am troubled; but I want to say to those things that trouble you and me this morning: ***"You Might Trouble Me Here, But You Can't Follow Me Home!"***

Now, I know that some of you feel defeated, discouraged, and disillusioned today. I want you to know that what you are going through will end some day and you will be home! The Bible tells us that it will be better then. **(Rom. 8:18; 2 Cor. 4:17)**.

Today, I want to take this passage and show you some of life's bullies that will not follow us home to glory. I want to preach for a few minutes on this thought: ***This Is Not Our Home!***

In Verse 4, we can see that **sorrow can't follow me home!** There is no denying that this life is a life of trouble, trials, and tragedies. Every day we hear accounts of diseases, distresses, discouragements, and deaths. But this is how the Bible said it would be. **(Job 14:1, Job 5:7; John 16:33)**.

There isn't a single reader who has come this far in their journey unscathed by life's troubles. In fact, many, if not all of you, bear the scars of your journey on your heart, in your mind, and in your body. Many things in your life have not gone as you planned them, and you know what sorrow is! That is the lot of every human being who has ever lived or will ever live on this earth!

According to **verse 4**, the troubles and trials of this life cannot follow us home! When we leave this world, whether by the rapture or the graveyard, there are just some things that cannot go with us! Think about it! In heaven, there will be no more:

1. **Death** – In heaven, no one will ever die, and no graves will be dug. Never again will grief stricken loved ones stand beside the body of a departed loved one. (Ill. **1 Cor. 15:53-56**)
2. **Sorrow** – This word refers *"to sorrow or grief of any kind."* It speaks of the all the pains, troubles, and heartaches we experience in this life. Disappointments, trials, problems, loss of friends and property, death of loved ones, persecution, and our failures are all in view here. Truly this life is a life of heartache and sorrow, but not one of the things that trouble us here will follow us there.
3. **Crying** – This word has the idea of *"an outburst or an outcry."* It refers to when we are overwhelmed and broken by life's events. It speaks about those times when we are at the end of our ropes and do not know what to do! Friend that will never happen in glory! Life may trouble you here, but it cannot follow you home!
4. **Pain** – This word refers to *"labor, toil or great trouble."* It refers to all the diseases, disappointments and disasters we encounter as we move through this world. Well, the good news is that none of these things will ever follow us home! No hospitals, broken homes, broken hearts, trials and tribulation will go with us to glory!
4. **Tears** – This is the sum of our blessed, promised state in Heaven. Everything that drives us to weeping and sorrow here will not be found over there!

Sorrow follows us today, but I want it you to know *"**You may have sorrow here. But it can't follow you home! This earth is not our home!**"*

In **Verse 8,** we see the **things of Satan can't follow you home!** While it is true that much of what happens in this life is just part of living in a sin-cursed world; it is also true that a being called *"the devil"* causes the saints of God much grief. Satan desires to defeat and destroy you, **1 Pet. 5:8**, and he will stop at nothing to see you fall and fail.

His names reveal his nature and his desires toward you and me. He is called:

1. **The Accuser of the brethren** – Rev. 12:10 (Ill. Job 1:9-11; 2:4-5)
2. **The Adversary** – 1 Pet. 5:8
3. **The Father of all Lies** – John 8:44
4. **The Devil** – Matt. 4:11
5. **The Murderer** – John 8:44
6. **The god of this world** – 2 Cor. 4:4
7. **The Tempter** – Matt. 4:3
8. **The Ruler of Darkness** – Eph. 6:12
9. **The Serpent** – Gen. 3:4
10. **The Wicked One** – Matt. 13:19

He has many other names, and they all tell us how evil he is. But the saints of God can call him *"missing, gone, displaced, no more, done."* Someday, because as evil as he is, he cannot follow us home! (Ill. **Rev. 20:1-3; 10; Rev. 21:27**) When the devil troubles you on this planet, you must remind him, *"You may trouble me here. But you can't follow me home! This earth is NOT my home!"*

Verse 2 tells us about the city of God, the New Jerusalem. **Verse 9-11** tells us this city is the Bride of the Lamb. As far as I can tell, the church is the Bride of Christ, **2 Cor. 11:2**. Here, the city is associated with the inhabitants. Here, the Bride of Jesus is pictured as a glorious, spotless, and sinless Bride, Ill. **Rev. 19:7-8**. This means that one of these days, we will be changed. This vile flesh will drop away and there will be no more appetite or ability to sin!

Let's face it, everyone reading this book, even those of us who are saved have trouble with this flesh we carry about. This was the experience of Paul in **Rom. 7:14-25**, and it is our experience as well.

You see, when the Lord saved us, He saved us from the ***Penalty of sin*** (**John 5:24; Rom. 8:1**). He also saved us from the ***Power of sin***, as in **Rom. 6:14.** We have also been saved from the Presence of Sin, but that great blessing will not be realized as long as we live in this world.

According to the Bible, there will come a changing day for the saints of God, **1 Cor. 15:48-54**. One glorious day, this flesh with all its appetites, affections and allurements will drop away forever. When that day comes, all the saints of God will be forever delivered from the presence of sin and will be in bodies that cannot possibly sin! We will be in a body and a land that is free from the blight and temptation of sin! We will be free! Free to worship. Free to praise! Free to live perfectly for the glory of God! I want to remind this flesh: *"You might trouble me here, but you can't follow me home!"*

In **Verse 8** we also see the **unsaved can't follow me home.** Everything I have told you about in this chapter is wonderful and glorious for those who are saved. But there is a sad note to this message. **Verse 8** tells us that those who die in their sins will not be allowed inside that city. That bothers me, but that is the price of refusing to believe on Jesus.

Notice the fifth word of **verse 8**. It is the word *"unbelieving."* This word refers to those *"without faith, to those without trust in God."* It speaks about those who have never been saved through a personal relationship to the Lord Jesus Christ. Jesus Himself said that those who would not believe in Him would not be saved, **John 8:24**.

My brothers and sisters, I hope your heart has been opened as I tried to teach about Heaven and some things that will not follow us to that perfect land. You might have thought, *"That's a place I would like to go to when I leave this world."* I want you to know that unless you come to saving faith in Jesus Christ, you will never go to Heaven! You will instead go to Hell. **(Psa. 9:17; 2 Thes. 1:8-9)**.

Friend, it does not have to end up that way for you! You can be saved, and you can be saved today. Let me tell you a story about a missionary to Africa!

Samuel Morrison was a faithful missionary who served 25 years in Africa. In failing health, Morrison returned to the United States. Also traveling home on the same ocean liner was President Teddy Roosevelt who had been in Africa for a three-week hunting expedition. As the large ship pulled into New York harbor, it looked as though the entire city had come out to welcome the President. Music filled the air, banners wafted in the wind, balloons flew to the sky, flashbulbs were popping, and confetti streamed like snow. As Roosevelt stepped into sight, the crowd exploded in applause and cheers. It was truly a reception fit for a king. While all of the eyes were on the President, Morrison quietly disembarked and slipped through the crowd. None of the applause was for him and nobody was there to welcome him home.

His heart began to ache as he prayed, *"**Lord, the President has been in Africa for three weeks, killing animals, and the whole world turns out to welcome him home. I've given twenty-five years of my life in Africa, serving you, and no one has greeted me or even knows I'm here.**"*

He then felt the gentle touch of God and sensed the Spirit say, *"**But my dear child, you are not home yet!**"* What a joyous thought to realize presidential receptions pale compared to the heavenly homecoming that awaits every child of God.

My friends, you might be troubled by many things today, but if you are saved, do not worry! We are not home yet! This world is not our home! None of the things that hinder and haunt our steps here can follow us home!

The question I have for you is where will you spend eternity?

THE END OF THE FINAL COUNTDOWN

Our study of the book of Revelation has taken us from the days of the early church in the past into eternity in the future. John has been faithfully fulfilling the divine purpose he shared in the first verse of the book, *"The Revelation of Jesus Christ, which God gave unto him, to show unto his servants things which must shortly come to pass; and he sent and signified it by his angel unto his servant John,"* **Rev. 1:1**.

John has been used of the Lord to reveal to God's people the God's plan for the future. We have seen the words of **Rev. 1:19**, where it says, *"Write the things which thou hast seen, and the things which are, and the things which shall be hereafter,"* fulfilled in the pages of this amazing book.

The Lord has shown us how the church age will end. It will end with the church in apostasy, cold and dead, with Jesus on the outside. We are steadily moving in that direction today.

He has shown us what will follow after the church is removed from the world. There will be a terrible tribulation period that will engulf the world. Billions will die from war, disease, and the tragedy of divine judgment. This age will also end with the Antichrist and Satan judged and sentenced to an eternity in the Lake of Fire.

We have even been given a glimpse of our future. We have seen a place called Heaven, where death, disease, sin, and Satan will be prohibited. We have been given a small foretaste of that wonderful place we will call Home someday.

We have arrived at the end of the book. Our text for this chapter is taken from **Rev. 22:6-21**

Let's read from the Word of God!

⁶ And he said unto me, These sayings are faithful and true:

and the Lord God of the holy prophets sent his angel to shew unto his servants the things which must shortly be done.
⁷ Behold, I come quickly: blessed is he that keepeth the sayings of the prophecy of this book.
⁸ And I John saw these things, and heard them. And when I had heard and seen, I fell down to worship before the feet of the angel which shewed me these things.
⁹ Then saith he unto me, See thou do it not: for I am thy fellowservant, and of thy brethren the prophets, and of them which keep the sayings of this book: worship God.
¹⁰ And he saith unto me, Seal not the sayings of the prophecy of this book: for the time is at hand.
¹¹ He that is unjust, let him be unjust still: and he which is filthy, let him be filthy still: and he that is righteous, let him be righteous still: and he that is holy, let him be holy still.
¹² And, behold, I come quickly; and my reward is with me, to give every man according as his work shall be.
¹³ I am Alpha and Omega, the beginning and the end, the first and the last.
¹⁴ Blessed are they that do his commandments, that they may have right to the tree of life, and may enter in through the gates into the city.
¹⁵ For without are dogs, and sorcerers, and whoremongers, and murderers, and idolaters, and whosoever loveth and maketh a lie.
¹⁶ I Jesus have sent mine angel to testify unto you these things in the churches. I am the root and the offspring of David, and the bright and morning star.
¹⁷ And the Spirit and the bride say, Come. And let him that heareth say, Come. And let him that is athirst come. And whosoever will, let him take the water of life freely.
¹⁸ For I testify unto every man that heareth the words of the

prophecy of this book, If any man shall add unto these things, God shall add unto him the plagues that are written in this book:

¹⁹ And if any man shall take away from the words of the book of this prophecy, God shall take away his part out of the book of life, and out of the holy city, and from the things which are written in this book.

²⁰ He which testifieth these things saith, Surely I come quickly. Amen. Even so, come, Lord Jesus.

²¹ The grace of our Lord Jesus Christ be with you all. Amen.

The verses in this chapter serve as the Lord's conclusion to the book of Revelation. So, let's move through these verses together and end our study of the book of Revelation and The Final Countdown. For me, this is a bittersweet end. I have enjoyed bringing you this series of lessons.

From the time God placed that old song from 1986 called The Final Countdown on my radio and inspired me (with some initial doubt) to preach on The Final Countdown and to begin it with one of the most theologically devastating sermons that preachers preach today, the sermon on Hell, it has been a journey. I started preaching this series on March 26, 2023 and ended on October 22, 2023. This was seven months of preaching. (Wow, there is that number of completions again!) I then received the (not-so-gentle) nudge to turn those sermon notes into the book you read now.

As the Lord closes out this book, He has a few final *statements*. I want to examine these statements and the final lesson and *The Conclusion of The FINAL COUNTDOWN*.

Verses 6-10 give us concluding words about the book of Revelation. As I write this, I get a little choked up. God doesn't say anything lightly. When he says something, that is it. There is no guessing.

Verse 6 tells us these verses are accurate. John is assured that everything he has seen is *"faithful and true."* There has not been a single exaggeration, nor has there been a single falsehood. Every prophecy in this book will come to pass in the Lord's time.

One of the names given to Jesus in the Book of Revelation is

"Faithful and True." (**Rev. 3:14; 19:11**). That name declares Him trustworthy and worthy of faith. The Lord can be trusted! When He makes a statement, it is truth. When He makes a promise, it will come to pass. When He issues a prophecy, it will be fulfilled. God has tied the truth of His Scriptures to the integrity of His Name! Hallelujah! Praise God!

You can believe the words of your Bible! When God speaks, He speaks the truth! Every word in this book is *"God-breathed."* (2 Tim. 3:16). You can trust your Bible!

Verses 7-9 tell us the scriptures have authority. With the statement, *"Behold, I come quickly"*, the Lord declares His authority! Man can say what he wishes about the Bible and about God's promises and prophecies, but **God will have the final say!!**

The Lord also reaffirms His promise to bless those who *"keepeth"* the words of the Revelation. That word has the idea of *"guarding, protecting, and attending to carefully"*. The Lord will bless the people who read, believe, and live out the words of this book. That was His promise at the beginning (**Rev. 1:3**), and it is His promise at the end.

The Bible was not given to us so we would have something to lay on the coffee table or in the car's rear deck. Many people died so that you can hold the Word of God in your hand and not go through someone else to learn of God's Word. The Bible was given to us to read, believe and live out. The Word of God has authority over our lives, and we are to heed its words. (**John 14:15; James 1:22-23**).

When John hears the promises of God given to him through the angel, he gets caught up in the moment and falls to worship the angel. The angel rebukes John, reminding him that he is a servant too. Then, John is advised that we all need to hear. He is told to *"Worship God!"* God and God alone is worthy and deserving of our worship.

It is easy to become like the world and become guilt of worshipping this person or that thing. The only person who is worthy to be worshipped is the Lord God Almighty! (**Matt. 4:8-10; Deut. 10:20**) Remember my word of caution I have used many times on the air, *"**DO NOT PUT YOUR PASTOR ON A PEDESTAL. HE IS STILL A MAN BORN UNDER THE SAME SIN OF ADAM AS YOU!**"*

Verse 10 tells us about the accessibility of the scriptures. John is commanded to *"seal not"* the book he has written. The word *"seal"* means *"to conceal or to keep secret"*. Many years earlier, the prophet Daniel was commanded to seal up a book he had written, **Dan. 12:4**. The time for fulfilling Daniel's prophecy had not arrived, and it was not time to share it with the world.

On the other hand, John should not hide these things and keep them secret. He is to publish them so that the world may hear the news that Jesus is coming, and judgment is about to fall on this world.

The Bible we hold is a living witness to the God of Heaven. It reveals Him in all His glory, power, and wrath. The Bible is not a closed book. It is open and its message is available to all who will pick it up and read with an honest and obedient heart! If this book is closed, it is closed to those who refuse to know the Lord and to those who have been blinded by the devil. **(2 Cor. 4:3-4)**.

One day, this book that is so hated by those who deny the Lord will be the standard of judgment. **(John 12:48)**. If I were you, I would read and heed this book! It is the Word of God, and it will stand for all eternity. (Matt. 24:35).

Verses 11-16 and 20-21 give us some concluding words about our Savior!

Verse 12 and 20-21 demonstrate the Lord's promise that He is coming again! That was His promise before He left this world, as stated in **John 14:1-3**, and that is His promise now. He is coming!

We know that the Lord's return will happen in two stages. First, He will return in the clouds above the earth to claim His redeemed Bride and take her home to Heaven. We see this clearly in **1 Thes. 4:16-18**. Then, He will return in power and glory to claim this earth for Himself. He will defeat all His enemies, establish His kingdom, and rule in righteousness in this world.

For the saints of God, the thought of our Lord's return offers peace and hope. Just the thought that we might be able to cheat death and leave here in the Rapture is wonderful. It is no wonder that John prayed for the Lord to come, **Rev. 22:20**. Every child of God who loves the Lord and believes the Bible is looking forward to leaving this world in the Rapture.

Verses 11-12 and 14-15 tell us about the awards of the Almighty!

According to **verse 12**, the return of Jesus will be a mixed blessing. He is going to reward every man according to *"his works."* Those who have received Him as their Savior will enjoy a time of blessing when He returns. He will reward them for their work and bless them for their service. Many faithful saints of God will hear Him say, *"**Well done, thou good and faithful servant: thou hast been faithful over a few things, I will make thee ruler over many things: enter thou into the joy of thy lord.**"* What a day that will be!

However, those who do not know Jesus will discover that the day of His return will spell their eternal doom. That is what He means in **verse 11**. When Jesus returns, there will be no time to *"get ready"*. When He comes, how He finds the souls is how that soul will remain throughout eternity. If I were you, I would be sure I was saved and ready to meet Jesus when He comes!

He pronounces a blessing on those who obey the Gospel in **verse 14**. He pronounces a curse on those who reject the Gospel in **verse 15**. Those who receive Him will enjoy the blessings of Heaven and everlasting life, **v. 14**. Those who choose sin over a relationship with Jesus will be shut out of Heaven, **v. 15**.

The question you need to consider today is this: where would you be if Jesus was to return today? Are you saved? Are you ready to meet Him? Has your soul been made fit for Heaven by the blood of the Lamb? Is your name in the Lamb's Book of Life? Jesus is coming! For some, it will be a time of rejoicing. For many more it will be a time of horrible rejection and retribution.

Verses 13 and 16 give us a word about His authority! In these two verses, Jesus declares His ability to make these statements and to bring them to pass. He reminds us that He was here when the world began and that He will still be here when all things are finished.

He reminds us that He is the King of Kings in **Verse 16**. He is the *"root"* of David. That is, He is David's ancestor. He is David's "offspring," too. He is David's descendant. Jesus is the ultimate authority! He founded the throne, and He will occupy the throne.

He is the *"**bright and morning star.**" In that culture, to be called a "star" was to be "elevated." The "morning star" signaled the advent of a* *new day. Jesus reminds* us that He, who is greater than all, will return to destroy the darkness of this world forever. The light of His glory will fill both heaven and earth when He comes again!

Jesus can make the promises He made because He has the power, and the authority to bring them to pass. He is coming, and He will rule and reign in righteousness and power someday!

Verses **17-19** give us a concluding word about the spirit! In Verse 17 we find the "*Spirit*" and the "*Bride*" inviting the Lord Jesus to "*come*".

The Spirit of God desires nothing more than the glory of the Son of God, **John 16:14**. The Spirit of God longs for the Savior to return so that He might defeat His enemies and occupy His rightful place on the throne of the universe. The Spirit desires the glory of the Son of God. Therefore, the Spirit says, "*Come*!"

The Bride of Christ echoes the invitation of the Spirit. There is a longing in the heart of the redeemed for the advent of the Redeemer. How many here can identify with that desire? There are times when the burdens of life press us down, and we long for Jesus to come. There are times when sin and Satan harass us, and they seem so strong, and we long for Jesus to come. Sometimes, this world seems foreign, and we long for Jesus to return. Well, hang on a little longer, sweet Bride of Christ; your Redeemer is coming again to take you unto Himself.

In **Verse 17**, there is an appeal to accept! Here on the last page of the last chapter in the last book of the Bible, the Spirit of God offers one last invitation to lost sinners to come to Jesus for salvation. Anyone who sees their need for a Savior and understands that Jesus Christ can save their soul can be saved. They can drink the water of life and "***pass from death unto life,*" John 5:24. *Even as the Lord brings things to a close; people are still being invited to come to Him for their soul's salvation.*"

Have you ever trusted Jesus as your Savior? If you haven't, let me invite you again to come to Jesus and trust Him to save your soul! If you come to Him, He will save you and prepare you for an eternity in Heaven, **John 6:37-40**.

In Verses 18-19, there is a clear warning! People are warned not to tamper with the words of this book. The Lord pronounces a curse on those who would add to or take away from the words of the Bible. This is not a new warning, but it is a warning that runs like a thread through the pages of Scripture, **Deut. 4:2; 12:32; Pro. 30:5-6**. The warning given here is two-fold. First, **men are warned not to add to the Bible** – The Bible is complete. When the Bible was finished, the revelation of God to man was ended. No more new revelations are being given today! Every person who stands up and claims to have a *"new word from the Lord"* is guilty of adding to the Word of God! They are bringing the threat of divine judgment upon themselves.

One of the hallmarks of the charismatic movement has been the inclusion of new revelation. Someone will stand in a service and claim to have a word from God. That is dangerous and it is heresy (here-e-see)! We have all the words from God that we will ever have, right here in the Bible!

These verses also let me know that every book written by a man that claims to be Scripture is a lie of the devil! The books by several religious cults, the so-called *"lost books of the Bible,"* etc., are all attempts by Satan to undermine our faith in the Word of God. I want you to think about this. If I were Satan and knew I was going to lose or thought I was going to lose, I would start planting blockers and false teachings in the way of God's people very early in the game. So, think about these things before you start to accept something that is not God's Will.

Those who add the Word of God will face divine vengeance and judgment. God does not want His Word tampered with!

Secondly, **men are warned not to subtract from the Bible**. Many people are guilty of picking and choosing what they want from the Word of God. They may not add to the Bible but are guilty of subtracting from its words. For too many are guilty of diluting the message of God. They deny its truth, water down its doctrines, and ignore its warnings. They, too, will face divine judgment!

Many years ago J.A. Seiss, in his commentary on Revelation, said, *"O, my friends, it is a fearful thing to suppress or stultify the word of God, and above all 'the words of the prophecy of this Book.' To put forth for truth what is not the truth,—denounce as error, condemn, repudiate, or emasculate what God himself hath set his seal to as his mind and purpose, is one of those high crimes, not only against God, but against the souls of men, which cannot go unpunished."*

God does not take it lightly when people tamper with His Word. And, neither should we!

I take this matter of handling the Word of God very seriously! I do not want to add to or subtract I want to present it just as it is given to us in the pages of the Bible. I want to preach and teach it clear and straight! If it makes people mad, so be it! I would rather offend you by preaching the truth than offend God by diluting and changing the truth.

Let every preacher of the Gospel, every Sunday School teacher, everyone who leads in a devotion, take heed to how you handle the Word of God! It deserves our best effort! We should study it, meditate over it and present it in the power of the Spirit. If you lack that power, prostrate yourself before the Lord until He gives you that power! When you have found the meaning of His Word, then stand forth and proclaim it in the authority of the Spirit, being careful not to add to or take away from its divine message!

Jesus wants you to know that he is coming again! He is coming to put down evil and raise up His kingdom. He wants you to be ready to meet Him when He does come. Are you? *Where will you spend eternity?*

THE INVITATION

And so, here we are, at the end. I pray that God has blessed you through this book. But the preacher is not yet finished. It is time for the invitation. And yet, the invitation cannot truly be given without remembering what Jesus Christ did for us on the cross. If you will bear with me for a few more pages, I'd like to remind you of the death of the servant Jesus!

Jesus left His home in Heaven and invaded this world, His arch-enemy's own territory, to redeem His people from their sins. Jesus Christ, who was, is, and ever shall be God, came to this world and became a man, **Phil. 2:5-8; John 1:1; 14**. He lived a sinless life, perfectly keeping the Law of God for those who could not keep it. Then, He was rejected by the very people He came to save, **John 1:11**.

Jesus came to this world to provide a way for the lost, to be saved. For Him to open this way of salvation, He had to die. He had to be nailed to a cross and executed, the innocent dying the guilty, **1 Pet. 3:18**.

Jesus was rejected by the Jews. They accused Him of blasphemy and declared that He was worthy of death. They beat Him, bound Him, and took Him to Pontius Pilate. Pilate refused to free Jesus and upheld the death sentence, turning Jesus over to his soldiers so that they could execute Him. Those soldiers took Jesus, and they mocked Him, they beat Him with a scourge, and they led Him away to a place called Calvary, where they nailed Him to the cross.

I want to open this view with Jesus on the cross.

Jesus has been on the cross for three hours. During those first three hours, He has suffered all the pain the cross can pass out. During that time, Jesus has also been mocked by the jeering crowds.

Those first three hours were painful, degraded, and shameful. During that time, humanity had its way with the Creator. The God Who made man out of the dust of the earth was dying for sin on a cross right before them and they had no more compassion for Him than they would have for a dog run over in the road.

Up to this point, Jesus has suffered greatly at man's hands. Now, it is time for Him to suffer at the hands of His Heavenly Father. **The cross was not about man having his chance to attack God. The cross was about God judging His Son for sin in the place of sinners.**

In the following lesson, we will see Jesus as He suffers for our sins on the cross. We will witness some of the price He paid that day so that we might go free. Let's enter the scene on the cross. As we enter this scene Jesus has been on the cross for three hours. Nails have been driven through His hands and His feet. The nails passing through His hands would have been near the median nerves. This would have caused acute spasms of pain to shoot through the Lord's body. The muscles of His body would be cramping from dehydration and from being forced to remain in such an unnatural position for a long period of time. The spasms in His body would have caused His back, which had been lacerated from the scourging, to writhe against the wood. A raging thirst would have gripped the Lord. We can only try to imagine the agony He endured that day as He died for us on the cross.

By noon, the Lord's physical sufferings were not even close to being over. By the "*sixth hour*", he had endured inconceivable physical agony, but his spiritual sufferings were just about to commence.

We are told that "*there was darkness over the whole land until the ninth hour.*" After humanity had abused and shamed the Son, God the Father turned the lights out. This was not an eclipse of the sun. That would not have been possible at the Passover, which was just after a full moon. This was not natural darkness; it was supernatural darkness. It also appears that this darkness was not worldwide but localized in Israel.

Why did God cause this darkness to fall upon Israel the day Jesus died? I want to offer a few possible reasons for this. One reason has to do with the people around the cross. For three hours they have laughed, mocked, and stared as Jesus Christ hung in nakedness and shame on the cross. Nakedness? Yes! The early church decided our savior was to wear a loincloth. The American Jewish University describes nakedness in the following manner. *Nakedness is different than nudity. "Nudity" is a state of personal intimacy and trust, without pretense or artifice. The nudity of a baby is beautiful and simple, lacking all guile. The nudity of a married* *couple is equally beautiful and trusting. "Nakedness", on the other hand, entails more than an absence of clothing – it is a mental state (both for the person lacking garments and for those observing the undressed body). To be naked is to lack an element of protection, to be stripped of dignity or decency. Nakedness is about objectification, reducing a person to a mere object to be appraised, to be used. In the Garden, Adam and Eve were nude and complete. Outcast, and with a consciousness of having sinned, they became naked.*[8] The Jews believed to be seen naked was to reveal one's shame.

Now, God brought about a dense darkness to prevent them from seeing what He would do to His Son. What Christ was about to endure was so holy that sinful humanity was not worthy to look upon it.

Another reason has to do with ancient prophecy. The Prophet Amos warned of God's coming judgment against Israel's sinfulness. In **Amos 8:9**, the Lord said this, *"**And it shall come to pass in that day, saith the Lord God, that I will cause the sun to go down at noon, and I will darken the earth in the clear day.**"*

Throughout the Bible, darkness is associated with the judgment of God. In **Exodus 10:21-23**, God sent darkness upon the land of Egypt as a sign of His coming judgment. The Egyptians worshiped a god named "***Ra***". He was the "***sun god***". God extinguished his power.

Jesus said that His second coming would be announced by darkness, **Mark 3:24-25**. In those days, the sun will not shine, the moon will not give its light and the stars will fall from the heavens. It will be a time of judgment.

When the darkness fell on Israel that day, God was signaling that the judgment of that nation was at hand.

A third reason has to do with the curse of sin. The lost are held captive in the darkness of their sins, **Eph. 5:8; Col. 1:13**. Jesus entered the very darkness of sin that we might be brought out of darkness into "***His marvelous light***", **1 Pet. 2:9**.

The darkness that covered Israel lasted for three hours. As far as we

---

[8] Rabbi Bradley Shavit Artson, American Jewish University

know, the darkness silenced the people around the cross. For three hours, there was little sound or movement. At the end of that time, from the depths of that oppressive darkness, Jesus cries, "***My God, My God, why hast Thou forsaken Me?***"

To understand why Jesus made that terrible cry, we must understand what happened during those three hours of darkness. While Jesus hung on the cross that day, the sins of those who would be saved were transferred to Jesus Christ. As Paul would later write in **2 Cor. 5:21**, "***For He hath made Him to be sin for us, Who knew no sin; that we might be made the righteousness of God in Him.***"

While darkness covered the nation of Israel that day, the blessed Lord of glory was plunged into the greatest darkness He had ever known. The holy, sinless, Lamb of God became sin on that cross. Peter would put it this way, "***Who his own self bare our sins in his own body on the tree, that we, being dead to sins, should live unto righteousness: by whose stripes ye were healed,***" **1 Pet. 2:24**.

Consider what this means. It means that every lie, every murder, every act of revenge, every word of blasphemy, and every evil deed committed by all those who would ever be redeemed by His blood was placed on Him. It means that all the pride, all the hatred, all the sexual sin, all the immorality, all the wickedness and all the ungodliness of His people was placed on Him. It means that every rape, every molestation, every injustice, and every evil thought or deed ever committed by those He would redeem was placed on Jesus.

Can you imagine how this must have repulsed His holy soul? Here is a man Who cannot sin. He was born without a sinful nature, and He had no desire or impulse to sin, ever! Here is a man who is accustomed to holiness and righteousness. Now, all the sins of His Bride are placed on Him. The spiritual agony Jesus endured that day far outweighed any physical torment He might have suffered.

When that transaction was made on the cross, God the Father focused all His wrath against sin into the body of His Son. God judged Him as if He were everyone who would come to Christ. God treated Jesus as if He were a murderer, a rapist, a whoremonger, or a blasphemer. In that moment, Jesus suffered the greatest agony of Hell itself. He suffered separation from the presence of His Father!

By the way, the greatest pain of Hell will not be the fire. It will not be the thirst. It will not be the gnashing of teeth. The greatest agony of Hell will be eternal separation from Almighty God, **2 Thes. 1:8-9**.

When Jesus cried "*Eloi, Eloi, lama sabachthani? Or My God, My God, why hast Thou forsaken Me?*" Some of the people near the cross thought He was calling on Elijah. An ancient Jewish legend said that Elijah would aid righteous Jews in their hour of need. One of them gave Jesus a drink of vinegar, a weak, tart wine that was said to take away thirst better than plain water. Jesus took this drink because it did not have the narcotic myrrh in it. The people thought they might see a miracle that day. They thought that Elijah might show up and save Jesus.

When Jesus cried like He did, He was not calling on Elijah. Jesus was quoting **Psalm 22:1**, but He was doing more than that! He was signaling that He had been judged in the place of sinners and for sin! Mark tells us in **verse 37** that He "*cried with a loud voice, and gave up the ghost.*" John tells us what He cried. **John 19:30** says, "*When Jesus therefore had received the vinegar, he said, It is finished: and he bowed his head, and gave up the ghost.*"

The phrase "*it is finished*" translates the Greek word "*tetelestai*". It was a common word that had many meanings in that society. The primary usage had to do with two parties agreeing on a price. When an agreement had been reached that was mutually satisfactory, the parties would say "*tetelestai*". It meant, "*the deal has been struck and both parties are satisfied.*"

When Jesus went to the cross, He went to satisfy God. Jesus did not die to pay the devil. Jesus died because "*the wages of sin is death*", **Rom. 6:23**. Jesus died because the only way we could ever be free was for an innocent man to give His life in our place. That is what Jesus did!

He took our sins upon Him, and He was judged in our place. He died when He knew the Father was satisfied. That is why the Bible says Jesus is "*the propitiation for our sins*", **1 John 2:2**.

The death of Jesus on the cross of Calvary was the ultimate expression of God's love for the lost, **Rom. 5:8; 1 John 4:10**. Jesus Christ died in physical and spiritual agony to save His people from their sins. He did it not because we deserved it, but because He loved us. He did it because we could not save ourselves. As the songwriter so accurately said, "He suffered *it all because He loved me!*"

The death of Jesus was attended by more supernatural miracles. When Jesus died, Matthew says this, *"And, behold, the veil of the temple was rent in twain from the top to the bottom; and the earth did quake, and the rocks rent; And the graves were opened; and many bodies of the saints which slept arose, And came out of the graves after his resurrection, and went into the holy city, and appeared unto many,"* **Matt. 27:51-53**.

Imagine that! There were earthquakes, rocks shattered, graves burst open, and long-dead saints got up and walked about the city. It was a miraculous moment.

The greatest miracle mentioned is in **verse 38** of our text. This is important! We are told, *"And the veil of the temple was rent in twain from the top to the bottom."*

The veil in Solomon's Temple hung between the Holy Place and the Holy of Holies. According to the Law, only the High Priest could go behind that veil and only go there one day each year. God promised Israel that He would dwell between the two cherubim over the Mercy seat. He promised that He would meet with His people there.

On the Day of Atonement, the High Priest, was to take the blood of a lamb and enter the Holy of Holies. He was to sprinkle that blood on the Mercy seat, which rested on top of the Ark of the Covenant, making atonement for the sins of the people. To enter the Holy of Holies at any other time, and without blood, was to violate the holiness of God and it meant certain death. The priests in Jesus' day did not need to worry about that; the glory of God had long departed from the Temple. He was no longer there; neither was the Ark of the Covenant or the Mercy seat.

That veil stood as a barrier between man and God. That veil said to all who entered the Temple, *"This far and no farther!"* The moment Jesus died, that massive veil, which was so thick it was said that a team of horses could not tear it apart, ripped down the middle, as if the mighty hands of God had reached down and ripped it in two from the top down. Note that this is not from the bottom up from the earthquake, as I have heard some preachers say (the ones that do not believe in the supernatural works of a

Mighty God – I'll let that one stand for today). The Mighty Hands of God reached down and grasped the veil ripping it in two from the TOP DOWN.

That rent veil signaled the end of the Jewish sacrificial system. That rent veil proclaimed that **the way to God was open for all who would come to Him**. That rent veil means that whosoever will, can come to Jesus and be saved by the grace of God. That rent veil means the way to God is open. **Rev. 22:17; John 3:16; Rom. 10:13**.

I remind you today that this text makes one crystal clear: There are not many ways to God; there is only one Way, and His name is Jesus, **John 14:6; Acts 4:12**. Muhammad did not die for sin. Buddha did not die for sin. Joseph Smith did not die for sin. There was only one man on that cross that day and His name was, and is, Jesus. He is the one Who died for sin and for sinners. All those who come to Him will be forever saved!

This may not mean much to you, but the fact that Jesus died possessing His mental and physical strength says a lot about His death. You do know that the Romans did not kill Jesus, don't you? You do know that the Jews did not kill Jesus, don't you?

The fact is, Jesus Christ did not release His Spirit, which is what the phrase "*gave up the ghost*" means, until He knew God was satisfied with the payment He had made for sin. Jesus chose the time; He chose the means; and He chose the place where He would lay down His life as a ransom for sin, **John 10:18**.

Jesus died for sin, but He died on His terms so that people might have a means of salvation.

Have you trusted Jesus Christ as your Savior? Have you looked at Jesus with eyes of faith and believed on Him? If you haven't, I beg you to come to Jesus today.

I praise Him that my spiritually blind eyes have been opened and that I have seen Him. I praise God that I have seen His life, love, death, and resurrection. I have seen it, and I have believed it! Thus, I am saved by grace and on my way to glory. How about you?

After every chapter, I have extended an invitation for the reader to either accept Jesus or return to Him. If you have read this book, you cannot say the plan of salvation has not been laid before you. You have received the true upright plan of Salvation in these chapters. You cannot say that you have not.

If you refuse to act on the words God speaks into your heart now, there is nothing more I can do. God has helped me present His Word. It is now up to you to make a decision. I hope you have carefully considered your decision along the way. If you are not saved, I urge you to reconsider. Eternity is just a heartbeat away. Don't surrender your eternal life when you can settle this right now. You don't need a preacher. You don't need an elder. There is only one other entity you need other than yourself. That is Jesus. You don't need an eloquent prayer. The only prayer Jesus is interested in is the one that comes from the heart. You can get down on your knees where you are, ask forgiveness for your sins, ask Jesus to come into your heart and receive the gift of the Holy Spirit. From that point, your life will change forever. You will never be alone. He will be there with you the entire time. The Christian life is not easy. But God promises us he will never give us more to bear than we can handle. All we have to do is trust in Him.

Maybe you are already saved, and that business was transacted long ago. But for whatever reason, you have fallen away. Maybe it was the circumstances of life. Maybe it was something a pastor said (we are far from perfect). Maybe it was something someone did at church. Please do not let someone else's sin keep you from returning to God. You are needed! There is much work to do, and people like you are needed to help bring others to Christ.

You have talents. There are things you can do for God. He will find those talents and help you bring them forward. Who knows? One day, you may find yourself driving down a country road, and a song called The Final Countdown, summoned by God may change your life and that of others forever!

May God bless you and keep you!
Amen!

Mike Letterman

June 15, 2024

CHRIST-LIVES.ORG MINISTRIES
PODCAST AND LIVE STREAMING

LIVE BROADCAST 6:00 a.m. CST 1460AM WXRQ radio or http://www.thewxrq.com
VISIT US ON THE WEB AT http://www.christ-lives.org or email us at ministry@christ-lives.org.
RSS.COM http://www.rss.com/podcasts/christ-lives
YOUTUBE https://www.youtube.com/channel/UC_ww90coIXB5AxRriTGx-uw/videos
APPLE https://podcasts.apple.com/us/podcast/pastor-mike-the-final-countdown-a-ministry-of/id1714168218
BOOMPLAY https://www.boomplay.com/podcasts/52540
IVOOX https://www.ivoox.com/the-last-supper-audios-mp3_rf_130429706_1.html

THE FINAL COUNTDOWN: Where Will You Spend Eternity?

Made in United States
Troutdale, OR
08/04/2024